D0476169

The Best of CRICKET

The Best of CRICKET

An anthology of stories reports and quotes

selected by Roy Peskett

HAMLYN

London · New York · Sydney · Toronto

Acknowledgments
The author and publisher thank all those writers and broadcasters whose stories, articles and comments make up this book. Every effort has been made to contact them. For permission to reprint this material they thank not only the writers but also the publishers of the newspapers, journals and books in which the items first appeared.

Published by
The Hamlyn Publishing Group Limited
London · New York · Sydney · Toronto
Astronaut House, Feltham, Middlesex, England.

ISBN 0 600 34674 9

Printed in Great Britain

Introduction

ROY PESKETT

Ever since I was a small boy many, many years ago, I have been interested in cricket. All sport, in fact – and in adult years I earned my living from knowledge and study of football. But all the time, in whatever part of the world big cricket is being played, there I am – in spirit.

I was eight years of age when my father first took me to the Oval, and from then on I haunted the ground. Virtually every day of my school holidays I caught a bus from Thornton Heath Clock Tower, preferably a Tilling/pirate, for then my threepenny ticket would take me at a faster rate to see my Surrey heroes, especially on that thrilling dash down Brixton Hill!

I knew all the great Surrey players ... my god, Jack Hobbs, who I never called anything else but 'Sir', the lovely Andy Ducat, who taught me to spin the ball both ways, and later became a colleague on the *Sunday Graphic*, Bill Hitch, Herby Strudwick, Percy Fender, E. R. T. Holmes, Alan Peach, the quickies I tried to emulate in run-up, but not pace: Fenley, Sadler and Gover. Also little Bob Gregory, with his whimsical sense of humour (he once chased a ball to the far corners of the Oval, and on his return was asked, 'Where've you been, Bob, they've run five?'... and produced a bus ticket to Victoria Station).

It was at the Oval that my interest was born, fanned and stimulated. Later I broadened out, and in my late teens was fortunate enough to be sent by an understanding Sports Editor, Lionel V. Manning, to cricket weeks, at Maidstone, Tonbridge, Canterbury, Chelmsford, and finally to the Olympian level of Test matches, where, at the age of 22, I 'ghosted' for the warm and friendly Maurice Tate.

That match, at Nottingham, I saw Eddie Paynter run Denis Compton to his first hundred in his first Test against Australia, and then get a double century himself; Charlie Barnett slaughtering the Aussie attack, and the incredible innings of Stan McCabe. I was even taken to the presence of the Don, by Maurice. I have so many wonderful memories which have remained to this day. I was lucky enough to see Mike Procter bowl to Barry Richards before a (then) Rhodesian crowd in Salisbury; to talk of Ramadhin and Valentine with Gerry Gomez in Trinidad over rum punches on Coronation Day ... 'two more and I would have *walked* like a leg break' ... and to have Willie Watson caught off a steepler for 99 at the lovely cricket ground across the bay at Rio de Janeiro.

Even while caught up in the world of reporting sport, mostly football, I spent quite a lot of my spare time, too, watching cricket. And all the time talking about it, and reading it.

I was lucky to sit next to, or near to, in the Press Box, masters like Jack Fingleton, Richie Benaud, Robertson-Glasgow, with his wonderful whimsy, the revered E. W. Swanton, John Arlott ('the umpire, a round and comfortable figure, is moving slowly to his destiny at square leg'), my colleague for so many years, Alex Bannister. And Bertie Henley. As a junior, as part of my sub-editorial upbringing, I was allowed to read his copy before a senior sub-editor was given the priceless work, closely written in ink on the pages from an exercise book.

All the time, magpie fashion, I was collecting cricket stories and incidents, pre-war, wartime – mostly at Lord's, sometimes at Service matches with famous names disguised in khaki or blue ('How long leave have you got?' 'Two 36 hours, a 24, and four hours the RAF owes me!' as Yorkshire's E. P. Robinson once told me) – and post-war.

Finally I was 'ordered' by Peter Arnold, of Hamlyns, to put all these stories together, or as many as would go into a book.

Then came the rub. I had to cut the copy down to size. I then found that the modern writings were as powerful, perhaps even more so, than those of the veterans of the past.

The command of Swanton's writings grew greater as he approached retirement; the musings of John Arlott were always a dream to read; then there were the sensible, authoritative prose of Alex Bannister, the pleasantries of Michael Melford, the authoritative sayings of Richie Benaud, whose incisive grasp of a cricket situation is still a joy, the pairing of Mike Brearley and Dudley Doust.

And there was the joy of reading the modern Neville Cardus, Ian Wooldridge, a shrewd, often whimsical, often deeply critical observer of cricket affairs and personalities.

I found great interest in the cricket columns of the *Sunday Times*, *Daily Mail*, *Daily Telegraph* and the coloured Sunday magazines. But the action was even better!

As the sight of the joy on Ian Botham's face as he straight drives yet another huge six starts to overframe past memories, I still see ... tubby George Duckworth explaining why he developed his shrill appealed 'HOWAZEE?' ... 'my first Lancashire captain frightened the life out of me in my first match: "if the ball hits pad, and the booger's Yorkshire, let's hear thee lad" '; Jim Parks *square cutting* Freddie Trueman into the pavilion at Hove; Bomber Wells at Bristol; Billy Griffiths and Hugh Bartlett, on leave from deadly glider pilot business, bravely blinking in the bright sunlight at Lord's after all-night celebrations; Bill Edrich, still wearing his RAF greatcoat in a shy attempt to hide the ribbon of the DFC, earned from a low level bombing raid; Percy Chapman, eager to follow up his hard hit 83 not out before lunch at Maidstone, answering my naïve question, 'Did you enjoy your lunch Mr Chapman,' ... 'yes, two large gin and tonics and a long distance telephone call!'; Trevor Bailey, who I saw grow from a precocious schoolboy, to a fine soldier, and to an even finer civilian ...

The rest will have to wait for the sequel. I hope you enjoy this new style anthology, with many of the stories printed as they were written on the spot, and not corrected, altered and embellished over the years.

Enjoy it as much as I enjoyed collecting it.

What Fred Told Me To Do with the Ball

BRIAN CLOSE

For too much of my career with Yorkshire, I had a love-hate relationship with Freddie Trueman. He was a truly great bowler when he wanted to be.

Peter Parfitt tells how, as a young batsman with Middlesex, he tried to hook Freddie, but ended up splattering his own nose and best part of his mouth.

After retiring for repairs, his captain sent him out again at the fall of the next wicket. Fred approached him, and with the appearance of solicitude, asked if he was all right.

'Yes, thank you ... why do you ask?'

'They don't usually come back when I've hit them!'

It took me nearly a year to convince Fred to accept that he was going to be a better bowler and a more useful bowler to the side if he was used in short spells. Like most bowlers, he liked bowling, and he most of all liked taking wickets.

At Scarborough in 1963, in a Festival match, he needed three wickets for his hundred. He took one quickly, but because it was a Festival match, and not the kind you wanted finished off quickly, I took him off.

He blew up. He languished at deep fine leg, expressing colourful views on the captaincy to anyone within earshot. At one stage, half the team couldn't field for laughing. Finally, when our opponents had reached 183 for 8, I called down to the boundary, 'Come on, Fred. Finish it off.'

He roared back: 'Stick your so-and-so ball. I'm not bloody bowling.'

'Fair enough,' I said.

In Fred's very first game for Yorkshire, a catch went straight to him and he tried to take it with hands held like crocodile's jaws. It went through, hit him in the chest and dropped down to the ground. When asked what happened, he replied, without a second's hesitation: 'That beggar hit it with a bloody steel bat.'

It is the first recorded instance of a Trueman instant epigram.

Adapted from 'I Don't Bruise Easily' by Brian Close, published by Macdonald and Janes, and highlighted in the DAILY EXPRESS, 20 AUGUST 1978.

The Ball that Won the Ashes

MIKE BREARLEY

The scene is set . . . Fourth Day of Headingley Test, 1977. England 436 (Boycott 191, Knott 57, Greig 43, Woolmer 37; Pascoe 4 for 91, Thomson 4–113) Australia 103 (Botham 5 for 21, Hendrick 4 for 41), and 248–9 (Marsh not 63, Pascoe not 0)

Christopher Martin-Jenkins, 15 August 1977, broadcasting to millions of listeners on Radio Two, B B C World Service and the Australian Broadcasting Company . . .

'And here's Hendrick again. Running in to bowl to Marsh. 63 not out. Marsh swings high on the offside. Randall's underneath it. This could be the Ashes for England. He's caught it. They've won. Randall turns a cartwheel. The stumps are seized by the players. The crowd comes on to the field, and England have regained the Ashes.'

And this is Mike Brearley's view from first slip, of this last fateful, historic ball which finished the 1977 Test series, with England going ahead 3–1.

Marsh, a trifle resigned, but pugnacious all the same, hunched over the crease. He would be taking the fifth ball of the over from Mike Hendrick, with Len Pascoe, a poor batsman, at the non-striker's end. Marsh was left with a choice; either nudge the ball for a single, and retain the batting at the other end, and then face Willis, or try to score fours. We were not worried about boundaries at this stage of the match. Yet the man must be got out.

Marsh hits the ball so hard that even when it goes in the air, you need a bit of luck to find a fielder.

I briefly considered my field placing. Were they set deep enough? Do I bring them in to cut off the single, or push them back for the big hit? I had Derek Underwood and Derek Randall at mid-off, and straight extra cover, orthodox enough to pacify Hendrick but still deeper than usual.

The ball was lobbed back to Hendrick.

What about short square leg? When Marsh plays defensively he pushes forward with his bat low and close to his pad. It might go bat–pad to short leg.

A quick snatch at the ball, and the Ashes would be won. Woolmer was there, waiting. Woolmer is unique.

He is the only bat–pad fieldsman I know who will take up a position *exactly* four yards from the batsman. The first time he does so in an innings, he will pace it out, make his mark, and stand there till Doomsday, and never complain. Woolmer is a brave fielder.

Hendrick began his stride towards the football stand end, reflexly shining the ball down the shine of his flannels. The second new ball was only one over old, and, for all that shining, the lacquer would show no useful wear on one side before a few more overs. It was comforting to know that, should we need it, the new ball would retain its fire until well after tea-time.

Hendrick is a big, gangling man with a big stride, and in the past he had been plagued with hamstring and groin injuries. Perhaps these breakdowns went a way towards explaining a view he expressed on bowling. 'Mike', he had asked a fortnight earlier, on being selected for the Third Test, 'could you limit my spells to six or seven overs?'

And now, here he was, striding back towards his mark, as fresh as a daisy, although earlier he had bowled ten overs in about an hour and twenty minutes, his longest spell in the series. Now I had to bring him back sooner than I hoped.

My admiration for Hendrick had grown innings by innings through the series, but that afternoon I had learned something surprising about him. I had suggested he bowl an over of in-swingers to Robinson. 'When I let the ball go,' Hendrick replied, 'I'm not sure which way its going to move, in or out!'

I was amazed that this was true of the finest medium-fast bowler in England!

Hendrick had now reached his mark. He turned and paused. He drew breath, and set himself. He told me later what went through his mind at the moment . . . Marsh is having a slog at almost everything, and if I bowl it anywhere near straight he will slog it into the air, or miss it altogether. He said to himself, 'decent line, decent length, off stump'.

Beside me, Alan Knott dangled down into position, feet together, gloves low, head up in that singular way of his. Woolmer went into his crouch, remarkably low, his eyes fixed on the roll of the front pad of the batsman. Tony Greig crouched. My hands were clammy. I wiped them down my flannels and crouched.

Hendrick came in. I remember thinking, as I often do, as he thunders towards us, 'Hendy, your stride looks too long to be comfortable.' He stretched himself to his full height, and bowled what he later said was a 'crap' ball. Knott, with his usual precision, recalls it as just short of a good length and headed eighteen inches outside the off stump. Woolmer, seeing Marsh swing, instinctively covered up, elbows up, eyes clamped shut. Marsh got a top edge, and skied the ball. He let loose a foul, Aussie oath.

That was it. As Hendrick said, everything went haywire. I watched Randall take two strides to get under the ball. Out of the corner of my eye I could see Underwood sprinting, possibly, half-skipping, towards him to congratulate him on the catch. As for the catch, I'm not certain I saw Randall take it. I had an eye on the stumps. Earlier in the over I had asked Knott to save me one, but, in the turmoil, I made certain of the souvenir myself by pulling it out of the ground.

Randall said later he thought he might finish the match, capture the Ashes with flair, by leaning forward to take the catch behind his back. He thought better of the idea. Photographs depict him grabbing the ball like grim death just above the breastbone. Then he did something which reflected his anxiety of the moment. He kept his grip on the ball a split-second too long so that when he threw it, or meant to throw it, high and ceremoniously into the air, it went over his shoulder.

Randall then turned his cartwheel, which doubtless will remain a prevailing image of the Ashes of 1977. I wish I had seen it. It is something I had been coaxing him to do at some opportune moment throughout the series. He had been afraid of both the selectors' and the public's opinion, but now, at the most opportune time, he had done it.

Underwood, in the meantime, had grabbed the ball and jammed it into his pocket. He recalls little else of the moment. To this day, for instance, he cannot remember whether he picked the ball clear out of the air, or caught it up on the bounce. More surprisingly, for weeks he believed that it was Willis, not Hendrick, who bowled the last ball. He had been unsettled throughout the match by a running joke, to the effect that if the Packer players, Greig, Knott and himself, hoped to be picked for the final Test at the Oval, England must intentionally lose at Headingley. Only in that way could the Ashes be kept in the balance.

Meanwhile, back at the crease, Knott was unperturbed at the moment of triumph. He plucked the bails off the stumps for the umpire to collect, and stood guard over the two remaining stumps.

At the other end, I'm told, Hendrick gathered up a wheatsheaf of stumps. Souvenirs were being reaped. The photographer, Patrick Eagar, later wondered why, at lunchtime we hadn't designated who was to get a souvenir. After all, there were eleven players, and eleven possible mementoes; the six stumps, four bails and a ball. The answer is we never thought of it. Perhaps we couldn't plan beyond winning the match, perhaps such a scheme would have courted disaster.

'THE RETURN OF THE ASHES', BY MIKE BREARLEY AND DUDLEY DOUST, PELHAM BOOKS, LONDON, 1978

EXCLAMATION MARK QUERY

Ray Robinson wrote this happy recollection of the late, incomparable Sir Neville Cardus in *The Cricketer*.

Sir Neville, being a meticulous cricket writer, invariably cabled words like 'comma' and 'semi-colon' to punctuate his brilliant despatches from the far-flung colonies.

Horrified at the expense, his employers once dared to instruct him: 'Please send story. We'll fix punctuation.' To which Sir Neville promptly replied: 'I'll send punctuation, you fill in words.'

My Only Trent Bridge Wicket

LINDSAY HASSETT

I have fond memories of Trent Bridge. It was here, in 1938, that I opened my short, but nevertheless, brilliant bowling career. Bradman finally succumbed to my continued pestering for the new ball . . . and I opened the Australian bowling for the first, and last, time.

My first ball to Walter Keeton was bowled wide outside the off-stump, and swung away wider still. Keeton, at full reach – he had never had such a shocking ball bowled to him – snicked a catch to Fleetwood-Smith at first slip.

Fleetwood-Smith caught it.

It is sad to relate that a bright-eyed sub-editor, on receiving the cable in Melbourne, corrected what he thought was a garbled report and the great event was finally published:

Keeton *c* Hassett *b* Fleetwood-Smith 0.

EVENING STANDARD, 12 MAY 1956

Catch with Snow on it

IAN PEEBLES

At Lord's, D. R. Jardine led England for the first time, and Leslie Ames and Bill Voce were playing their first English Test match. For me it was the first and only Test match I played there.

The New Zealanders batted first on a beautiful wicket, and we did well to get them out for 224, the most memorable feature of their innings being Ames catching I. B. Cromb off one of the highest hits ever seen.

I was the bowler, and shouted 'mine', but after quite a lengthy debate Jardine called 'Ames', whereupon the latter trotted gently to my end, and, after a long pause caught the ball beside the bowler's umpire! EVERYBODY'S WEEKLY 1950

SWINGERS

Stuart Surridge arrived at a charity cricket match at Newmarket, together with Tyson, Tribe and Manning, three Northants stars. Said the harassed hostess, vastly relieved, 'I'm ever so glad you've arrived, three of our players have dropped out.'

Surridge: 'Who are they?'

'The Hedley Ward Trio!'

Ireland v *West Indies*

ULICK O'CONNOR

There are only 35 senior cricket clubs in Ireland, and for the Irish international cricket team to take on the current West Indies side last week in Dublin seemed almost impertinent. Yet it had to be remembered that Ireland had put the West Indies out last time they travelled to Ireland for 25 runs ... in 1969.

The Irish won on that occasion, and not for the first time. They had beaten the West Indies in 1928, when the legendary George McVeagh, an international at hockey, squash, tennis and cricket, made 103 and took four catches.

This time the West Indies won by 204 runs; but the Irish made 41 more than the English had made last week-end.

The glorious hitting of the West Indies had the crowd cheering themselves hoarse. Decently the visitors had not forced the follow-on after a first innings lead of 268, and batted again to declare at a further 114–4. Afterwards Ireland made a grand stab at a draw.

At one stage they were 170 for 5, with Ivan Anderson making 79. Then, alas, the spinner Raphick Jumadeen knocked down four of the last five wickets. He finished with 5 for 29 and Ireland added only five runs to the innings.

Recently, on television, Lord Killanin, President of the International Olympic Committee, remarked that cricket was not played in Ireland. This result may enlighten him. But it must be admitted that the game has a different flavour there. Anything could happen during week-ends in the old days at country matches organised by Lord Dunsany, Sir Stanley Cochrane and others.

At Dunsany Castle, Co. Meath, if you failed to score a mechanical duck waddled out to meet you after it had been wound up by his Lordship. Dunsany was the best snipe shot in Ireland and used to demonstrate his skill at cricket lunches by shooting the wasps off the top of champagne bottles and summoning the butler by firing at the bell push. Once he bowled a hand grenade instead of a cricket ball because he considered the match was slowing up.

SUNDAY TIMES, 18 JULY 1976

TONS MISSED

Dennis Amiss, Majid Khan and Mushtaq Mohammed made Test history when they were all dismissed for 99 in the England–Pakistan Test in Karachi in March 1973.

What was (is) MikroPul Ducon?

IAN WOOLDRIDGE

The only problem about MikroPul Ducon, as advertised at the Oval cricket ground and, therefore, on BBC television, is whether you purchase it by the quart, the yard, the kilo or in packets of three?

'No doubt about it' said my informant, 'it's the most brilliant coup of the year. It's a Greek firm, you know. Trust the Greeks to think up that "environmental protection" line.'

The implications, of course, were huge. If the BBC have banned Grand Prix motor-racing from their screens because some of the cars roar around with Durex written all over them, how could they conceivably televise the fifth Test from the Oval with MikroPul Ducon staring you in the face every time the ball ran down to the Vauxhall Stand boundary?

Well, millions of bewildered televiewers *did* see it on Wednesday when BBC screened the one-day Surrey–Essex match. So, bristling with puritanical outrage, one felt it only right to telephone the Surrey County Cricket Club and castigate them for the offensive tastelessness of their boundary advertising.

'Oh my God' said a Surrey spokesman. 'Is *that* what they are? It never occurred to us. I say, you're not going to print this, are you? You realise that the Fifth Test will be blacked out on television?'

'It is the duty of a free Press to protect young children and elderly ladies from being affronted by this kind of nauseating advertising' we boomed. 'Motor racing? Cricket? What's the difference?'

A low moan from The Oval indicated they knew all was lost.

To conclude our inquiries we called at a chemist's in London EC4, waited until two lady typists had bought some shampoo, gestured a male assistant to the end of the counter and whispered: 'Three MikroPul Ducons, please'.

'I'm afraid I've never heard of the product, sir,' said the assistant.

'Really,' we replied nastily, 'of course, they *are* the very latest and presumably only very up-to-date stores stock them for really discerning clients.'

'Possibly, sir,' said the assistant.

So the search widened.

'Awfully sorry,' said a worthy-sounding man at the Family Planning Association, 'we don't seem to have them on our recommended list.'

'What on earth,' demanded a businesslike lady at the Association of British Pharmaceutical Industry, 'are you talking about?'

'Very sorry, old boy,' said a jolly chap at the Ann Summers Establishment up near Marble Arch, 'can't help you out at all.'

'If they're rivals of ours,' said a big wheel at the London Rubber

Company somewhat brusquely, 'we've never heard of them.'

'I've just searched through all our reference books,' said an infinitely helpful secretary on the "Chemist and Druggist Directory", 'and they don't appear to be here. A Greek firm, you say?'

'Yes, a Greek firm,' we replied testily, and promptly rang our correspondent in Athens to track down, once and for all, these Hellenic environmental protectionists whose cunning advertising was about to wipe cricket off the English television screens.

He drew a blank.

It was fast approaching teatime on the cricket grounds of England when we received a telephone call from a man in Shoeburyness, Essex.

'I understand from Surrey County Cricket Club,' he said pleasantly, 'that you wish to buy an air-conditioning unit?'

'Are you some kind of nutcase?' we demanded. 'Get off the line.'

'No,' he replied, 'I am the managing director of MikroPul Ducon, manufacturers of filters for cleaning dirty industrial and domestic air.'

'Do you sell *anything* in packets of three which have been sent out under plain cover,' we asked weakly.

'Certainly not,' he retorted, 'air filters is our business and we are cricket fans to a man.'

'Thank you for calling,' we said. 'Forgive us our trespassing.'

'Not at all,' said Mr MikroPul Ducon. 'I'll send you a price list.' DAILY MAIL, 11 JUNE 1976

Two Prince Richards: 1. Barry from Rhodesia

RICHARD GORDON

When Hampshire played Lancashire in the John Player League on the second Sunday in June, I travelled from London to Bournemouth to watch. It was no chore. I once travelled from London to Australia to watch a cricket match.

And I was to meet Barry Richards, the greatest batsman in the world. The invaders of my compartment at Southampton talked about him all the way through the New Forest.

Barry Anderson Richards is six foot tall, pushing 29, with a complicated hawk-nosed profile, and long, wiry fair hair. He wore a red jersey, a white polo necked shirt and black shoes as scruffy as my schoolboy son's. He had at the time scored over 20,000 runs in first-class cricket, averaged a century one innings in every seven, a fifty every other innings, and held 200 odd catches at first slip. At five wickets a year his bowling is not too hot. But beside being a prolific source of runs, his superb timing and wide range of strokes combine to make him one of the most attractive batsmen to watch in action in the world.

We found a tiny, empty and sadly unopened bar upstairs in the Dean Court ground's doll-like pavilion. He was approaching the interview with the wariness of the bomb squad approaching a car parked in the middle of Belfast.

'I like to keep my interviewing and my cricket apart,' he explained. 'There are few good cricket reporters, the game's too technical. They write headlines instead. They just stick labels on me, which is embarrassing.'

There are two Achilles heels beneath his Barry-Richards cricket boots. He is a South African. Nothing wrong with that. 'I'm ridiculously patriotic,' he told me. But being a South African sportsman today means running into the well-relished highmindedness of the rest of the world.

Richards is, of course, as much against racial segregation in sport as Calvin Coolidge's preacher against sin. He explained that he was a liberal, a word with a dirtier meaning in Capetown than in Cornwall. Earlier this year, Richards, and the Rhodesian all-rounder, Mike Procter, who plays for Gloucestershire, were in the Gilbertian situation of trying to play charity matches in India for flood relief, and finding themselves banned through Indian Government policy towards their countries. He has no time for the Peter Hain sort of fuss.

Nobody plays cricket with South Africa any more. Richards represented his country only four times, against the Australian touring side under Bill Lawry in 1970.

From them he took 500 runs, starting with 94 on the first day of the first Test, and before lunch. He was obliged to achieve an international reputation without the support of any international cricket. Which developed the Achilles heel on the other foot. Money.

Richards is the highest paid cricketer in the game. He achieves this partly by sunlighting. In the English summer he opens for Hampshire; in South Africa he captains Natal. He can sell his services round the world.

'No gentleman discusses money at a cricket match,' I murmured, coughing apologetically. 'But . . . well . . . I mean, old chap, you do rather have this reputation of being a "mercenary", don't you know, the batsman who keeps his score in the cash register.'

He defended himself with the patient forbearance of President Nixon at his best. A cricketer and a model girl, he pointed out, both have to think of their old age.

'I gather you make . . . ahem . . . ten thousand smackers a year?'

'That's about right.'

'And English taxes?'

'I get PAYE knocked off, like everybody else.'

Hampshire became fashionable only by swinging their way to the

Championship in 1961. When Richards joined, in 1968, they were still among the poorest clubs. He is supposed to have demanded £1,000 over the odds. 'It wasn't a definite figure,' he demurred. Two anonymous cricketomanes put up the money, and at 2,395 runs in the season got a good bargain.

During the South African summer of 1970 Richards shocked Natal by hiring himself out to South Australia instead. This was through a pleasant arrangement with the Coca-Cola Company, who topped his salary with an Australian dollar a run (the season cost them A$1,538). To keep him at home the following year, a Durban ice-cream merchant offered four rand a run, and bought £2,000 worth.

'I'm selling runs on a commission basis,' Richards put it. 'It isn't a new idea. In 1962 Gary Sobers was sponsored in Australia. Anyway, sponsors aren't all that easy to find.'

He makes a bit more on the side. Like all top cricketers, his soul, or his ghost, is in writing. *Attack to Win* (Pelham Books, 1973) made him £400, more than most highly praised first novels. He gets £750 a year from signed cricket bats. And about £1,000 from his two columns, which span the world from his South African *Sunday Times* to the *Southampton and Bournemouth Echo* ('I speak into a tape recorder, and they take what they want.')

Run of the mill awards – Man of the Match and the like – are shared under club rules. Up to £30, you keep it – anything above is one-third to you, two-thirds to the pool. Richards never buys a car. Showrooms in England, Natal and Australia are eager to lend him one. He owns the semi-detached house he occupies in Chandlers Ford, and has an interest in a block of flats in Durban. Hardly international investments on the London scale. 'What I earned in five years wouldn't be as much as Chris Drysdale earns in half a year in tennis.'

That is Barry Richards' sin. He is a cricketer. As our country moves swiftly from selfishness to rapacity, in desperation we respect our cricketers as white-flannelled incorruptibles. Even that paragon of many virtues, Colin Cowdrey, courted displeasure in plugging cigars. Making money from cricket is not cricket.

During the final Test against the Australians at the Oval in 1896, the professionals literally refused to play the game and went on strike for higher pay. The dispute was solved in a typically English manner, because it started to pour with rain and so render the stoppage pointless. By the time the pitch had dried all but two of the strikers had turned blackleg. (England won, 145 and 84, Australia 119 and 44.)

The captain of England that match was, of course, an amateur. In commercial acumen he compared to Barry Richards as Sir Charles Clore to our sub-postmistress. He was W. G. Grace.

Of the eleven Graces – including Mother – listed among Wisden's memorable cricketers, Dr W. G., Mr G. F. and Dr E. M. all played as amateurs and took fees. G. F. was found out and excluded from the Gentlemen *v* Players match. 'A gentleman ought not to make a profit from playing cricket,' MCC admonished him. His shrewder elder brother, W. G., took the money as expenses, including the salary of his *locum tenens*.

The Victorian MCC hardly discouraged shamateurism in 'the sport of the people, open to all, from the prince to the peasant'. They resolved in 1877 'that taking into consideration the extraordinary play of Mr W. G. Grace and his great services to cricket . . . a national testimonial to Mr Grace ought to be supported.' The doctor got £1,458 and a 40-guinea clock.

When W. G. Grace was sixteen years older than Barry Richards he captained Lord Sheffield's 1891 team to Australia. There was no MCC tour to 1903 as everything depended on sponsorship by the aristocratic equivalent of Coca-Cola. Grace played in almost every match, headed the averages, and collected £3,000 plus expenses. When he achieved his century of centuries in 1895 (he got 2,346 and nine centuries that season) *The Daily Telegraph* started a second national testimonial which brought in £9,073 8 3d.

Tucked away at the rear of the north staircase in the pavilion at Lord's is Max Beerbohm's comment. His cartoon shows the bearded doctor, in one hand a tiny cricket bat and in the other a large cheque, the distance filled by a cricket ground and a pair of gaily cantering hearses with plumes flying and weepers trailing, 'To dear old W. G.,' says the caption, 'To the left, the grandstand; to the right, the funeral of one of his patients.'

The bar where we sat that Sunday afternoon having filled with eager ears, Barry Richards and I moved to a slit under the pavilion tiles. I asked how he amused himself.

'I play golf and squash to keep fit. I don't smoke. I drink lager. I go to a disco, but only with a crowd I know. I've had girlfriends, nothing serious, none at the moment. I bet, maybe £20 to £25.' Hardly the George Best of Bournemouth.

Richards was born in the Morningside suburb of Durban, where his father ran the municipal market and played rugby. He discovered a talent for the bat aged about eight or nine, endlessly hitting a golf ball against the garage wall. That was how the infant Bradman started. 'I went to Durban High School but I spent more time in the nets than anywhere. I'm not academic. I don't mind English, but I couldn't take maths or science. I never matriculated. I didn't want to go to University. Nor could I have afforded it.'

He first came to England with a South African Schools XI in 1963, and returned with Mike Procter to scrounge any sort of cricketing work. I asked if he thought of settling here. He laughed: 'I can hardly survive the English summer, let alone the winter!'

'The weather, and the cost of going out, keeps everyone confined to their homes here. Just reading the sports pages and watching television, which we haven't got in South Africa. Besides, I don't care for the lack of discipline, which goes under the name of progressive freedom. All the schoolkids smoking and fooling about. Anyway, there's no incentive. Those who work hard get heavily taxed, and though your social security is good, it's abused.'

Perhaps all that was the effect of working in Bournemouth.

'I've mellowed a lot. I used to get furious when I got no runs; now I accept it as one of the trials of life. I think I learned a captain's skills between the ages of 21 and 23, getting the players to respect me. I welded together a young Natal team under pressure, and we won the Currie Cup. I think that's my highest achievement.'

That, and what the Hampshire Secretary told me afterwards – his inestimable example to young English cricketers.

I learned something else about him. Like another distinguished South African, Professor Christiaan Barnard, Barry Richards has exercised his profession under the threat of arthritis.

Richards went to change for the match. Shortly I was standing by the sightscreen watching him bat. He has an ability I have seen only in the most expert surgeons – to make his job look amazingly easy. He hit six runs with his favourite cover drive, then was bowled middle stump in the third over by the Lancashire seamer Lee.

Distrustful of the Constable-like clouds, I made for the station. Spectators were still queueing. Had I shouted 'Richards is out,' some of them would have turned away. That would have happened with W. G. Grace. With the doctor he shares also star quality.

I had looked into the dressing room to commiserate with him. He was watching Notts. *v* Worcester on television, and reading the *Investors Chronicle*. He had charged £50 for the interview.

SUNDAY TIMES MAGAZINE, 10 AUGUST 1974

CLASSY BOWLING

This story came from the days when the West Indies thought *our* bowlers were fast.

Frank Worrell, Gary Sobers and Conrad Hunte, who claimed he was caught off his boot, all told me how unplayable was Statham's early spell.

'Man, he was swinging that little ball so far I couldn't believe my eyes,' said Hunte.

Said Sobers: 'We got blamed for bad batting. But, boy, I'm telling you that was some classy fast bowling from both ends. Brian Statham was bending them, and Freddie Trueman was upping them!'

KEITH MILLER, DAILY EXPRESS, FEBRUARY 1960

2. *Vivian, from Antigua . . .*

PETER JACKSON

The most electric batsman in the world will be arriving at Lord's today behind the wheel of an emerald green Capri when he might have been some 3,500 miles away mending fuses in a dark corner of New York City.

In all probability, Isaac Vivian Alexander Richards will turn up for the Gillette Cup semi-final against Middlesex with the car's dashboard vibrating to the sounds of Radio One.

By the time he leaves Lord's will have been privileged to witness the young master practising a craft which offers a rather higher entertainment value than anything he could have achieved as an electrician in America.

If it hadn't been for the persuasion of a particular Bath bookmaker, Len Creed, now Somerset's chairman, Richards would have flown from his native Antigua to enrol in a New York college as a budding electrical engineer and perhaps spend his week-ends watching the Yankees.

'Who knows where I might be today if Somerset hadn't asked me to go to England? I learned then that when one door opens, another closes,' said Richards.

'Everything was set up for me to go to New York to study electrical engineering. My family were leaving Antigua to join my grandmother's relatives in America, and my father had made arrangements for me because he wanted me to have some qualification. I never had any ambition to earn my living from cricket. The thought had never occurred to me until Somerset came along, and in the end I had to plead with my father to change his mind about my future.

'I said: Let me go to England and if it's no good after two months I'll come home and go to college. Just let me give it a try.'

In the four years since Creed, the bookmaker, made the most spectacular gamble of his sporting life, Viv Richards has become the biggest thing in world cricket.

The cricketing public know him simply as a West Indian who scores more runs more excitingly than anyone else. Arguably, he is now a better player than the other Richards, Hampshire's Barry. But there's another side to Viv Richards, a man with much more than merely a magnificent collection of big scores and an enormous batting average.

His ambition 'to keep enjoying myself' means more than hitting into the next parish every bowler who dares confront him.

He likes discos, the Detroit Spinners and other soul music, and at Weston last week, after the Surrey match, he was listening to pop music in preference to Test Match Special.

He enjoys a glass of lager and an occasional vodka and lemonade, although his friends all agree that the only thing Viv does to excess is to score runs. He has a soft spot for Starsky and Hutch, fish and chips and pretty girls. He doesn't smoke and passengers wishing to smoke in his car are instructed to wind down every window and to lean as far out as possible.

He follows English football, watches Bristol City whenever he can, and clings to Pelé and Bobby Charlton as his favourite players. He admires Sidney Poitier, Muhammad Ali, and names Sir Garfield Sobers, Sir Donald Bradman and the three W's – Weekes, Worrell and Walcott – as his boyhood idols.

His is the most instantly recognisable face in Somerset. A five-minute walk down the main street of Taunton from his rent-free club flat to the bank has been known to take two hours, and his following down Milsom Street, in Bath, makes the Pied Piper of Hamelin sound out of tune.

'I am the same person now as when I first came here,' said Richards. 'Some players let success go to their heads, but I'm the same, success or failure. I make sure that nothing ever goes to my head.'

The Somerset players nicknamed him 'Black Magic'. In the world's Press he has been called, among other things, 'The Black Bradman.'

'I was always confident, that, given the opportunity, I could do it well. I fancy myself,' he added.

Richards is already looking ahead to when his cricket career finishes, although at 25 he has a long way to go. He runs a sports shop in Antigua with Andy Roberts, plans to build a house on the island and will definitely go back there one day . . . 'you always go back to your roots.'

His immediate task is to help win the Gillette Cup for Somerset. Richards, clearly Kerry Packer's top attraction for his Supertests, has signed a three-year contract with Somerset, subject to next month's High Court ruling on the TCCB's two-year ban on the cricketing pirates.

There are even whispers round the Quantocks that, given freedom to carry on playing, he will succeed Close as captain.

DAILY MAIL, 25 AUGUST 1977

NEW RULE OK

Viscount Cobham, speaking at the Football Writers Dinner, Criterion Restaurant, 3 May 1956, said he was playing in a county cricket match (as The Hon C. J. Lyttelton) for Worcestershire during the first season of the new lbw rule. The umpires were Bill Reeves and George Brown.

'When we batted we had *six* lbw decisions against us, and Maurice Turnbull said, non-committally, "Not a bad rule." But when they batted, they had *seven* against them.

At the fall of the thirteenth, Bill Reeves said to Brown, "Steady on, George, otherwise you'll get your thousand wickets in May!"'

Varsity Match, 1827

ROBIN MARLAR

Whatever views we may have on this and related subjects this is the week to raise a glass to Charles Wordsworth, nephew of the poet, and Herbert Jenner, captains of Oxford and Cambridge University in the first match between the Blues 150 years ago.

Wordsworth took the dark blue of Harrow to Oxford, Jenner the light blue from Eton to Cambridge. Wordsworth had to get leave from his tutor by pleading a trip to the dentist. The person who suggested this deception subsequently became Archbishop of Canterbury. Two years later Wordsworth was in poor shape for the cricket match after organising and rowing in the first Boat Race on the previous day.

Jenner kept wicket to Alfred Mynn without pads or gloves, but in those days hacking at football was allowed and shins were more used to bruises. If a cricket match survives for 150 years it is worth perpetual reinforcement, and Brearley's presence on the England balcony last week is a reminder of all the talent which has emerged, and which is hopefully still to come forth, from The Parks and Fenners, two of the most prolific cricket nurseries in the country.

SUNDAY TIMES, 26 JUNE 1977

Randall's Wonder Catch

JACK FINGLETON

Auckland, New Zealand, Third Test with England, First Day, 5 March 1978: New Zealand, First Innings, 113–3, M. G. Burgess c *Randall* b *Botham 50*

Burgess batted well, and played some splendid strokes. He was out to a blinder of a catch squarish on the off-side by Randall, who covers so many positions that often one is pushed to know where he is.

It would be interesting to slip a pedometer on to Randall's foot and find out just how much ground he covers in a day, but I guess he would wear out a few pedometers in a season.

As one who once fielded in the covers in a Test match I marvel at the ground he devours. He moves in many yards with his typical skip, as the bowler runs up, and he is at full speed when the ball is hit to him.

Thus yesterday he 'flew' yards, and dived to intercept a hard slash from Burgess, who had just got to his fifty in 137 minutes with five fours.

It was one of the best cover point catches I have seen.

SUNDAY TIMES, 5 MARCH 1978

Mid-wicket Decision

Southgate, the North London club, are due to play Streetly, Notts, this afternoon in a semi-final of the John Haig Trophy. One of their earlier matches, against Bedford Town, produced an interesting point.

Chris Payne, the Southgate skipper, played at a ball and most of the fieldsmen thought he had tickled it on to his pad. The batsmen ran a single. The umpire then, unexpectedly, signalled a leg bye. The bowler said, 'If you've ruled that he didn't hit the ball, how's that for lbw? The umpire gave Payne out. A correct decision?

It was. Many cricketing hawks know that any appeal is valid 'prior to the delivery of the next ball' (Law 47). What they may not know is that Payne could still have been given out had the umpire signalled the leg bye and immediately called 'Over.' A call of 'Time' at the end of a session invalidates an appeal, a call of 'Over' does not.

David Whiley, of the Association of Cricket Umpires, and the author of a witty umpiring book, has encountered such a case. 'I was sure the batsman had tickled the ball to the wicket-keeper,' he says. There was no appeal. I called 'Over.' The wicket-keeper and the bowler met in the middle of the pitch, chatted, and only then appealed. I gave the batsman out.' SUNDAY TIMES, 7 AUGUST 1977

One Day Cricket

JIM LAKER

For as long as I watch one-day cricket I cannot seriously believe I shall see a more dramatic day's cricket than the Gillette Cup semi-final played at Old Trafford between Lancashire and Gloucestershire on 28 July 1971.

Apart from an hour's delay at lunchtime through rain, play continued from 11 am to 8.50 pm in front of a crowd officially estimated at 23,520, who paid receipts of £9,738.

I am sure the latter figure is a correct one, but remain unconvinced of the attendance figure which would never take into account the hundreds of 'free-loaders' coming in over the top.

The vast crowd was still streaming in and jockeying for position as Tony Brown won the toss for Gloucester, and decided to bat on a perfect pitch of easy pace. Nobody was more anxious to do well than David Green, formerly of Lancashire, who, in the company of Ron Nichols, weathered the early attack of Lever and Shuttleworth. An opening stand of 57 gave Gloucester the necessary base before Green was run out.

Nichols battled on for an admirable fifty, but it was the mighty Procter who held the stage; a string of superb drives brought him nine fours and a six before Farokh Engineer took a brilliant catch to dismiss him.

The score was then 150 for 3, and Gloucester were ahead on points. Not for the first time Lancashire turned to the burly Jack Simmons to provide an answer. His immaculate off-spin brought his side back into the game, bowling his twelve overs for only 25 runs and a couple of wickets.

At 210 for 6 the odds now favoured Lancashire and despite an aggressive 29 not out from Mike Bissex, a final score of 229 left me feeling that the visitors were 30 or 40 runs short and a score of 230 was well within Lancashire's compass on a pitch unaffected by the rain, and offering no help to the bowlers.

As is their wont, Lancashire looked for a solid start from David Lloyd and Barry Wood, and this they duly supplied. Although the first fifty had taken seventeen overs, and eleven runs later Lloyd fell to Tony Brown, Harry Pilling and Barry Wood saw them safely into three figures, and it seemed that the game was their's for the taking. John Mortimore had different ideas. After the departure of Wood and Pilling, the Gloucester off-spinner, in a fine accurate spell, clean bowled Clive Lloyd and induced Farokh Engineer to hit his wicket.

With Davey accounting for Sullivan, Lancashire had slumped to 163 for 6, and the game was wide open. This enormous and vibrant crowd who had previously been cherishing and cheering every run went quiet. That clock had crept past the 7.30 pm mark, and the light was gradually worsening. Umpires Bird and Jepson consulted and play went on.

The new batsmen in charge were 'Skipper' Bond and Jack Simmons and they badly needed to right the ship. With typical Lancashire commonsense, and no trace of panic, they went about their task skilfully and professionally, and the colour gradually began to come back into the faces of the Lancashire supporters. These two added 40 runs, defying all the bowling changes made by Tony Brown, until Mortimore broke through again and bowled Simmons to make it 203 for 7.

Twenty-seven were wanted, three wickets in hand and six overs left. By this time it seemed impossible that the game could be finished that day. It was now very, very dark, the pavilion light casting shadows on the enclosure, and in the background Old Trafford Station had been ablaze with lights for some time. The umpires only needed a nod from Jack Bond for the play to be suspended when down the pavilion steps appeared David Hughes, unnoticed for more than one reason.

The focus was now on Bond. Would he decide to call it a day? He goes on record as saying that his first thought was to ensure that this noisy, excitable crowd would not be deprived of a finish that day. It would be a terrible anti-climax to come back the following day and complete the final twenty minutes or so in front of ten men and a dog. Jack Bond is an extremely honest man and I believe his thinking would be along those lines. Perhaps it was also supported by the fact that Gloucester had already been in the field for well over three hours and the strain was beginning to tell. Of the six overs left Procter and Davey had to bowl four of them, and after a night's rest may well be a different proposition next morning. Any lingering doubts were dispelled by the confidence of David Hughes who maintains that he purposely sat in a dark corner of the dressing room 'to become accustomed to the light!'

His reply to Bond's instructions to look for the singles was 'if I can see them skipper, I think I can hit them'.

In view of what followed it must have been the understatement of the year. Most people will forget that Hughes came within a whisker of being bowled first ball by John Mortimore and batted through a fine over from Davey, who was extremely difficult to pick up at all. In this light their only hope was to attack the slow off-spin of Mortimore.

What followed must go down as one of the most remarkable overs of all time. The unfortunate Mortimore was hammered for 24 runs in his next over, in a wonderful exhibition of shrewd and skilful hitting by David Hughes. There was no wild slogging or hitting across the line and it seemed that it was almost premeditated execution.

By dint of excellent footwork the first ball was hit over extra cover safely for four and the second ball deposited in the crowd at long-on for a mighty straight six. The crowd was going wild, up and down in their seats as Hughes, running like a hare, put the third ball through the off-side for two and the fourth wide of mid-on for two more. The cover drive off the fifth ball for another four was the shot of the match, and nobody could have bettered it. To crown it all the last ball was hit handsomely for six over mid-on, and unbelievably the scores were level.

Appropriately it was left to Bond to nudge Procter wide of gully for a single and the crowd erupted. The entire playing area was invaded. Lancashire had won a famous victory with David Hughes so rightly judged Man of the Match. The same people who had been queueing for a seat at eight o'clock that morning were rushing to get the last bus home from the ground after ten o'clock that night.

Jack Bond asserts that it took weeks to get over it, and no doubt David Hughes is still accepting drinks for his memorable achievement!

In acclaiming Lancashire's great day one cannot help but sympathise with Gloucester and John Mortimore, in particular. I can think of no reason for John to reproach himself or believe that he was responsible for his side's defeat. The fatal over did not include a solitary bad ball, although one could possibly argue that he might have pushed the ball through quickly on a fuller length round about the leg stump. This has never been John Mortimore's method. Praise be that he always goes down in my book as an attacking bowler, and did he not previously account for Lloyd, Engineer and Simmons in this manner?

For three minutes in that match he was unlucky to run across a man totally inspired to produce half a dozen shots worthy of being ranked with the greatest of our time, and when that happens, no matter who the bowler is, there is precious little that anyone can do about it.

One of the least publicised facts about this game and one which I am sure, in retrospect, had a profound bearing on the result, concerned the final period of play. The Gloucester side in fact must have achieved some kind of record with an unbroken spell of four hours on the field. There would be a public outcry if any side were asked to field from start of play at 11.30 am right the way through until the tea interval which, of course, is the equivalent of Gloucester's marathon effort in the field. A twenty-minute break in that final period would have allowed them vital breathing space, a chance coolly to assess the situation and break the Lancashire concentration, all of which must have been very much in their favour.

If the players unanimously agreed that it was some time before they recovered from their efforts, the same may also be said of the TV commentary team. For some time our producer in charge of BBC One cricket, David Kenning, had the happy knack of selecting the best of the one-day matches but on this occasion he was, for once, thwarted by the weather. Believing that the thrills and excitement of the semi-final would come from the other game between two evenly matched sides, Kent and Warwickshire, he took himself off to Canterbury, along with Peter West and Richie Benaud, and posted me north to complement the main coverage from Old Trafford. Only as an afterthought did he book Tony Lewis to help me out and make his TV debut as a commentator.

The inevitable happened, of course. Old Trafford was bathed in sunshine most of the day, and Canterbury was awash with overnight rain. A little after 10 am Tony and I took up our positions in the commentary box, and, apart from a short break when a shower held up play, recorded just about every ball bowled until we finally descended the scaffolding shortly after 9 pm. For obvious reasons we sat cross-legged over the last three hours!

Soon after 8 pm we had a call from the Controller of BBC One, Paul Fox, asking if there was any chance of play still being in progress at 8.50 pm. Peering through the gloom I replied that there was no chance unless the game was transferred over the road to the floodlights at the other Old Trafford. As everybody knows play did go on, and at 8.50 pm I received a message that on a ten-second count down the game would be taken live into the National News. Thus cricket history was made.

No one-day game that I have ever witnessed was more deserving of the immense publicity that surrounded it.

'ONE DAY CRICKET' BY JIM LAKER, B. T. BATSFORD LTD., LONDON, 1977

How One Wave of My Pencil Nearly Ended the Innings!

BASIL EASTERBROOK

Cricket, as Winston Place, the Lancashire opening batsman, once observed, is a wonderful thing for keeping the head small. The moment you cease to concentrate or take liberties is invariably the one when you get rolled over.

I remember vividly the 1953 Test at Old Trafford with Australia, our visitors this summer. Manchester was in one of its monsoon moods, and by late afternoon of the fifth and final day of the match each side had completed only one innings. Once England had saved the follow-on, only one result was possible – a draw, and it was written up as such by all present.

Our stories filed, the London-based writers left the formalities after tea to be taken care of by the agencies and departed to catch the early evening train. I think it was in the region of Crewe that the late Bruce Harris of the *Evening Standard* stuck his head into my compartment, where six of us were enjoying a convivial journey, and said: 'There's a fellow just joined the train who has been listening to the radio and he says Australia are 31 for 8.'

This was greeted with considerable ribaldry and cries of 'Push off, you old idiot,' or words to that effect. Sometime later the ticket collector arrived, and as he inspected our pieces of pasteboard, said conversationally, 'What about those Aussies losing all those wickets for 30-odd runs then?'

When the train drew into St Pancras a clutch of cricket writers emerged in a very fair imitation of the start of the Greyhound Derby, emitting agonised cries of 'Taxi, Taxi'. The *Sporting Chronicle*, still an all-sports national daily publication, was kind enough to retain my byline, but my intro appeared halfway down the second column.

Only the year before I had run foul of the Sports Editor of the *Evening Chronicle*, Manchester, on the Saturday afternoon of the Leeds Test. At this time the Press Box was at the back of the rugby stand where the telephones were. Time for copy was over when India began their second innings, but I sent through a message to be fudged that India had lost her first three wickets without scoring a run. Moments later my telephonist leant over my shoulder to say there was an urgent demand for me to speak to Manchester. I picked up the instrument and had said no more than 'Hello' before Jack Smith launched into a veritable tirade. He could, he told me, take a joke with the best of them, but not on a Saturday evening when he was trying to put his main sports edition to bed.

At this point came an ear-splitting roar that the said Mr Smith would probably have heard across the Pennines even without the aid of the telephone. 'What's that?' he asked sharply. I informed him my previous message was now out of date and should be altered to read: India nought for four.

The noises at the other end grew incoherent. Happily at this point confirmation of the score came from the Press Association. Jack was soon restored to his usual gentle, unassuming self. Freddie Trueman, the architect of that remarkable piece of cricket, found the story appealed to him so much that you will find it in his autobiography.

My first Test was against the New Zealanders at Lord's in 1949. It was a rather dull, inconclusive affair, but I shall never forget it for only a month or so before on the same ground I had created a line of journalistic and cricket history by becoming the only cricket writer ever to declare at headquarters or anywhere else if it comes to that. In those days the Press Box was next to the visiting team's balcony and I was talking to Norman Preston of the PA. As I talked I sharpened a pencil on to a pad of copypaper. When I finished I waved the pad to and fro outside the window to get rid of the chippings of wood and carbon.

Suddenly the current Editor of Wisden's Cricketers Almanack gripped my arm and said:

'My God, they are all coming in – you've declared!'

Bill Sime, the Nottingham captain, later to be appointed one of Her Majesty's judges, rushed out on to the balcony next door and by frantic signalling indicated the innings was to continue. There was one awful moment when after checking, the cavalcade of fielders, batsmen and umpires started to come again to the pavilion. Slowly, reluctantly, it seemed to me, they about turned, went back to the middle and the world went rightside again.

Crawford White backed away from me with the look on his face of a man who wanted the world to know he had never been friends with Benedict Arnold or Guy Fawkes and said slowly: 'I would not want to be in your shoes, mate.'

Another dear colleague made a swift gesture across his throat with a forefinger. But MCC are not so egg and strawberry as their tie might suggest, and no action was taken. It's a question in cricket quizzes nowadays, and Norman Preston went on dining out on the story, but I can tell you it was anything but funny that far off afternoon when the darling buds of an English spring were making their usual late appearance. TREND, JUNE 1977

How Football Saved England at Lord's

ROY PESKETT

The time is 6.45 pm, the date 30 June 1953. Lord's, scene of one of the most exciting days in its long Test history is almost deserted. Under the trees, near the Father Times Stand, a young couple slowly walk, deep in conversation. The man is Willie Watson, 32-year-old Yorkshire left-hander whose first Test century had just foiled Australia. The woman, his 30-year-old wife, Barbara. They were 'snatching' a few minutes together, the first since Watson took the field against the Australians last Thursday.

Mrs Watson had stayed at Lord's all day, missing three trains to see her husband become the hero of the hour. But Watson did not know that she was watching although her seat was only twenty yards from the England dressing room.

Mrs Watson told me: 'If Willie had been out early this morning, I would have gone back to Sunderland, where we live and have a sports shop, on the three o'clock train. When he was still in at lunchtime, I booked a seat on the 4.45. At the tea interval, when Willie wanted only sixteen runs for his century, I let my reservation go and decided to catch the 5.35 to Newcastle. Finally I said, "Oh hell, there's always another train, but this hundred I must see!" '

After their brief stroll together under the trees the Watsons separated, as they have done so many times this season, the cricketer to catch the 7.50 to the West Country where today he plays for Yorkshire against Somerset, the wife to a London hotel for a night's rest before the train home to take charge of Graham, their two-year-old only child, at the moment staying with grandmother.

'When will you next see Willie?' I asked.

The attractive Mrs Watson sighed: 'I don't really know. I shall have to look at the cricket fixtures. He is in London again over the week-end. I even have to travel when he is playing at home for Yorkshire!'

During the winter, Watson, one of the select band of men who has played for England both at cricket and football – he has played in seven Tests, scoring his first Test century yesterday, and four soccer internationals – is a professional with Sunderland. But, as he told me, 'Not even playing for England against Wales on my home ground of Roker Park, gave me such a thrill as I had today.'

It was a soccer players' day at Lord's. First Watson partnered Denis Compton (Arsenal Cup finalist and England) for 105 minutes, when Compton was out for 33. Then came the long stand with Trevor Bailey, amateur international who has played for Walthamstow Avenue in an Amateur Cup Final at Wembley.

Watson told me that the worst part of it all was the 'terrific concentration'. He said, 'I knew I mustn't get out especially after Denis Compton went. All I was concerned with was keeping my wicket intact. Neither Trevor nor I enjoyed our light lunch because we knew that the new ball, and Ray Lindwall, were due about three o'clock! The crowd knew it too, and I could feel the tension as the overs were slowly counted away. Then came the new ball, and Lindwall at his fastest. Finally, Lindwall was taken off and the crowd's relief, freely expressed, was nothing to mine!

'When I did get a chance to relax momentarily, I glanced in the direction where I knew my wife ought to be sitting. But I didn't know whether she had seen me get the hundred until we met afterwards.'

I can vouch for the freshness of this fit young international. After a quick bath and a hastily gulped soft drink, Watson – known as one of the best dressed players in football – changed and came out to answer my questions, looking as if he was just starting, not finishing, a five-day Test.

Trevor Bailey, hero No 2, who plays for Essex today against Middlesex, decided to 'nip home' to Southend last night, 'for a huge meal and a sleep in my own bed'. Bailey who, like Watson, received a tremendous ovation from the crowd on returning to the pavilion, batted in great pain for a considerable part of his innings, being three times hit on the hand from balls from Lindwall.

There was no time for celebration among the England players at the magnificent feat of saving a hopeless cause against the Australians (at the start of play England were 20 for 3; at the close, 282 for 7).

As soon as the kit was packed, the eleven split up to join their county sides for today's games. Watson, Wardle and Hutton travelled to Taunton; Graveney went by road to Bristol for the game with the Australians; Statham to Manchester; Brown to Chesterfield, and Kenyon to Worcester. Compton and Bailey will be at Lord's, Alec Bedser at Guildford – and Godfrey Evans has three lovely days rest!

DAILY MAIL, 1 JULY 1953

NO CRISPS?

All present were delighted by Freddie Brown's reply to a solemn question at the inaugural sports debate organised by the Lord's Taverners.

Brown, lately the MCC President, when a slim young cricketer on the notorious 'bodyline' tour of Australia in 1932–33, was perennial twelfth man, and was responsible for carrying drinks on to the field during intervals.

'Today,' he said, 'I understand they take orangeade. My order always included two brandies and soda, one whisky and soda, three glasses of champagne, two pints of beer for Larwood and Voce, and a glass of milk for Eddie Paynter.'

The team for which he carried the tray won the Ashes.

E. W. Swanton . . . the New Pope

It was quiet and peaceful in the Press Box at Lord's. The game of cricket out in the middle was being played without excitement or quarrel. Not even an appeal broke the cloistered calm.

Outside the world went about its business; war and pestilence; the balancing of the dollar and mark against the pound; electing a new Pope in Vatican City, after which, as you have probably read, they burn the election papers of the Cardinals in a great burst of white smoke.

Suddenly from the giant chimney stack alongside Lord's (now demolished) came smoke, white smoke.

And with it a voice like John Arlott's, 'Its okay boys, you can relax . . . they have elected E. W. Swanton as the new Pope.'

Gentlemen v *Players · the Only Tied Match*

This was the only tie in the history of the Gentlemen v *Players matches, which were played between 1806 and 1962, when the series was abolished as amateur status was removed from first class cricket. Scores: Players 203 and 181, Gentlemen 235 and 149.*

On Saturday, after a wonderfully exciting struggle, the match, at Kennington Oval, ended in a tie. Overnight the Gentlemen had been left with an innings to play and 150 runs to win. For so good a team, the task did not seem a heavy one, and had the wicket been as hard and fast on Saturday as it was on Friday the runs would, no doubt, have been obtained.

The violent storm of Friday night however, had a considerable effect on the ground, and batsmen were thereby placed at an obvious disadvantage. From the commencement of play until the fall of the last wicket the game never flagged in interest, but as a full description is given below, only a few points need here be mentioned.

The prominent cricketers of the afternoon were Mr A. P. Lucas and Flowers. Mr Lucas went in first and took out his bat for 47, his innings lasting as nearly as possible three and three-quarter hours. No finer display of steady batting has been seen this season. Half a dozen bowlers were tried, four of them more than once, but Mr Lucas mastered them all, his defence being as stubborn as his patience was inexhaustible.

When he had scored eight a curious incident occurred. Barlow was bowling round the wicket at the Pavilion End, and Mr Lucas made a sharp cut very low down to point. Lockwood took the ball and there was a general appeal for the catch. Jupp was the umpire at the Pavilion wicket, but, as Barlow had been in front of him at the time of the hit he could not give a decision and an appeal was made to Street. The latter was equally unable to decide the point and Mr Lucas, of course, went on with his innings. Flowers bowled as well as he ever bowled in his life and took six wickets at a cost of only forty runs, a great performance.

The attendance was smaller than that on Thursday and Friday, intending visitors having no doubt fancied that the Gentlemen would gain an easy victory. There had not been a tie game at the Oval since Surrey *v* Middlesex in 1876.

Play began soon after midday, the Gentlemen's task being commenced by Mr Lucas and Mr Hornby. Peate and Flowers were entrusted with bowling. From Peate's first ball Mr Lucas made a cut for four, and in his second over Mr Hornby made an off drive of the same value. After this, however, runs came rather slowly, a dozen overs being sent down for seven singles and a leg bye.

Then, with the score at eighteen, the batsmen were parted, Mr Hornby being brilliantly caught by Shrewsbury at extra mid-off. The hit was a hard one, but the fieldsman, springing up, took the ball with one hand. This was as good a piece of cricket as anything in the afternoon. Mr C. T. Studd went in first wicket down, and the bowling was quickly changed at both ends. Barnes displaced Peate at 25, and Barlow took the ball from Flowers at 29.

Under the influence of bright sunshine the wicket was evidently becoming more difficult, and Barnes bowling bumped very awkwardly. Barlow's first five overs were all maidens and it was in his fifth over that the question arose as to Mr Lucas being caught at point. The total was then 33, and Mr Lucas had scored eight. The batsman immediately afterwards drove Barnes to the off for four, a splendid hit. Mr Studd drove the same bowler for three and the total quickly reached 49. Emmett then went on to bowl in place of Barnes, and from his first ball Mr Studd was caught at long-off. Robinson had been purposely placed very wide for the Cambridge captain's favourite stroke and the ball, although hit hard enough to reach the boundary, went straight to him; two wickets down for 49.

With the score unaltered, Lord Harris was completely beaten by a ball from Barlow, and Mr Wright only made a single before having his leg stump bowled down by Emmett. The Gentlemen had now lost four wickets for 50 runs, and the Players had all the best of the game.

However, on Mr Steel joining Mr Lucas there followed a marked change, and the batting that followed being some of the very best of the match. Mr Lucas continued to play in the most correct and careful fashion and contented himself with a defensive game, but Mr Steel adopted quite a different method and punished the bowlers severely. Twice he sent Barlow to leg for four, and then, in one over from Emmett, he made cuts for four and three, the first going through the slips and the second past point. Ulyett and Barnes were put on at 72, but it would have been a wiser course to have tried Bates and Peate. Mr Steel showed himself completely master of the fast bowling, and after hitting Ulyett to leg for four, he cut Barnes for the same number.

At the adjournment the total was 86, Mr Steel being 30 not out and Mr Lucas not out 19. Out of the 36 runs put on since he went in, Mr Steel had thus scored all but six. Mr Lucas had made one hit, a cut for three off Emmett, and there had been three leg byes. On the game being resumed at a quarter to three, the bowling was shared by Peate and Flowers. The former bowled three maidens, and two singles and a three were scored from Flowers. Mr Steel was then out *lbw* for a brilliant and invaluable innings of 31; five wickets for 91. With half their wickets down, the Gentlemen wanted 59 to win the match. Mr Forbes was the next batsman and in the course of about ten overs he carefully scored four singles. He attempted to drive from Flowers bowling and was easily caught by Shrewsbury at extra mid-off; six wickets for 99.

Mr Leslie came in, but after making a single and a splendid on drive for four, he was also caught at extra mid-off by Shrewsbury. There were now seven wickets down and the score was only 104. All this time Mr Lucas was playing as steadily as ever, but naturally enough the slow bowlers with their greater spin and break caused him more trouble than the fast ones had done. Mr Kemp, the next batsman, showed no lack of confidence but was far from comfortable with the bowling. Mr Lucas got Flowers through the slips for three, and two overs later glanced him finely to long leg for four, but at 115 a good catch at long-on dismissed Mr Kemp. With only two wickets to fall the Gentlemen wanted 35 to win, and the chances seemed all against them. Mr Frank joined Mr Lucas and from that point to the finish the game was watched with ever increasing interest. Seven runs having been added, Barnes was tried again, in place of Peate, and in his first over Mr Frank gave a sharp chance at the wicket. The catch, had it come off, would have been a good one. The two batsmen played with great nerve and the bowlers and fieldsmen were, of course, thoroughly on their mettle.

Unluckily for the Players a bye went to the boundary, and just afterwards Mr Lucas hit Barnes splendidly to the boundary for four. This made the total 134, or only sixteen to win. Barlow went on for Barnes at the Gasworks end. A maiden was bowled from each end, and then Mr Lucas scored a single.

Now followed three more maidens, the bowling being wonderfully straight and good. Another single was scored, but at 136 a ball from Flowers beat Mr Frank and just took the bails. Though he only made six runs the Yorkshireman had played sound cricket at a most trying time. With fourteen runs wanted Mr Rotherham, the last man, went to the wicket. He got a two in the slips off Flowers, and with four singles the score was quickly carried to 142, or only eight to win. Mr Rotherham then made a lofty hit to long-on and looked certain to be out, but to the intense disappointment of the Players, Bates missed a palpable catch, getting the ball into his hands and then letting it drop.

Two maiden overs were bowled and encouraged by his good fortune Mr Rotherham sent a four through the slips off Barlow. Mr Lucas then scored a single off Flowers, the hit being a possible chance to Robinson at short mid-on, and from the last ball in the same over a single to Mr Rotherham brought the scores level.

This fact was announced by an enthusiastic cheer, the excitement having reached the highest level.

The Players held a consultation and as the result of their deliberations, Peate was put on in place of Barlow. The change was successful for Mr Rotherham, after playing the first ball, was bowled by the second, and in this way a most splendid match ended in a tie.

Needless to say, there was plenty of cheering!

None of the Players bowlers were ever collared as these figures show:

	OVERS	MAIDENS	RUNS	WICKETS
Peate	30·2	16	25	1
Flowers	44	24	40	6
Barnes	13	7	29	0
Barlow	23	11	26	1
Emmett	7	5	10	2
Ulyett	4	2	7	0

For the record, the full details:

PLAYERS

FIRST INNINGS		SECOND INNINGS	
1. R. G. Barlow *b* Steel	47	*c* Forbes *b* Steel	31
2. G. Ulyett *c* Kemp *b* Steel	63	*c-b* Rotherham	10
3. S. Shrewsbury *b* Studd	11	*b* Steel	0
4. E. Lockwood *b* Rotherham	18	*b* Steel	8
5. W. Barnes *c* Steel *b* Rotherham	20	*st* Kemp *b* Steel	28
6. W. Robinson *c* Forbes *b* Studd	8	*c-b* Steel	6
7. W. Bates not out	19	*b* Frank	76
8. W. Flowers *c* and *b* Rotherham	0	*c* Lucas *b* Steel	7
9. T. Emmett *b* Rotherham	8	*b* Steel	0
10. E. Peate *b* Rotherham	0	*c-b* Frank	3
11. M. Sherwin *b* Rotherham	3	not out	2
bye 1, l-byes 5	6	byes 4, l-byes 6	10
TOTAL	203		181

GENTLEMEN

1.	Lord Harris *b* Bates	38	*b* Barlow	0(4)
2.	Mr A. P. Lucas run out	8	not out	47(1)
3.	Mr C. T. Studd *c* Sherwin *b* Emmett	30	*c* Robinson *b* Emmett	20(3)
4.	Mr A. W. Wright *c* Bates *b* Barlow	21	*b* Emmett	1(5)
5.	Mr A. N. Hornby run out	20	*c* Shrewsbury *b* Flowers	11(2)
6.	Mr A. G. Steel *b* Barnes	21	*lbw* *b* Flowers	31(6)
7.	Mr W. F. Forbes *st* Lockwood *b* Barnes	28	*c* Shrewsbury *b* Flowers	4(7)
8.	Mr M. C. Kemp *b* Barlow	6	*c* Barlow *b* Flowers	2(9)
9.	Mr C. F. Leslie *lbw* *b* Barnes	12	*c* Shrewsbury b Flowers	5(8)
10.	Mr J. Frank *b* Flowers	16	*b* Flowers	6(10)
11.	Mr H. Rotherham not out	13	*b* Peate	11(11)
	byes 19, l-byes 2 wide 1	22	byes 7, l-byes 4	11
	TOTAL	235		149

THE STANDARD, 28, 29, 30 JUNE 1883

Giant in a Floppy Hat and Specs

IAN JARRETT

There will be a moment today at Lord's when an England batsman will play the ball into the covers, look up ... and stop dead in his tracks. Coming at him, all arms and gangling grace, will be that familiar stooping, swooping figure of the player they call the Supercat.

Clive Lloyd is still not a man to be trifled with, even when age and a couple of knee operations may have shaved a split second or two off his speed of reaction.

At thirty-four, and approaching the end of a brilliant Test career, the man in the white floppy hat is determined that no one will be fool enough to take liberties, least of all England in today's Prudential World Cup Final.

Supercat. Supercool. And a Superstar. Lloyd, the West Indies captain, will be the player whom the crowd will warm to as World Cup emotions boil over.

Smokin' Viv Richards may provide an hour of violence with the bat. Andy Roberts or Michael Holding could cause mayhem with the ball. Ian Botham or David Gower may for a time snap back for England.

Nothing is likely to compare with big Clive's contribution if he can get his eye and 6ft 4in frame in tune early on. He will walk out all lithe lazy elegance, intensely peering up at the sky through rimless spectacles and holding his bat in massive hands which make it appear more like a matchstick. This is the formidable black figure who has the crowds on their seats from Lord's to Lahore, from Melbourne to Madras. If we are lucky we will see the full Lloyd repertoire. The seemingly effortless levered six; the cover drive which you miss if you blink; the leg glance which is whipped away at the last possible moment.

Shots such as these brought Lloyd a searing century in 82 balls when the West Indies won the first World Cup at Lord's four years ago. Lloyd's innings was near perfect that day. It combined style and savagery to such remarkable effect that it won him the Man of the Match award when a momentous struggle against Australia came to a thrilling climax just before nine in the evening.

Lloyd, the left-hander from steamy colour-splashed Guyana, now says about that epic innings, 'When I went out to bat it was a tense situation. But I had a feeling even then that it was going to go well.'

It went well, all right. Lloyd met everything in the middle of the bat from the very first ball, playing as straight then as he has always done in his leadership of the West Indies side.

After 65 Tests – thirty as captain – eight overseas tours and 4,594 runs, Lloyd is understandably running out of ambitions in first-class cricket. 'There is not much more that I can want to do,' he says.

You will find his remarkable record in any cricket annual ... a debut century against England in Port of Spain ... a debut century against Australia in Brisbane ... an unbeaten 201 in 120 minutes for the West Indies against Glamorgan. The record goes on and on.

But what you won't find among the facts and figures is the real effect of Lloyd's leadership on the bubbling West Indies. There was a time when the men from the Caribbean had little stomach for a fight. Shoot the chief and the braves would run away. Not now though. There is backbone and character in this side. It has steely resolve to match the talent of the players.

However much England huff and puff today, Clive Lloyd's West Indians won't all fall down without one helluva fight.

THE SUN, 23 JUNE 1979

COMMENTARY BY JIM LAKER

Jim Laker, during chat on past players while rain held up a TV commentary ... 'Denis Compton was the most difficult English batsman I ever bowled against. During that 1947 season I suppose I got the same sort of average as the others. I trapped him once at the Oval, caught at long off for 176!'

Headingly, fourth Test: As Geoff Boycott's leg glance took him from 187 to 191 (the total at which he was out) TV commentator Jim Laker said: 'The ball went like a marble on a skating rink.'

Companions of Honour

The *Daily Telegraph* announced on 9 September 1980:

'John Arlott, who retired from the BBC radio broadcasting, has been made an honorary member of the MCC.' These are the companions of honour who join him:

Honorary members, *United Kingdom*: D. B. Close, B. L. D'Oliveira, R. Illingworth, G. Pullar, F. J. Titmus, J. V. Wardle, M. J. C. Allom, R. A. C. Forrester, R. E. S. Wyatt, N. W. D. Yardley. *Australia*: F. W. Bennett, T. C. Coldwell, J. W. Gleeson, N. J. N. Hawke, G. D. McKenzie, A. P. Sheahan, K. R. Stackpole. *East Africa*: Major H. A. Collins. *Hong Kong*: E. H. Wilson. *Singapore*: J. C. Cooke. *South Africa*: J. L. Pamensky, M. R. Verschis, K. J. Funston, A. J. Pilley, A. M. B. Rowan. *USA*: J. R. Gardiner. *West Indies*: B. St. E. Atkinson, C. Griffith, R. B. Kanhai. *New Zealand*: B. E. Congden, B. F. Hastings, V. Pollard. *India*: C. G. Borde, F. M. Engineer. *Pakistan*: Saeed Ahmed.

Geoffrey Reaches the Ton

The good-humoured but dramatic scene as Geoffrey Boycott reached his hundredth 100 in first-class cricket came on his favourite ground at Headingley, in the Fourth Test *v* Australia, 11 August 1977.

The bowler was Greg Chappell. Boycott straight drove the ball past him and it sped on to the boundary. Before that, however, Boycott dropped his bat and raised both arms to the sky. Within seconds he was mobbed. When a policeman finally restored order it could be seen that he had had his England cap whipped off his head. Another policeman brought out two Yorkshire caps, and he chose one. The game proceeded with Greg Chappell bowling a bouncer!

Then over the barriers came a prancing youth waving Boycott's England cap which, snatched by Australian Hookes, was handed to the English hero, who passed on the 'White Rose' cap to the umpire – and the game went on. But not before Boycott had shaken hands with the youth, who confessed he was a Lancastrian!

Boycott was last out for 191 made in 627 minutes from a total of 436, and England finally won by an innings and 85 runs, as his autographed card shows.

YORKSHIRE COUNTY CRICKET CLUB

CROWN PAINTS were used to redecorate this ground

HEADINGLEY CRICKET GROUND, LEEDS

FOURTH TEST MATCH

8p **ENGLAND v. AUSTRALIA** 8p

THURSDAY, FRIDAY, SATURDAY, MONDAY & TUESDAY, 11th, 12th, 13th, 15th & 16th AUGUST, 1977

ENGLAND WON BY AN INNINGS AND 85 RUNS

ENGLAND

	First Innings		Second Innings	
*1	J. M. Brearley c Marsh b Thomson	0		
2	G. Boycott c Chappell b Pascoe	191		
3	R. A. Woolmer c Chappell b Thomson	37		
4	D. W. Randall lbw b Pascoe	20		
5	A. W. Greig b Thomson	43		
6	G. R. J. Roope c Walters b Thomson	34		
7	I. T. Botham b Bright	0		
†8	A. P. E. Knott lbw Bright	57		
9	D. L. Underwood c Bright b Pascoe	6		
10	M. J. Hendrick c Robinson b Pascoe	4		
11	R. G. D. Willis not out	5		
	Extras...	39	Extras...	
	Total...	436	Total...	

FALL OF WICKETS

	1	2	3	4	5	6	7	8	9
First Innings:	1-0	2-82	3-105	4-201	5-275	6-398	7-398	8-412	9-422
Second Innings:	1-	2-	3-	4-	5-	6-	7-	8-	9-

Bowling Analysis	Overs	Mdns.	Runs	Wkts.	Overs	Mdns.	Runs	Wkts.
J. R. Thomson	34	7	113	4				
M. H. N. Walker	48	21	97	0				
L. S. Pascoe	34.4	10	91	4				
K. D. Walters	3	1	5	0				
R. Bright	26	9	66	2				
G. Chappell	10	2	25	0				

* Denotes Captain † Denotes Wicket-Keeper

Umpires: W. E. ALLEY & W. L. BUDD

Scorers: E. I. LESTER & D. SHERWOOD

PREVIOUS RESULTS IN THE SERIES

First Test — Lords — MATCH DRAWN.
Second Test — Old Trafford — ENGLAND won by 9 wickets.
Third Test — Trent Bridge — ENGLAND won by 7 wickets.

AUSTRALIA

	First Innings		Second Innings	
1	R. B. McCosker run out	27	c Knott b Greig	12
2	I. C. Davis lbw Hendrick	0	c Knott b Greig	19
*3	G. Chappell c Brearley b Hendrick	4	c Greig b Willis	36
4	D. W. Hookes lbw Botham	24	lbw Hendrick	21
5	K. D. Walters c Hendrick b Botham	4	lbw Woolmer	15
6	R. D. Robinson c Greig b Hendrick	20	b Hendrick	20
†7	R. W. Marsh c Knott b Botham	2	c Randall b Hendrick	63
8	R. Bright not out	9	c Greig b Hendrick	5
9	M. H. N. Walker c Knott b Botham	7	b Willis	30
10	J. R. Thomson b Botham	0	b Willis	0
11	L. S. Pascoe b Hendrick	0	not out	0
	Extras...	6	Extras...	27
	Total...	103	Total...	248

FALL OF WICKETS

	1	2	3	4	5	6	7	8	9
First Innings:	1-8	2-26	3-52	4-57	5-60	6-77	7-87	8-100	9-100
Second Innings:	1-31	2-35	3-63	4-97	5-130	6-167	7-179	8-244	9-245

Bowling Analysis	Overs	Mdns.	Runs	Wkts.	Overs	Mdns.	Runs	Wkts.
R. G. D. Willis	5	0	35	0	14	7	32	3
M. J. Hendrick	15.3	2	41	4	22.5	6	54	4
I. T. Botham	11	3	21	5	17	3	47	0
A. W. Greig					20	7	64	2
R. A. Woolmer					8	4	8	1
D. L. Underwood					8	3	16	0

Hours of Play: First Second Third and Fourth Days, 11-30 a.m. to 6-30 p.m.
Fifth Day, 11-00 a.m. to 5-30 p.m. or 6-00 p.m.
Lunch: 1-30 p.m. to 2-10 p.m. Tea: 4-15 p.m. to 4-35 p.m.

NEXT MATCH IN YORKSHIRE
YORKSHIRE v. LANCASHIRE at Bradford
20th, 22nd and 23rd August, 1977

This was his record to that date:

In England	
for Yorkshire (county championship)	57
for Yorkshire (outside championship)	8
for England (in Tests)	9
for England XIs	5
for T. N. Pearce's XI	1
for D. H. Robin's XI	1
	81

Abroad	
for England (in Tests)	5
for MCC	13
for Transvaal	1
	100

And this was the list of the immortals he joined:

Jack Hobbs (Surrey) 1905–1923	197
Patsy Hendren (Middlesex) 1907–1928	170
Wally Hammond (Gloucestershire) 1920–1935	167
Philip Mead (Hants) 1905–1927	153
Herbert Sutcliffe (Yorkshire) 1919–1932	149
Frank Woolley (Kent) 1906–1929	145
Len Hutton (Yorkshire) 1934–1961	129
W. G. Grace (Gloucestershire) 1865–1895	126
Denis Compton (Middlesex) 1936–1952	123
Tom Graveney (Gloucestershire) 1948–1964	122
Don Bradman (Australia) 1927–1947	117
Andy Sandham (Surrey) 1911–1935	107
Colin Cowdrey (Kent) 1950–1973	107
Tom Hayward (Surrey) 1893–1913	104
John Edrich (Surrey) 1956–1977	102
Leslie Ames (Kent) 1926–1950	102
Ernest Tyldesley (Lancashire) 1909–1934	102
Geoffrey Boycott (Yorkshire) 1962–	100

Twenty-six years earlier another great Yorkshireman neared his 'ton' in a Test match. He was Len Hutton, and he was on 99 hundreds when he began his second innings against South Africa in the Third Test at Old Trafford in 1951.

England needed just 139 to win and Jack Ikin (38) and Simpson (4 not out) gave Hutton most of the strike. He was 94 not out when one run was required. He had to hit a six, but could only manage a four.

ROY PESKETT

Wilf Wooller · Fighter

PETER JACKSON

Wilf Wooller's colourful career as one of the most consistently controversial figures in British sport during the past 40 years, ends a trifle prematurely this week with his retirement from Glamorganshire County Cricket Club.

At around 4.30 tomorrow afternoon the longest serving Secretary in first-class cricket will raise a glass of sherry with the office staff at 6 High Street, in Cardiff's City Centre, lock the door behind him for the last time and leave the county club he has been serving since 1938.

Wooller goes three weeks before his 65th birthday, to spend his last month in Glamorgan's employment on holiday and doubtless reflect on a lifetime as the all-rounder who took on all-comers.

'I have no regrets, none at all,' Wooller said, 'I thoroughly enjoyed every minute of what has been a marvellous experience. My attitude to life is to do what I think is right.

'You lose a hell of a lot in life by sitting on the fence. No, if I had my time all over again, I wouldn't change anything. I have never believed in backing away because you think you are going to get hurt.'

Wooller played eighteen times for Wales, one of the great three-quarters. He made one appearance for Cardiff City (as centre-forward), spent three and half years as a prisoner of the Japanese, captained Glamorgan to their first county championship in 1948, and helped select England cricket teams for five years.

He could have been a Test cricketer himself had he been able to tour South Africa in 1948 and India in 1951.

Wooller's off-the-field activities have been every bit as spectacular, right from the day in June 1936 when Cambridge magistrates fined him £5 after Wooller and another undergraduate went out to celebrate end of examinations, got 'pretty plastered' and were spotted removing the receiver, valued at 14s. 6d. (72½p.), from a telephone kiosk.

In his time Wooller has lambasted an array of formidable opponents, ranging from Government Ministers to the Archbishop of Wales, and anyone who did not support the maintenance of sporting links with South Africa.

He even provoked a row among educationalists by writing in the 1967 Varsity rugby match programme: 'The inflexibly high academic entrance level ensures that the greatest number of pimply swots enter Oxford and Cambridge, presenting a barrier often too high for the individual who has spread his energies at school over the wider front of sports as well as study.'

Wooller has been the central figure in some of the most outrageous events ever to take place on a cricket pitch.

At Trent Bridge in 1951 Nottinghamshire captain Reg Simpson, incensed by Wooller's slow batting, bowled underarm and appealed for lbw when Glamorgan's captain padded up.

He once sued a Sunday newspaper over allegations of gamesmanship, giving the £250 out of court settlement to his wife to do out the kitchen, which then became known in the Wooller household as the '*Empire News* Kitchen.'

Wooller is the only county cricket secretary to fill a town hall over a threatened resignation, and the only one to offer a crowd their money back to protest at Brian Close's batting on into the second day at Swansea.

He also has the dubious distinction of being the only secretary the late Arthur Fagg almost threw a bowl of soup at during his umpiring career. 'I don't care if it costs me my job,' Fagg said. 'I'll never umpire again while that man is secretary.'

Wooller said: 'Anyone can avoid criticism by sitting on the fence, but if you do nothing, you tend to end up a nobody.'

Wooller may be retiring from Glamorgan, but as a member of the National Union of Journalists he intends to concentrate more on his rugby and cricket writings.

'Might even do a book or two as well as the garden,' he says, 'I can even save myself £500 a year making my own wine and beer. I've had a very full life. I'm grateful for good health and a fine physique, but, Good God alive, I can't retire completely.'

Woollerisms

Wooller on Denis Howell during an Oxford Union debate on politics and sport: 'He is not unlike a 50p. piece – double faced, many sided and intrinsically not worth a great deal.'

On the opponents of the 1970 South Africa cricket tour which never took place: 'They are either lefties, weirdies or odd bods. Some of them may be all three.'

On South Africa's right to play international sport: 'Do you ever hear of a Jew in Soviet football? No, because they are all screwed up.'

On former Conservative Sports Minister, Eldon Griffiths: 'I'm not very impressed by him. He is a politician playing at sport.'

In reply to the Archbishop of Wales's threat to resign his Glamorgan membership if they played cricket against South Africa: 'Its time the church confined itself to spiritual matters which I find sadly lacking in this permissive era.'

DAILY MAIL, 17 OCTOBER 1977

Computer Names Thomson Fastest

Australian fast bowler Jeff Thomson is the fastest and most accurate bowler in world cricket – according to the computer.

Thomson scored highest on November 22 at Perth when most of the top pace bowlers were invited to be measured by camera and computer. Missing were Australia's Rodney Hogg and England's Bob Willis.

Each bowler had eight balls – a computer printed out the speeds to 100ths of a second. Thomson's fastest was 91·86 mph, well clear of Michael Holding (West Indies) with 87·76. The full results:

1. Jeff Thomson (Australia)	91·86 mph
2. Michael Holding (West Indies)	87·76
3. Imran Khan (Pakistan)	86·77
4. Garth Le Roux (South Africa)	86·58
5. Colin Croft (West Indies)	86·45
6. Andy Roberts (West Indies)	86·08
7. Dennis Lillee (Australia)	84·72
8. Wayne Daniel (West Indies)	82·90
9. Len Pascoe (Australia)	81·73
10. Richard Hadlee (New Zealand)	80·62
11. Mike Procter (South Africa)	79·87
12. Sarfraz Nawaz (Pakistan)	78·88

REUTER, 22 NOVEMBER 1979

KEEPING IT DARK

What does Geoffrey Boycott, England's only world class player, think of the present kerfuffle and the MCC bowlers in the West Indies.

As usual, the Greatest Living Yorkshireman's mind has been concentrating on cricket matters, and he told a friend the other day:

'I'd like to paint my face black and go in for this lot against our bloody attack ...' NIGEL DEMPSTER, DAILY MAIL 4 MARCH 1981

Apochryphal story attributed to Lord Tennyson, martinet captain of Hampshire. With Yorkshire dashing about trying to finish off the match in two days, the good Lord appealed against the light, it seemed, every other ball, only to be turned down.

Finally, No 11, Lofty Herman, came in to bat. Lord Tennyson called down the wicket, 'Terrible light, Herman', to get the astonishing, but loyal, reply, 'My Lord, I can hear your voice, but I cannot see you.'

Even the umpires had to come in after that.

Ode (Owed) to Bannister

For Sportsmail cricket writer Alex Bannister, the final day of the final Test in Sydney yesterday was his last report from a cricket tour. The England team, led by manager Doug Insole, marked the occasion by presenting him with a gold travelling clock inscribed:

> 'Australia 1978–79. To Alex – thanks for the memories – from the England Touring Party.'

Then Insole read out this poem to the man from the *Mail*.

> You've suffered in Jamaica,
> Freaked out in Bangalore,
> You've done your stint in Auckland,
> For thirty years or more.
> You've gnashed your teeth in Sydney,
> In Cape Town you've been tough,
> Wept buckets in Karachi,
> Where you've filed some lovely stuff.
> But now we hear your touring days
> Are drawing to a close,
> No more shall we be privileged
> To read your trenchant prose.
> We thought we ought to tell you
> We shall miss you when you've gone
> And that we've had no cause at all
> To doubt whose side you're on.
> So we trust that as you reminisce
> When all is said and done
> You'll reckon that its been worth while,
> And 'best of luck, old son'.

DAILY MAIL, 15 FEBRUARY 1979

CASE AND BATSMAN DISMISSED

During the hearing of the assault charge against Ian Botham at Grimsby Crown Court, in September 1981, the following dialogue took place between England's then cricket captain and the prosecuting counsel.

Mr Richards: 'To kick a man when he is on the ground is cowardly.'

Ian Botham: 'That's one thing I am not.'

Counsel: 'In sport you have to have an aggressive spirit.'

Botham: 'That doesn't mean I hit the umpire when he gives me out!'

Compton · Part of England's Summer

NEVILLE CARDUS

From time to time, in most walks of life, a man appears who rises above his particular job and attracts the attention of people who are not intensely interested in his vocation. He has the appeal of what we conveniently call 'personality', though few of us are able to define the term. 'Handsome is as handsome does' is an old and very sensible saying, so true indeed that even a Denis Compton is obliged to prove his skill day after day, as he and the rest of us have found cause ruefully to realise only yesterday. It is apparently not enough that he should 'look well' and embody charm and appeal in all his actions in the field. Some cricketers, on the other hand, may show abnormal technique perpetually, breaking records by rote: yet they fail to achieve 'glamour' in an age that insists on it.

He was baptised Denis Charles Scott Compton, and he was born only a mile or two from Lord's in the month of May, the month when the cricket season blooms and blossoms; and his father not only loved the game but was good at it himself. Denis was endowed with sturdy loose limbs, square shoulders and strong wrists enlivened with suppleness. He was born with an inexhaustible flow of spirits and an eye that sees swiftly and can usually seek out the bright lining of a cloud; and not only that, it is an eye that wins friends at a glance. He is not tall but not short; just the right build, mingling the physical attributes of cricketer and footballer.

Nature came to him with her cornucopia pretty full, and she let him help himself to it – for a while. Best of all, she brought to him a modest mind, without which the straight bat is only a symbol of vanity – not that Compton's bat is always straight. As we shall see, he has his own way of rendering first principles up to date.

Only the other year, it seems – time flies quickly in the cricketer's life, with wars ripping out whole chunks of summers – people going to Lord's and entering the ground at the W. G. Grace gates were buying score-cards from a bright-eyed boy, and he was Compton.

Yes, his career has contained all the romantic ingredients; upward flight from the bottom rung. But no writer of a boy's story would risk a sudden eclipse of his tyro at the height of his fame, in Australia too! Let us keep to the main pattern – 'card of the match, sir?'; then, at the age of eighteen, our hero is playing for Middlesex at Lord's, the historic place shaded by great ghosts; and all London around him on a June day, all granted him without a hard fight, gift added unto gift, the plant in the proper soil from the start. For his first season he scores 1,004 runs, average 34·62. He gets a century in his sixth match.

At the age of twenty he is chosen to play for England, and facing Australian bowling in a Test match for the first time he gets a century.

War merely gives him the schoolboy's second wind; there seems no summit beyond his reach. He lowers the record of the one and only Jack Hobbs, eighteen hundreds in one memorable summer. After beating at home the record aggregate in a season of Tom Hayward, 3,816 runs to the Old Master's 3,518, he goes on to score two centuries in a Test match against Australia when he first plays there.

Today he is thirty-four years old and should have been rather in need of crutches. He throws off vicissitude without a shrug; he even throws off a sudden dreadful blow from his deceitful fairies, and throws it off without spite. He sometimes seems to trust his stars dangerously, grateful if they are ascendant but apparently scarcely aware if they are not. But genius – even genius – needs to choose the right moment.

Compton came to the high summer of his renown in a period when we all badly wanted the like of him on our fields, for the purpose of rejuvenation. His cricket, in 1947, gave a nation-wide pleasure which was somehow symbolical. In a world tired, disillusioned and threadbare, heavy with age and deprivation, this happy cricketer spread his favours everywhere, and thousands of us, young and old, ran his runs with him. Here at any rate was something unrationed. There were no coupons in an innings by Denis Compton. He was contagious; he liberated impulses checked for long amongst all sorts and conditions of English folk – women as well as men, girls as well as boys. He embraced a new public in search of entertainment and release, a public which knows nothing of the old divisions that restricted sport to 'men's games'. Denis hath his fans not less dewy-eyed than those of Hollywood.

Is he a great batsman? I would prefer to describe him as a richly gifted one who is a stroke-player of distinction and some originality. He certainly isn't Hutton's equal in technique, and nature didn't intend that he should be. Hutton is obviously the more organised batsman of the two; he possesses what I shall here call power of conception, ability to see a long way ahead in an innings. A big score by Hutton is thought out, or is the consequence of deliberation, either before or during its execution.

Compton seems frequently to play according to mood, or what once on a time was called the inspiration of the moment. Hutton's cricket is old in the head, rational and responsible. Compton's cricket is never old in the head; for all its schooling and skill it simply will not grow up. If Hutton had run into half of Compton's appalling misfortunes in Australia during the Test matches of 1950–51 he would have extricated himself by a severe bracing of the mind and will. Compton was soon at a loss – an Aladdin who had forgotten how to rub the lamp and pronounce the necessary Abracadabra.

It is the failing of all sorts of criticism to consider an artist's or performer's technique apart from the individual who is using it, and to regard skill as a thing in itself which moves of its own volition and always in the same way. The truth is that if the technical equipment of Hutton could somehow be given to Compton, inoculated into his bones and being one night while he slept, and his own taken away from him, we should see little essential difference in his cricket next day.

With Hutton we have the order and fulfilment of science; with Compton we have the short-cuts and spontaneous illuminations of temperament. Compton one day is so quick on his feet, and in and out of the crease, that the bowler seems now and then to have to change his mind while running ball in hand to the wicket. Sometimes Compton prances down the pitch, only to find a length altogether too short for a forward stroke; he will run back to cut it, and sometimes it is a scurry to save himself.

He is a superb driver between the left-hand of mid-off and point. He is not always too particular about placing his left foot near the line of the ball; he is trustful of the enormous power and steering-wheel suppleness of his wrists.

But on his ill-starred days he may very soon be caught because his bat has gone out to seek the ball on the off-side with no guidance apparently from Compton himself; it is as an artificial limb. On these inexplicable days he falls under that evil spell which reduces others not fit to tie his laces to immobility of the right foot, so that he, Compton, yesterday as impertinent and ubiquitous of movement as a young terrier tackling a mastiff, is bird-limed. Or his bat has become leaden. Not often, though, is he so reduced and chap-fallen.

Yet, you see, the margin of error is there. He needs always to be 'seeing' the ball with the clearest and most rapid and comprehensive eye. A Hobbs or a Hutton, because of sound grasp of the fundamentals, is able to go on and on until the age of spectacles and ear trumpets. Compton's cricket at his best belongs to youth. As youth leaves us – and no man lives for ever – we must overhaul our catechism. He has already proved his harder metal.

In Australia, five years ago, on his first visit there he was put under the obligation of adopting a method and outlook foreign to his nature as then supposedly known and revealed. He found himself bowed down somewhat in heavy armour, his job grimly to 'hold the fort'.

Nobly, if not grimly, he obeyed the orders of the day, and at Adelaide on a perfect wicket he was professionally clever enough to score 43 in two hours and a quarter, and compile two centuries in one Test match.

At Trent Bridge in 1948 he defended a broken bridge for England for six and a half hours against Australians 'on the kill', while darkness fell on the earth from the sky. This innings was one of the greatest ever played in all the annals of Test cricket, both for extensive skill judiciously applied and for disciplined mind and temperament. His wonderful year, as we all know, was 1947, in a season of glorious summer. When he came down the pavilion steps at Lord's on his way out to bat, the schoolboys crowed like cocks.

An innings by Compton played in this year against Kent takes its place on the sunlit frieze of all that memory holds of gallant, accomplished and beautiful batsmanship. Kent declared on this enchanted afternoon and Wright bowled at his very best. Compton consumed him, leg-spinners, 'googlies' and all. His strokes were as shooting stars, gliding and skimming according to an astronomy of their own. The same sort of ball was treated in different ways and sent to different parts of Lord's. No effort, all grace; no flamboyance, but brilliance in the dress of courtesy.

When he got out, Kent quickly won the match, and so this great innings assumed the lustre which shines on bravely lost causes.

For my part I don't wish to think of Compton as one of the persistently masterful players. In spite of what recent trials and ordeals may have taught him, and in spite of the technical adjustments demanded by increase of years and some inevitable check on physical elasticity he will never, I am sure, surrender to middle age.

He will continue, at least this is the hope in the hearts of thousands of us, to convey the impression that he is capable, while batting, (1) of making a superb stroke with his feet in the 'wrong' place; (2) of making a mighty pull while falling flat on his stomach; (3) of suddenly achieving a flawless execution so that the textbook black-and-white examples of Hutton seem to be given the illumination of colours; (4) of getting out to the easiest ball because after having gone half-way down the pitch he has forgotten exactly what he had ventured so far to do; (5) of running himself out or somebody else by yards; or (sixth and last) of performing all these remarkable actions at one and the same time.

Denis Compton contributes to English life and holiday at the crown of the year; he is part of an English summer. *Extracted from 'Cricket All The Year', published in* EVERYBODY'S WEEKLY, 1952.

Souvenir of 1947
Denis Compton, 29-year-old Middlesex and England cricketer, beat Jack Hobbs' feat of 16 centuries in a season – a record that had stood for 22 years. He finished with 18 centuries. Here are his centuries of 1947 and the highlights of an astonishing career:

for Middlesex
112 *v* Worcester, Lord's
110 *v* Sussex, Lord's
154 *v* S. Africans, Lord's
151 *v* Leicestershire, Leicester
129 *v* Essex, Lord's
110 *v* Northants., Northampton
100 not out *v* Sussex, Hove
106 *v* Kent, Canterbury
137 not out *v* Surrey, Oval
168 *v* Kent, Lord's
178 *v* Surrey, Lord's
139 *v* Lancashire, Lord's

for England v *S. Africa*
163 First Test, Nottingham
208 Second Test, Lord's
115 Third Test, Manchester
113 Fifth Test, Oval

for South of England
101 *v* S. Africans, Hastings

for Champion County
246 *v* Rest of England, Oval

Milestones
Born: Hendon, London, 23 May 1918
1936: First played for Middlesex, scoring 1,004 runs
First county game: *v* Sussex at Lord's as No 11
1937: Test debut *v* New Zealand (65, run out)
1938: First Test *v* Australia, at Nottingham (102)
1946: Had season's highest aggregate (2,403 runs)
1947: *February*: Scored century in each innings at Adelaide – third England player to do so against Australia (others were Hammond 1928–29, Sutcliffe 1924–25)
September 2: Equalled Hobbs' record of 16 centuries in a season with 139 *v* Lancashire at Lord's
September 4: Beat record *v* South Africans at Hastings with 101, which gave him total of 1,157 in 13 innings against tourists, for average of 89
Season's total: (naturally a record) 3,816 runs

And as a tailpiece – a tribute from his great batting partner Bill Edrich.

Bill Edrich had a close-up view as a Ray Lindwall bumper split open Denis Compton's forehead in an Old Trafford Test match. He says: 'I remember it as though it was five minutes ago, instead of it happening in 1948. Denis was aiming to hit Ray out of the ground, but got a top edge. The ball crashed into his head and Denis staggered about with blood pouring down his face.'

Eventually he was persuaded to go off. After having the wound stitched, Compton came back with his head swathed in bandages to resume battle with Lindwall and Keith Miller.

Edrich recalls: 'They were really after Denis, but he never flinched and played some glorious attacking shots. He finished up 145 not out.'

Middlesex 'twin' Edrich saw more of Compton's great innings for county and country than anyone and he rated that knock . . . 'the bravest I've ever witnessed'.

Edrich said of Denis: 'He had all the normal strokes and a repertoire all of his own as well.'

But the moment Edrich really savoured was when he and Denis took England to victory at The Oval in Coronation year. The famous Compton leg sweep sealed it and brought the Ashes home for the first time in twenty years. LONDON EVENING NEWS

Sundries

Don't Call Us – we'll try and call you: Mike Brearley, recalled as England's captain after the departure of Ian Botham, was not surprised to get the selectors' vote. But he hardly expected to have to pay for the phone call that put him back in the driving seat.

He said yesterday: 'The phone to my London flat started to ring. I kept hearing the pips at 8.30 last night and obviously somebody was having difficulty with a pay phone.

'In the end, the operator came on and asked me if I would accept the charge, which I did, and that's how Alec Bedser, chairman of the selectors, broke the news.' DAILY MIRROR, 9 JULY 1981

'A captain's innings – one match too late.' Ian Botham's message to the Press after his astonishing 145 not out at the Headingley Test against Australia, 20 July 1981, the first match he played after resigning the England captaincy.

Advertisement in the National newspapers, 4 August 1981:

NATIONAL BREAKDOWN RECOVERY CLUB

Congratulates its 11 members who recovered so well at Headingley and Edgbaston.

The best fast bowler I ever saw was, without doubt, the great Ray Lindwall; he had a superb action, super balance and rhythm in his run-up.

It has often been said that if Tchaikovsky had seen this man with his approach to the wicket, the slow start, the beautiful acceleration coming into his point of balance, and delivery, he would have written a symphony to commemorate him. 'THE THOUGHTS OF TRUEMAN NOW,' MACDONALD AND JANES, LONDON, 1978

Peter May, one of the world's greatest-ever batsmen, always fancied himself as a bowler, so John Warr, the Gentlemen's captain, put Peter on to bowl the last over before lunch against the Players at Lord's. As they walked off the field together, Warr said:

'Peter, you had a lot of bad luck. You had their top scorer dropped off successive balls by the same bloke . . . the man in the brown suit at the back of the stand!' R. C. ROBERTSON-GLASGOW

When I went along to Lord's the other day to play against the Public Schools, 'positively my last appearance, Ladies and Gentlemen', memories came crowding. There was Sir 'Plum' Warner, who persuaded me to turn out for the Lord's XI, to remind me of a great county game some twenty years ago. It was his last match and he was carried off shoulder high – skipper of a championship winning team.

What a match! Surrey had to beat us if they were to have a championship chance; we had to win to be certain of finishing in front of Lancashire, another county in the championship with a chance.

We left Surrey to get runs at eighty an hour for three hours. Tom Shepherd looked set, and we were worried. The game turned when Percy Fender, always ready to gamble boldly, gave Shepherd the order to hustle. Tom lashed out, and I held a sky-high catch near the Nursery sightscreen. That was the end of Surrey.

PATSY HENDREN, SUNDAY EXPRESS, 18 AUGUST 1940

In a book published in August 1979, Jim Laker tells of a funny umpire story he experienced in India: We were staggered at the start of the match to see an elephant between the shafts of the heavy roller, but what came later was even funnier.

It concerned the continual difference of opinion between the bowler, George Tribe, and a diminutive umpire over Tribe's constant appeals for lbw against the Maharajah of Patiala.

Finally, when yet another appeal from the distraught Tribe was turned down, the bowler picked up the umpire by his shirt front, shook him, and shouted: 'Don't be such a bloody fool, have another look.'

The trembling umpire, took a quick look at the giant maharajah, then at the raging Tribe, and taking a deep breath to calm himself, said: 'My word, Mr Tribe, you're right. I am sorry, sir, but you are out!'

'A SPELL FROM LAKER', HAMLYN, LONDON, 1979

Hot Gospellors: Reuter reports from Melbourne: 'In a church cricket competition, Albert and Middle Park Presbyterians needed eighty-five runs to win, with eighteen minutes left. They got them, and one batsman scored 31 off the last over.'

From an Australian cricket report . . . 'At the close of play Ponsford was 429 not out, made from 1059 for 6. As he left the crease, he said, "Goodnight fellows, we'll meet here again in the morning."'

Ten Foot Catch

ROY PESKETT

Hove, Sussex *v* Australians, 15 June 1968: Sheahan received increasing help from the lower order batsmen. Joslin helped him add 64 for the 5th wicket, Freeman 49 for the 7th, and McKenzie 59 for the 8th. That both of his later partners out-scored him was greatly to the delight of the sun-drenched 9,000 crowd.

It all happens when Eric Freeman, the 23-year-old pace bowler is around. Freeman finds contact lenses help his batting. He has had a most eventful first tour so far. His first innings brought him 116 against Northampton. Then he got a duck.

Last week, on the way back from the Manchester Test, he crawled out of a totally wrecked car on the M1 without a scratch.

And yesterday, after scoring 26 in seven scoring shots (2 sixes, 3 fours and 2 singles) he was out to one of the most exciting catches ever seen on the Hove ground. Freeman hit Mike Buss for a towering 6 over the pavilion. Next ball he attempted to repeat the feat to deep long-on. Standing one pace inside the boundary, Tony Greig, the giant South African, judged an extraordinary catch with simplicity. As the ball was roaring overhead Greig, who stands 6ft 7in, jumped 2ft off the ground with his arms full stretch above his head. So that when he made the clean catch, he took the ball at least 10ft in the air.

SUNDAY MIRROR, 16 JUNE 1968

You Can't Bat with One Eye

COLIN MILBURN

At 11.50 pm on Friday 23 May 1969 Colin Milburn was in a car crash near Northampton. He lost one eye completely, and damaged the sight of the other. One of the most spectacular careers in Test cricket was over. Milburn, capped eight times for England in two years, now lives in a bachelor flat and has not been able to choose another career.

How would I describe myself now? It's a really good question. I have no idea. It is about time, after nine years, that I settled down into some sort of regular job. I have had a lot of offers. It is a case of getting it into my mind that I have got to accept one of them.

But it is very difficult to clear right out of the game. People come up to me and say, 'What do you fancy doing?' What can I do? Since I left school, I played cricket. In the summer I played here, and in the winter I played abroad.

It never crosses your mind that at 27 years old you are going to have an accident and you are never going to be able to play again. You still think you are going to play till 40-odd, which you can do as a batsman, easily.

I still remember all of the accident. I was perfectly conscious at every stage. I walked out of the car. I can remember the surgeon forcibly trying to open my eye, but he couldn't manage. I was feeling sick and swearing like mad.

In the morning the sister came and said: 'Colin, I have got some bad news. We have had to remove your left eye.' I said: 'How's the right one?' She said: 'That's been damaged as well, but we are hoping it will get back to 100 per cent.'

There was a clock on the wall and every morning when I woke up I looked to see if my sight had improved. At first the clock was very blurred ... it kept improving. But on the last day in hospital it still wasn't clear.

I think if they had got that to normal sight, I could have played to the first standard again. But in poor light it is like watching a television set which isn't in focus. It has never got any better. As long as it doesn't get worse, I suppose that's the main thing.

It never sank in for a long time that I wouldn't be able to play cricket. I was busily going round doing television commentaries, writing for newspapers and whatever. But after a while the Press were nagging at me all the time. 'When are you going back in the nets?'

So I got everyone together one day and did 10 minutes in the nets at Northampton. I tried everything. I wore special glasses to ease the haziness. But it was hopeless.

Since that day I haven't really settled into anything. Everything I have done has been one-off things. A couple of months of this and that.

I have only got really depressed once. That was a couple of years afterwards when a travel agency employed me to take a party out to Australia to watch a Test. Seeing the lads there in front of a big crowd at Sydney I felt very low. TV TIMES, MAY 1978

ARLOTT ARTISTRY

Ian Botham, Somerset's last hope to salvage something for 1978's unlucky county, slashed at a high-rising bouncer from Essex's Lever at Taunton, and the ball sped through the cleverly set field.

Exclaimed John Arlott: 'None but the brave deserves the four.'

'He didn't so much hit it as wave it goodbye!'

John Arlott, John Player match, Glamorgan *v* Lancashire, 28 July 1979, as Clive Lloyd pulled Swart for six, at Swansea (on the same ground where Gary Sobers took six successive sixes off Malcolm Nash).

100 Years of Tests

IAN WOOLDRIDGE

One hundred years ago on March 15, at one o'clock Australian time in the afternoon, a bearded Englishman named Alfred Shaw turned his back on the ornate pavilions of Melbourne Cricket Ground and ran in to bowl at a moustachioed Australian named Charles Bannerman.

So began a relationship unique in the history of sport. One century later England and Australia are still periodically playing cricket Test matches against one another in the same atmosphere of uncompromising hostility and inherent mutual respect.

Only Armageddon or nuclear holocaust, should there be any difference, will terminate a continuing contest incomprehensible to the outside world in its intensity.

You have to be born either English or Australian to understand that any weakening in the resolve to win would render the whole exercise as pointless as perpetuating a grudge in the wake of defeat.

The mere first 100 years of this special relationship will be celebrated with a single Test between England and Australia starting tomorrow week in Melbourne Cricket Ground.

It is now a vast tiered concrete colosseum, cruel of aspect and devoid of hiding places. The Olympic Games were staged there in 1956 and it is now capable of holding 100,000 spectators, which makes it three times the size of the average Test arena.

To commemorate this genuine Match of the Century we invited two of the most eminent contestants of the first 100 years – Sir Leonard Hutton of England and Keith Miller of Australia – to choose their strongest All-Time XIs to represent their respective countries in a mythical Test. Each was asked to select himself.

Hutton had 318 players to choose from, Miller 250. Neither sought to confuse the issue by considering William Midwinter, the only man who played for each country against the other.

One thing is certain: their choices will generate many heated discussions on such eternal questions as how would Donald Bradman have fared against Wilfred Rhodes, and how is the 125-year-old Charles Bannerman likely to cope with the pace of the 72-year-old Harold Larwood?

Serious students of cricket will be intrigued and possibly alarmed by one fact. Hutton and Miller chose their respective All-Time XIs independently. Neither man chose a single cricketer currently playing the game.

Sir Leonard Hutton's English XI

	E. *v* A. TESTS	INNS.	N.O.	RUNS	H.S.	100S	AV.	BALLS	MDS.	RUNS	WKTS.	AV.
John Berry Hobbs (Surrey) *b. Cambridge, Dec. 16, 1882; d. Hove, Dec. 21, 1963 61 Tests*	41 (1907–1930)	71	4	3636	187	12	54·26	124	5	53	0	—
Herbert Sutcliffe (Yorks.) *b. Summerbridge, Nidderdale, Nov. 24, 1894 54 Tests*	27 (1924–1934)	46	5	2741	194	8	66·85	—	—	—	—	—
Maurice Leyland (Yorks.) *b Harrogate, July 20, 1900; d. Harrogate, Jan. 1, 1967 41 Tests*	20 (1928–1938)	34	4	1705	187	7	56·83	395	10	223	1	223·00
Walter Reginald Hammond (Glos.) *b. Dover, June 19, 1903; d. Durban, July 2, 1965 85 Tests*	33 (1928–1947)	58	3	2852	251	9	51·85	3958	136	1612	36	44·77
Leonard Hutton (Yorks.)† *b Fulneck, June 23, 1916 79 Tests*	27 (1938–1955)	49	6	2428	364	5	56·46	54	1	60	1	60·00
Frank Edward Woolley (Kent) *b. Tonbridge, May 27, 1887 64 Tests*	32 (1909–1934)	51	1	1664	133*	2	33·28	3590	129	1555	43	36·16
Leslie Ethelbert George Ames (Kent)‡ *b Eltham, Dec. 3, 1905 47 Tests*	17 (1932–1938)	27	2	675	120	1	27·00			33 ct., 4 st.		
George Herbert Hirst (Yorks.) *b. Kirkheaton, Sept. 7, 1871; d. Huddersfield, May 10, 1954 24 Tests*	21 (1897–1909)	33	3	744	85	0	24·80	3469	118	1585	49	32·34
Wilfred Rhodes (Yorks.) *b. Kirkheaton, Oct. 29, 1877; d. Branholme, Dorset, July 8, 1973 58 Tests*	41 (1899–1926)	69	14	1706	179	1	31·01	5796	234	2616	109	24·00
Sydney Francis Barnes (Staffs.) *b. Smethwick, April 19, 1873; d. Chadsmoor, Dec. 26, 1967 27 Tests*	20 (1901–1912)	30	5	210	38*	0	8·40	5749	262	2288	106	21·58
Harold Larwood (Notts.) *b. Nuncargate, Nov. 14, 1904 21 Tests*	15 (1926–1933)	22	2	386	98	0	19·30	4053	120	1912	64	29·87

† Captain *‡ Wicket-keeper* ** Not out*

England

Sir Leonard Hutton announced his all-time England team with the portentous deliberation of some Bradford electoral returning officer. Then he stayed silent, counting the seconds it took you to spot that five of the 11 were Yorkshiremen.

It wasn't long, but experience warns you against engaging Hutton in the intricate swordplay of cricket theory.

In any case, only one was a contentious selection and Hutton, sensitive to accusations of northern chauvinism, already had the gloves on waiting to defend his choice of Maurice Leyland ahead of Denis Compton, Peter May or the early-or-mid-career Colin Cowdrey.

'Since it's inconceivable that any all-time Australian team would go into the field without Bill O'Reilly,' he said, 'I've picked Leyland as the horse for the course.

'O'Reilly was the best bowler Australia ever had: aggressive, unbelievably accurate to the right-handers. Well, Leyland was a left-hander and he also had the jinx on O'Reilly.

'I remember him saying: "I've got that O'Reilly in my pocket and, what's more, he knows it." I've never heard another England batsman tempt fate by saying anything like that. But it was true and that's why Leyland is in.'

Hutton's *de rigueur* inclusion gave him the initial problem of where to bat himself. 'It wasn't a big one,' he said. 'Hobbs and Sutcliffe were not only great players of fast bowling but had a magnificent understanding running between wickets.

'I'd be quite happy to go in No. 5, particularly in Melbourne, where opening an innings can be a literally frightening experience.'

After explaining Leyland's presence, he knew that no justification of Walter Hammond's inclusion was required. 'He was simply the best cricketer I ever played with.'

Woolley, towering, commanding and also left-handed to challenge O'Reilly, was a natural. And although there was sorrow that he could not include Godfrey Evans – 'a friend, a marvellous team man and great reader of batsmen's weaknesses' – he chose Leslie Ames as wicket-keeper.

Much of Hutton's own character was revealed by his selection of bowlers. Not only did he require wickets, but he also wanted men who could bat.

'George Hirst was fantastically accurate and could also swing an old ball. What's more, he was a very aggressive batsman.

'It's also impossible to leave out either Wilfred Rhodes or Syd Barnes. They represent genius. Barnes could bowl anything.

'Rhodes was the complete cricketer, a very great bowler who began batting No 11 for England and finished up opening the innings.'

It was only after much analysis that Hutton chose Harold Larwood as his spearhead fast bowler. Tyson, phenomenally fast, had won him a series in real-life cricket against Australia but Hutton said: 'I think Larwood just had the edge over Tyson for speed. He had the finest action I've ever seen.'

It was obvious that Sir Leonard Hutton had given many hours to his selections.

'I shall probably be criticised for the fact that it isn't a great fielding side,' he said. 'I know that. Given the choice I would have chosen Peter May or Colin Cowdrey as 12th man as well. But I gather the idea is to beat Australia in Melbourne. It's never easy.'

Australia

Keith Miller, inveterate horse-player, party-goer and probably the most glamorous figure ever to play for Australia at anything, immediately renounced the responsibilities of captaincy. It was almost as though he couldn't trust himself to get to the ground in time to toss-up.

His team is more controversial than Hutton's, but it is his voluntary decision to play under the captaincy of Sir Donald Bradman that will cause most comment in Australia. They were always seen as incompatible figures and there are many legends of bad blood between them.

'It is quite true,' admits Miller, 'that we had a couple of blow-ups during Test matches. One was at Lord's when I flung the ball back and refused to bowl for him. But that never lessened my respect for him as a captain dedicated to winning and since this match is against England there can be no other choice.'

Those with some knowledge of cricket may feel that Miller has gambled with his very first selection in his all-time Australian team.

'I probably have,' confesses Miller, 'but I'm a bit of a romantic as well. Obviously there's nobody alive today who ever saw Charlie Bannerman bat, but he faced the very first ball ever bowled in England–Australia Tests and he scored 165 before he had to retire hurt and Australia won by 45 runs. He must have been as tough as nails.

'It's bloody hard choosing Australia's opening batsmen because there have been so many great ones: Ponsford, Woodfull, Barnes, Morris and Bobby Simpson, who was also the greatest slip-fielder I've ever seen. It's hard to leave any of them out.

'I couldn't contemplate leaving Ponsford out altogether so I've chosen him to bat No 4. That means Victor Trumper opens the innings with Bannerman. I never saw Trumper either, but the stories can't all be wrong. Anyway, my father saw him bat and said he was as good as Bradman and that will do me.'

No one would challenge Miller's own selection and few that of Stan McCabe at No 5. It was while McCabe was scoring his 232 at Nottingham in 1938 that Bradman summoned Australia's players from a dressing-room card game to the pavilion balcony with the words: 'Come

Keith Miller's Australian XI

	E. *v* A. TESTS	INNS.	N.O.	RUNS	H.S.	100S	AV.	BALLS	MDS.	RUNS	WKTS.	AV.
Charles Bannerman (N.S.W.) *b. Woolwich, Kent, July 3, 1851; d. Sydney, Aug. 20, 1930 3 Tests*	3 (1877–1879)	6	2	239	165*	1	59·75	—	—	—	—	—
Victor Thomas Trumper (N.S.W.) *b. Sydney, Nov. 2, 1877; d. Sydney, June 28, 1915 48 Tests*	40 (1899–1912)	74	5	2263	185*	6	32·79	348	18	142	2	71·00
Donald George Bradman (N.S.W. & S. Aus.)† *b. Cootamundra, Aug. 27, 1908 52 Tests*	37 (1928–1948)	63	7	5028	334	19	89·78	92	2	51	1	51·00
William Harold Ponsford (Vic) *b. Melbourne, Oct. 19, 1900 29 Tests*	20 (1924–1934)	35	2	1558	266	5	47·21	—	—	—	—	—
Stanley Joseph McCabe (N.S.W.) *b. Grenfell, July 16, 1910; d. Sydney, Aug. 25, 1968 39 Tests*	24 (1930–1938)	43	3	1931	232	4	48·27	2585	84	1076	21	51·23
Keith Ross Miller (Vic. & N.S.W.) *b. Melbourne, Nov. 28, 1919 55 Tests*	29 (1946–1956)	49	4	1511	145*	3	33·57	5717	226	1949	87	22·40
Montague Alfred Noble (N.S.W.) *b. Sydney, Jan. 28, 1873; d. Sydney, June 22, 1940 42 Tests*	39 (1898–1909)	68	6	1905	133	1	30·72	6845	353	2860	115	24·86
Raymond Russell Lindwall (N.S.W. & Qnslnd) *b. Sydney, Oct. 3, 1921 61 Tests*	29 (1946–1959)	43	7	795	100	1	22·08	6728	216	2559	114	22·44
Donald Tallon (Qnslnd)‡ *b. Bundaberg, Feb. 17, 1916 21 Tests*	15 (1946–1953)	20	2	340	92	0	18·88			38 ct., 4 st.		
Clarence Victor Grimmett (S. Aus.) *b. Dunedin, N.Z., Dec. 25, 1891 37 Tests*	22 (1925–1934)	34	6	366	50	0	13·07	9164	427	3439	106	32·44
William Joseph O'Reilly (N.S.W.) *b. White Cliffs, N.S.W., Dec. 20, 1905 27 Tests*	19 (1932–1938)	32	6	277	42	0	10·65	7864	439	2587	102	25·36

† *Captain*   ‡ *Wicket-keeper*   * *Not out*

and watch this. You may never see anything like it again.'

Miller delves back to the turn of the century for Monty Noble, a huge first-generation Australian all-rounder who defeated England little short of single-handed in several Tests with either a batting onslaught or a swing-bowling technique which he had developed as a young baseball player.

His choice of Ray Lindwall, his own new-ball partner and inseparable drinking buddy, as the greatest of all Australian fast bowlers will cause no controversy. Nor will his choice of Bill O'Reilly 'the greatest bowler of any type the game has ever seen'.

'Also I had no hesitation,' said Miller, 'about choosing Don Tallon. He was the best batsman-wicket-keeper I've ever seen.'

Miller's final selection, spin support for O'Reilly, caused him his only lost sleep. 'It was a straight fight between a very good friend, Richie Benaud, and Clarrie Grimmett. In the end I decided to go entirely on the evidence of the record books: Benaud 248 wickets in 63 Tests, Grimmett 216 wickets in only 37 Tests.

DAILY MAIL, MARCH 1977 RESEARCH BY IRVING ROSENWATER

England's Life in Greig's Hands

PAT GIBSON

Every policeman in Leeds should have been on duty guarding the Headingley pitch last night to make sure no one dug it up this time.

For the six hours remaining of one of the most fascinating, unpredictable contests of all time, England need only 114 runs and West Indies just five wickets to win a famous fourth Test match.

And everyone is waiting for the sting in the tail of an epic that has taken so many twists and turns in four days it might have been scripted in Hollywood and given a ragtime theme.

The plot has been incredible, the best and the worst of both West Indian and English cricket chasing each other in such giddy confusion that even the most knowledgeable crowd in cricket must have been hard pressed to keep up with it all.

The set-up when England began their fourth innings was that they needed 260 to win.

They had nine hours 20 minutes to do it, but they were haunted by the fact that they had not made that many to win a Test since 1902 when they scored 263 for 9 to beat Australia at the Oval.

Now everyone awaits the sting – because although England made yet another miserable start, first Bob Woolmer and Peter Willey and now skipper Tony Greig have kept alive their hopes of a sensational victory.

With their first five batsmen gone, they are still the outsiders. Yet, when Greig was thrusting a long left leg down the pitch last night and driving through the covers even more commandingly than he did in the first innings, no one could write them off.

What a climax we had reached. With Greig unbeaten on 35, Michael Holding foolishly bowled a chest-high bouncer at night watchman Derek Underwood, and the umpires, showing far more sense, ended play for the day five minutes early on the grounds of bad light.

And what a day it had been, beginning with a characteristic show of West Indian panic.

But for Collis King, the smiling 25-year-old from Barbados who expected to spend his English summer playing League cricket for Nelson, England might have won by now.

He came in at 72 for 4 – a lead of only 135 – and batted as though it was a Sunday afternoon thrash. He smashed 10 fours and reached his 50 from only 39 balls.

He put on 49 in 34 minutes with Clive Lloyd, 57 in 47 minutes with Deryck Murray, and seemed to have put the match beyond England's reach.

Then Bob Willis, the much-injured fast bowler playing his first Test for two seasons, shattered the tail with the last four wickets for three runs in 24 balls to return his best England figures of five for 42.

Once again England were full of hope, but briefly. Andy Roberts got rid of David Steele (second ball) for his 100th wicket in only 19 Tests, then added Frank Hayes and Chris Balderstone to make England 23 for three. DAILY EXPRESS, JULY 27, 1976

At this point, wrote Brian Scovell in the *Daily Mail*, umpire David Constant admonished the West Indies fielders preparing to dispute a decision when England were 23 for three.

Andy Roberts' first ball to Peter Willey struck him on the pad and when Constant turned down the chorused appeal several waved their arms about. Constant pointed a finger and said: 'Cut it out, get on with the game.'

Constant appeared to speak to Michael Holding later when he bowled two successive short deliveries at Willey.

Now came another fightback. Woolmer, easily the most impressive England batsman this summer even when he has not been making runs, and the marvellously forceful Willey added 57 to drive away the gloom once more.

But when he had made 37 Woolmer was lbw to Holder and, with the England captain coming in at 80 for 4 for the second time in the match, everyone suspected the outcome was in his hands.

And when Willey, having thumped nine fours in 45, clipped a ball from Holding to Roberts just behind square leg, we all knew it was. And because it was Greig we knew too that this game is not over yet.

Footnote: This is how Wisden saw the following day: Although full admission was charged over 9,000 spectators turned up on the last morning to see England's hopes dashed, not by Roberts or the partially fit Holding but by Daniel. In his first 23 balls the young fast bowler disposed of the night watchman Underwood, Knott and Snow, all caught off the outside edge from forward prods. Greig, pinned down by three maiden overs from Roberts, watched helplessly. Greig then threw the bat, forcing Lloyd to man the boundaries, but although Ward stayed while 46 were added, he and Willis finally fell to successive balls from Holding, leaving Greig unbeaten with a valiant 76. So West Indies won by 55 runs to establish a winning lead in the series.

Greig not out	76
Underwood *c* Murray *b* Daniel	6
Knott *c* Murray *b* Daniel	2
Snow *c* Greenidge *b* Daniel	8
Ward *c* Murray *b* Holding	0
Willis *lbw* Holding	0
B 12, lb 5, w 7, nb 8	32
	204

Fall: 6/146 7/150 8/158 9/204

	O	M	R	W
Roberts	18	8	41	3
Holding	14	1	44	3
Daniel	13	0	60	3
Holder	11	3	27	1

'WISDEN'S CRICKETERS ALMANACK', 1977

TV ASIDES

Tuesday, 2 September 1975, 11.45 am on the sixth day of the last Test.

Tony Greig caught behind. Ian Chappell arms upraised. Greg Chappell stands motionless, arms folded. Richie Benaud says: 'He's got the look of a man who's been away from home for four months, and who knows he's booked on tonight's plane to Australia.'

As Gary Sobers ambles back to the pavilion, after another tremendous innings, and the crowd rising to a standing ovation, John Arlott says . . . 'What can you say about Gary Sobers?

'He can bowl finger spin; wrist spin; quick seamers; he is a wonderful batsman; fine cover point; great hitter; fine captain.'

What a testimonial!

Scored Century · Lost £65

MAURICE LEYLAND

No need to think when my greatest sport thrill happened. It was at Melbourne in 1929, when I scored a century in my first Test for England against Australia.

It was the fifth and last Test, the first four of which England had won under A. P. F. Chapman's leadership.

My score stood at 99 after five hours' batting against the bowling of Tim Wall, wily Clarrie Grimmett, Hornibrook, Oxenham and the rest of Australia's star attack.

One to get and Hornibrook bowling his usual immaculate length just outside the off stump. I began to despair of ever getting a ball short of a length.

Four or five overs, it seemed an age, yet it was only 15 to 20 minutes, and still the scoreboard mocked me.

All this time I was living the innings over again: wondering whether the silent crowd wanted me to get my 100, or whether they would prefer to see my wicket spreadeagled. I marvelled that so many thousands of people could make so little noise.

Hornibrook again. No, again a good length – just another temptation to take a chance and end the terrible silence. Then I received a shortish delivery and promptly drove it through the covers to register my eighteenth boundary hit and realise a lifelong ambition.

As the ball left my bat something happened I shall remember all my life. It seemed as if a vast wall had risen around me. Forty or fifty thousand spectators rose to their feet. The applause was almost a rebuke that I should ever have doubted their reception.

On my way back I reflected on the start of the innings, and the kindly help generously given me by Patsy Hendren. I often wonder how many cricketers owe a debt of gratitude to the big-hearted Middlesex player.

When I joined Patsy he said: 'The first ball you hit – run. Don't worry where or how far it goes.' I played the first ball defensively. It went about four yards. Hendren was up at my end almost before I had remembered his advice.

I was off the mark and Patsy knew how tremendously important that is to any young player facing the ordeal of his first Australian Test innings.

If I said Patsy Hendren was the most loved and likeable character in sport I don't think it would be an exaggeration, and certainly wouldn't be challenged in first-class cricket circles.

SUNDAY EMPIRE NEWS, AUGUST 1943

Leyland collected 53 not out in the second innings, which gave him 190 runs for once out.

Of his Melbourne performances, Wisden records that: 'Leyland distinguished himself by two really delightful displays, in one of which he joined the band of cricketers who have made 100 on their first appearance in one of these encounters.

'His exhibition of powerful, well-timed driving past cover will long be remembered by those who saw it.'

But something took the gilt off the gingerbread. That day Maurice 'lost' his wallet containing about £65 when the dressing room was robbed while he was batting.

Pre-War Stories

Confession by Brian Valentine, former Kent cricket captain, of attack of nerves during his first Test match at Johannesburg (he went in with the England score 95 for 6, and only a few minutes left to play): 'When I hit the first ball I was nearly sick, and told Walter Hammond at the other end that I would be if I had to go on. All he said was "Don't do it on the wicket!"

'Next morning I went out chewing gum and feeling fine, but the moment I made a stroke, the gum fell out and I was sick on the spot!'

Duckworth on Tate, 10 July 1938: As a personal note it may interest you to know that Maurice Tate was the most difficult bowler I ever had to take. Tate, though only medium fast, came off the pitch with the speed of a really fast bowler and I alone used to stand up to him.

Jack Fingleton was out in curious fashion after scoring his second century of the Australian tour at Cambridge yesterday. Kaye came on as the new bowler, and from his first ball, the batsmen ran three.

Then Paul Gibb, the Cambridge University wicket-keeper called the umpire's attention to the wicket, which, upon examination, showed that one of the bails had been dislodged. Fingleton was given out 'bowled' and the three runs deleted. DAILY SKETCH, 12 MAY 1938

Two newspaper contents bills, side by side:

'Read R. C. Robertson-Glasgow in the *Morning Post*.'

'Read *The Times* and see what really happened.'

Hobbs (the Bowler) Hits 100 in 44 Minutes

BRIAN SCOVELL

45 Balls....4..12...4..4464....4444.14661466.6121.614 (100 Runs)

Robin Hobbs, self-confessed non-batsman, yesterday scored the fastest 100 since 1920. He hit Australian spinners Jim Higgs and Ashley Mallett for seven sixes and 12 fours at Chelmsford in an innings lasting 44 minutes and 45 balls.

It was all so hectic that he couldn't remember much about it afterwards. But it counts as the quickest 100 since Percy Fender's 35-minute century scored 55 years ago against Northamptonshire.

'I've never considered myself a batsman and I still don't,' said Hobbs. 'I didn't go out there thinking about records or even making runs. The ball just came up and I hit it. Don't ask me where, I can't remember.'

Hobbs, who played his first match for Essex in 1961, added: 'I could have been out first ball. The Aussies were great, entering into the spirit of it. They tossed it up and I had a go.'

Two balls were lost – one deposited in a river by Hobbs, and another struck into the crowd by Keith Boyce (11), the previous holder of the fastest hundred recorded in 1975.

Boyce made his in 58 minutes on the same ground against Leicester in May.

Said Boyce: 'I didn't mind Robin beating my record. I'll get it back here tomorrow.'

The fastest century carries a £250 prize and the winner each season is awarded the Lawrence Trophy.

Essex, needing to make 353 to beat the Australians, were 109–5 with Keith Fletcher and Brian Edmeades unable to bat when Hobbs, one of the best-liked cricketers on the circuit, came in to join opener Brian Hardie.

Hobbs, who had made only one century in his career, took four balls to get off the mark, reached his 50 in 33 minutes and his second in 11 minutes. He went from 29 to 100 in 22 balls.

Hardie was 88 not out when the Essex second innings finished at 254–8. So Australia won by 98 runs.

But the day belonged to Robin Nicholas Stuart Hobbs, aged 33, educated at Raine's Foundation School, Stepney and born at Chippenham, Wiltshire.

Fender, the Surrey and England all-rounder who scored his incredible century in 1920, said last night that he had to race the clock and his captain.

Fender, who was 83 last Friday, said: 'It was 4.07 when I went in to join 'Podgy' Peach.

'I was convinced that our captain, C. T. A. Wilkinson, would declare at tea, so I had to get on with it. I had scored 91 in 23 minutes by the interval.

'I was delighted when Wilkinson permitted us to carry on after tea. I passed my century in 35 minutes and scored 113 not out in 42 minutes.

DAILY MAIL, 26 AUGUST 1975

Woolley Says Goodbye-e-e-e-e

When Frank Woolley, then 51 years of age, announced his retirement during the 1938 season, an amazing series of farewell matches followed. At every ground, including that at Oakham in Rutland (used by Leicestershire for the first time), cricket fans paid homage to a figure who will become as legendary as W. G. Grace, if not as colourful.

On his final appearance, at Folkestone, during the festival, Woolley was presented with a magnificent radio-gramophone – and the cricket world settled down once more. REYNOLDS NEWS, 10 MAY 1940

Don Bradman

BRIAN CHAPMAN · LINDSAY HASSETT

1 Brian Chapman

Recently Londor. had the honour of welcoming one of the greatest figures in any sport of any time. I mean, of course, Sir Donald Bradman, indisputably the most prolific runs-scorer world cricket has known, 'The Don' to a vast public, 'Braddles' to the modern Australian cricketer.

So it sounds a pleasurable as well as easy assignment to describe what manner of man was this squarely built fellow with the granite features who devastated England's fields in the seasons each side of the war.

Yet it is not as easy as all that. There must be fewer stories about Bradman than any other top-ranking sportsman. No after dinner speaker ever set the tables aroar with a string of sidesplitting anecdotes about him. He was not easy to laugh with, and, during his career, you laughed *at* him at your peril – especially if you were a bowler.

I could fill a page with yarns about W. G. Grace or Compton or Trueman or Miller. Take, for instance, one Miller classic. As captain of New South Wales he led his team out at Sydney when some observer remarked that 12 men were taking the field. Miller had a novel way round the problem. 'Will one of you guys do me a favour and get lost?' he said. That, to Bradman – and perhaps rightly – would have been to profane the high altar of captaincy.

It was his unbending approach that won him boundless respect but something which stopped just short of affection. If you like, that has been his life-style. You could use Bradman as an example to point a moral but hardly to adorn a tale. He plays golf – he could have been a professional at that game or at lawn tennis – with the same utter determination, even in a 'friendly'.

I remember a match, Australia versus England, one Christmas at his beautiful home club, Kooyonga, in Adelaide. He was drawn against Compton, conceding half-a-dozen strokes against Denis's eight handicap. Even at Lord's, more deadly battle could not have been joined and they finished all-square.

Jack Fingleton, who studied Bradman from close quarters of under 22 yards, records that in one charity match that much-loved character, Arthur Mailey, then well past his best as a googly bowler, came up against Bradman whose wicket had fallen to him in the past. Somebody had tipped Mailey to 'do' Bradman again. Mailey knew what he was in for as a result. Bradman 'murdered' him. The tiger would turn into a rabbit to oblige nobody and in no circumstances.

In perhaps the acutest summing up of Bradman, Fingleton wrote: 'His fundamental thinking and love of cricket were, I am inclined to think, basically sadistic. He carried no soft feelings with him to the middle. He loved to murder bowlers and make the opposing skipper look futile and foolish. Every bowler, every fieldsman, every spectator in Bradman's heyday sensed that he was using not a bat so much as an axe dripping with the bowler's blood and agony. He didn't know pity.'

It was not for nothing that Bradman's favourite Test ground in England was Headingley, where he scored close on 1,000 Test runs including 334 in 1930 and 304 four years later. The Yorkshire crowd took him to their hearts. He was their sort of cricketer. Deep called unto deep. He was, they were prepared to concede, a Yorkshire player raised to the ultimate power – Herbert Sutcliffe and Wilfred Rhodes rolled into one. To quote a stirring poetic line: 'They exulted in him and knew their mighty king.'

But there is one human story concerning the Don I can tell, a story of which he was the centre rather than the hero or instigator. The setting was Canberra, the occasion a match between a team raised by Australia's cricket-loving premier, Robert Menzies, and Ted Dexter's touring team of 1962–63. Bradman had retired from cricket after that final duck on his last appearance against England at the Oval in 1948. When he wrote 'Finis' it meant just that, but Menzies persuaded him to change his mind.

The ground was packed for the maestro's reappearance. Many Aussies travelled hundreds of miles from the outback to see him and him alone, and anything below an innings of 50 would have been a dreadful anti-climax. Another duck was monstrous to contemplate.

The England Test players, of course, knew the form. They had marked the Don's card, not to get him out but to keep him in. He was given a tremendous ovation as he walked, slightly stiff-legged, to the wicket. His opening shot, a four down to leg, set minds at rest. That, we all thought, was the old magic.

Then Brian Statham wheeled up a 'safe' ball. It was just outside the off stump, of a fair length, medium-paced. The slips were too well briefed to catch a snick. The wicket-keeper, Alan Smith, was not within stumping distance. If it broke back, an appeal for leg before would have required a following appeal for mercy at the hands of an irate crowd.

But one disaster had not been foreseen. Playing forward, Bradman edged the ball on to his foot and then into the stumps. The umpire was the Australian fast left-hand bowler, Alan Davidson. 'Davo' alone, if he had acted promptly, could save the day by shouting 'No ball'. But Davidson, perhaps horrified by the wreck of Bradman's wicket, remained dumb. And the great man walked out amid a stunned silence.

So England's well-plotted scenario, written for the first time in recorded history under the title of 'Don't be beastly to the Don', came unstuck. Their one consolation was that Bradman finished not with a duck against England but with four runs. That might be good enough for a trick question in your local!

In a candid appreciation of Bradman printed in Wisden at the time of his retirement 'Crusoe' Robertson-Glasgow, fine cricketer and fine writer, had this to say: 'By his very nature he was bound to have admirers rather than friends.' That was the price London's famous guest paid for greatness.

2 Lindsay Hassett

'The Don was the greatest of them all.

'The Don's record spoke for itself. He made a hundred every third time he went to the wicket.

'Not even Jack Hobbs, Wally Hammond or W. G. Grace got anywhere near that ratio. There has never been another batsman like him.'

Those were the words of Lindsay Hassett, highly popular skipper of the Australians in the 1950s, who endured a painful introduction to the power of Don Bradman's batting.

The dapper Victorian batsman, who was to share later in many match-winning partnerships with the Don, will never forget his first encounter on the field with the great man.

He said: 'I was 12th man at Melbourne when we were playing New South Wales. Our No 1 fast bowler broke down early on. "Braddles" was just settling in when I was put in the covers, in those days being a fairly agile fielder.

'I tried to count up the number of times my hands were left stinging from stopping his drives.

'I worked out that for the times I got to the ball there were another ten occasions that I picked it up as it rebounded off the boundary fence.

'It was humiliating. I felt like a ball-boy retrieving it for him to hammer another boundary.

'He was master of all types of bowling, a great placer of the ball. He wanted to dominate every bowler and he had tremendous concentration.

'I still maintain he could have handled Jim Laker when he took 19 wickets against us at Old Trafford. His footwork was so good even at the end of his career.

'Back in the 1930s the Victorian wicket-keeper, Stan Quinn, swore that during one of the Don's brilliant innings he never had to take a single ball behind the stumps!'

Hassett insists that Bradman did not deserve the image he sometimes portrayed of being selfish or self-centred.

He recalls how Bradman went out of his way to spend time over dinner during a Test when one of Lindsay's employers wanted to meet the Australians.

Nor does Hassett agree that the reason why Bradman was sensationally bowled by Eric Hollies for nought in his final Test at the Oval in 1948 was that he was overcome with emotion.

'I was at the other end and he was composed and concentrating as hard as ever when a googly got him second ball.

'But Braddles insisted the best ball that ever got him in a Test was a leg-cutter from Alec Bedser which pitched leg-stump and removed the off at Adelaide in 1947.'

For The Record: The Don finished his first Test series in England with an incredible average of 139·14. His full career record was 28,067 runs (average 95·14) in 338 innings, 117 of which were centuries. He topped 200 on 37 occasions and six times passed the 300 mark, with a personal best of 452 not out against Queensland in 1929–30. In 52 Tests he scored 6,996 runs at an average 99·94. DAILY MIRROR

LUCKY CENTURY

The best innings I've ever seen at Lord's? Very difficult, but I'll take a chance on Bradman's knock against Middlesex in 1934. Jim Smith had Australia's opening pair, Woodfull and Ponsford, back in the pavilion for a couple of ducks. It was twenty-five minutes past five when Bradman arrived. In the first over Jim Smith all but bowled him twice. At the end of that over Bradman said to me, 'Pat, it looks like my lucky day, so I'll have a bang'. And Bradman banged ... to have a hundred against his name before half-past six. PATSY HENDREN, SUNDAY EXPRESS

Pom-Baiter in an MCC Tie

MICHAEL PARKINSON

Visiting our Australian cousins for the first time recently, and preparing myself for the call that never came from Alec Bedser, I happened upon the city of Canberra.

Actually, I was invited there by the National Press Club, and a right jolly time was had by all until it came my turn to sing for my lunch. Even that part of the proceedings was passably OK. Where things took a turn for the worse, and a reasonably balanced discourse on the respective sporting merits of the two countries deteriorated somewhat, was during question time.

It was then that an elderly gentleman sporting an MCC tie (just to be provocative) and a grizzled drawl (just so he could never be mistaken for an Englishman), took to his feet and asked a question which lasted five minutes, and stripped all formality from the occasion with the speed and efficiency of locusts demolishing a green valley.

The point of his question, as I recall, was that although he didn't much like whingeing Poms, he was prepared to accept that those who came from Yorkshire were not as bad as the normal variety, even if this one did come from Barnsley which, as everyone knew, had the highest incidence of illegitimacy in the Western world. And while on the subject of illegitimacy which Yorkshire son of a bitch was it who sabotaged the Headingley wicket so that Fred Trueman made the ball talk and England beat Australia? Or rather, the Poms fixed it again so the Aussies didn't have a sporting chance.

All this and more poured forth, delivered in the flat, deadpan manner that I, for one, have much missed on radio and television in recent years. Moreover, the wry, tongue-in-cheek content was a joyful reminder of the style he displayed as a journalist, particularly in these columns, until he retired. I'd heard he'd not been too well, but I was delighted to see, as I faced his wit in that Canberra club, that Jack Fingleton looked and sounded fit enough to keep on chivvying the Poms for a few years yet.

Not all the cricket news out of Australia lately has been good, but to see Fingo in the pink, and to sit and yarn with him was not only a joy but a reassurance that not everyone to do with cricket Down Under has gone completely crackers.

In retirement, he lives in the Australian capital where he reported the goings-on in the nation's parliament for 25 years, and is writing a book about his life, which has lasted more than 70 summers. He started in the golden days of Australian batsmanship, played with Bradman and observed cricket through its many changes and crises until today, when, like me, he can barely bring himself to gaze upon some of the more extreme developments which have been forced on the game we love.

He is a reminder, too, that once there was humour and character in the game when it wasn't afflicted with a few surly, bad-tempered, foul-mouthed louts whose permanent scowls are designed only to accentuate the narrowness of their foreheads.

For instance, we talked about the verbalising that goes on today on the field of play. Not the usual pleasantries ('Good morning, fellow workers,' Charlie Harris of Notts used to say to his comrades as he settled down to a day's batting by first hanging a Do Not Disturb sign on his bails), but the kind of cursing that has led to Australia's captain designate, no less, being banned from all cricket for three weeks.

Fingo's point is that 'sledging', as it is known in Aussie, is not new. It was simply done with much more style when he was a lad. He reckons that the nice thing about cricket is that, because of its shape and structure, it lends itself to the application of more subtle and effective pressures than the mere crudities of a slanging match.

To this end, he told me a lovely story of the great and good Charles Macartney, who opened for the club Jack joined as a raw hopeful. To the young Fingleton Macartney was a god, already a Test player and, on the days his fancy took him, a murderer of any attack in the world.

It was with some trepidation that Fingleton made his debut as an opener with his new club in the company of Mr Macartney. As they walked to the middle ready to face the opening overs, Fingleton was as alert as a grasshopper, eager to please his partner, desperate to learn. Macartney said nothing until they had reached the centre, then, turning to Jack, said 'Think on, young man, be ready first ball.'

This set Jack's mind at a gallop. What did it mean? He decided that Macartney was warning him that he liked a quick single from the first ball, and so, as the fast bowler came charging in, new ball gleaming, Jack was on tip-toes, backing up and ready to go.

The next few seconds are a blur in Jack's mind. As the bowler thundered in and Jack began backing up, Macartney came sauntering down the wicket. As the bowler delivered, Macartney, still on the advance, hammered the ball head-high back down the wicket. Fingleton, the bowler, and the umpire saved themselves from serious hurt by flinging themselves to the ground. The ball screamed overhead, hit the sightscreen without bouncing and came back 50 yards on to the field. Untangling himself from the heap of shell-shocked manhood, the young Fingleton looked up to see Macartney standing above him, gently gardening the pitch.

The great man looked at his partner on the floor and said: 'You see, young Fingleton, always try to hit the first ball straight back between their bloody eyes. They don't like it.' He addressed the bowler, who was scrambling to his feet: 'Isn't that right, mate?' Needless to say, he made a ton before lunch, after having demolished the opposition with one stroke and one quote.

The virtue of people like Jack Fingleton, you see, is that they stand not as cobwebbed monuments to the past, but living reminders that there was a time, not so long ago, when the game was hard and competitive but played, nonetheless, with a humour to it.
SUNDAY TIMES, 18 NOVEMBER 1979

Todd Sets the Pace

MICHAEL MELFORD

Running between the wickets stands high on most lists of things in which English cricket could be improved. To those cricketers old and young who are currently struggling in defiance of the weather to get fit for a new season, I would therefore commend as a spur to ambition the following startling fact from the 'Guinness Book of Records': The fastest time recorded for running four runs with full equipment is 12·3 seconds by R. Todd in Melbourne in 1940.

This bald and alarming statement will, I think, have prompted two questions from most readers: Who is or was R. Todd? And how did he come to be timed racing full-accoutred over this unusual course?

Ray Robinson has kindly supplied me with the answers. The details of Todd's sporting career will be some consolation to the ordinary batsman, appalled by the thought of anyone covering about 68 yards with three stops, stoops and turns in less time than it takes to read this paragraph. For Ron Todd was no ordinary batsman.

As a cricketer he made hundreds in Victorian first-grade cricket for Northcote, the club which Bill Lawry now captains. He was on the fringe of the Victorian XI when the war caused a suspension of Sheffield Shield cricket.

His talents did not end there. He was one of the most prolific goal-kickers which Australian Rules football has produced and he was a good enough sprinter to compete in Australia's greatest professional race, the Stawell Gift over 130 yards. He did not win it, but the race was not run for four years when he was in his prime.

He was 23, 6 foot 1 inch, and of willowy build, when in 1940 members of clubs in the Victorian Cricket Association held a series of contests with students from the University of California – throwing the cricket ball, fungo hitting (a baseball exercise meaning throwing the ball in the air yourself and hitting it) and running between wickets.

There were eliminating heats and eventually Todd, representing Northcote, won the final in 12·3 seconds. Thus was earned his place in the Guinness Book between Denis Compton's 300 in three hours and Godfrey Evans's 0 in 97 minutes.

He later ran a sports shop in Melbourne, but since being bought out by Lindsay Hassett has been the proprietor of a seaside hotel.

Ray Robinson, commenting that Todd's time could only have been accomplished by a trained athlete with the agility to stop and turn quickly, doubts if such as Colin Cowdrey could challenge it.

Cowdrey expresses himself in full accord with this view but has been good enough to have himself timed over the distance in his garden. He returned 14·5 seconds. The rain and mud on his lawn were something of a handicap, he says, but not to be compared, for example, with that of having Compton as a partner.

Two of the liveliest runners between the wickets nowadays are M. Barnard and P. J. Sainsbury, who obliged me last week by running up and down the indoor school at Southampton. Neither is fit yet and the Hampshire secretary, whose watch showed 14·2 seconds for both, thinks that in high summer they might be under 13½ seconds if pressed.

A fast time for a comfortable middle-aged batsman seems to be about 17½ seconds, as revealed by tests made last week by Brian Johnston and myself. It is only fair to add, however, that neither of us would have been able to run again for some ten minutes afterwards.

Johnston, moreover, emphasises with laudable honesty that this time is for running four runs struck off his own bat. In the unlikely event of his being persuaded to run four for anyone else's hit, he thinks another five seconds might be needed.

Anyhow, the target is there. Off to the starting blocks.

SUNDAY TELEGRAPH, 21 APRIL 1963

HOWS THAT?

In 1936 Messrs Ashdown and Wensley were invited, and accepted, to play a match against eleven of the Isle of Oxney to commemorate the centenary of the match when Messrs E. G. Wenham and Richard Mills of Benenden, Kent played against eleven chosen players of the Isle of Oxney at Wittersham on 4 and 5 September 1834, the match being won by the two players.

On 5 September 1936 history repeated itself when the two players again defeated the chosen eleven. The eleven were all out for 153 runs made in 24·4 overs. Ashdown and Wensley made 186 before Wensley was out for 96, leaving Ashdown 83 not out, made in 36·4 overs. Well over 2,000 people attended and all proceeds from the match were devoted to charities in the Isle of Oxney.

THE CRICKETER, OCTOBER 1970

Two Goodbyes to John Arlott

GLENN GALE · HENRY BLOFELD

1 Retired, Not Out (by Glenn Gale)

Cricket without John Arlott will be like bread without butter, strawberries without cream, as the greatest cricket commentator retires.

John Arlott is on form. A batsman beaten by sheer pace looks like 'a little boy caught stealing jam'. A bowler approaches the wicket like 'Groucho Marx chasing a pretty waitress'. The umpire signals a bye with the 'air of a weary stork'.

Tony Lewis, his colleague in the box and BBC Radio 3's new boy, exclaims: 'When Arlott is in full flow it makes me wonder why the rest of us try.'

At the end of this Centenary Test, Test Match Special's team of commentators – collectively termed a *waffle* by Brian Johnston – will try to replace the irreplaceable. There's Johnston clowning and kidding; thoughtful Trevor Bailey, once of the stonewalling bat; earthy Fred Trueman, formerly fierce, fast and furious; chatty Tony Cozier; articulate Christopher Martin-Jenkins; and meticulous Bill Frindall, the statistician.

They are going to miss Arlott. Brian Johnston sums it up: 'He has the knowledge of cricket, especially cricket lore, and brings a tremendous sense of cricket into everything. I don't think any of us can match his power of description. And of course he has the wit as well.'

The most famous voice in radio was launched in 1946. Arlott was Poetry Producer with the BBC's Eastern Service. When the Indians came over on their tour, the BBC decided to transmit a 10-minute live programme on the tour each day, and Arlott was despatched with the brief to 'make sure the names of the players are pronounced correctly'.

'Everything went well in the first two matches,' he recalls, 'and my bosses at Bush House were so pleased that they asked me to carry on.'

The next year he covered a whole season's cricket, including Test Matches. 'Since then I've been a commentator at every Test Match played in England.

'I feel slightly nostalgic this season, but it's my own decision so I've no real regret. I think a man must end a thing like this one day – and so do it with dignity. I don't want to stay around until I have to go.'

Back in the box for another stint in the commentator's chair, Johnston tips a glass of wine over his trousers and generates muffled laughter. Fred Trueman says: 'We have fun. We're more like a happy family having a day out at the cricket than a commentary team.'

Listeners phone in. The questions send Bailey and Johnston diving for Wisden. Frindall says, 'Basically, John needs no prompting.'

Rain, as much a part of the summer as Arlott's voice, sends players scurrying back to the pavilion, leaving Lewis with every commentator's nightmare – keeping up the chatter until the studio is ready to take over. Bailey recalls a similar situation when Arlott was at the mike. 'He went on to give a marvellously flowing 20-minute account of the covers being moved. It was one of the finest pieces of broadcasting I've witnessed.'

Arlott's loss will not be felt here alone. Test Match Special has millions of listeners around the world. Within minutes of it going off the air a telephone call comes from a listener in Saudi Arabia, who complains that TMS went off just as they were receiving their daily 30-minute transmission.

Earlier in the day a letter arrived to say that TMS was being received loud and clear in Indonesia.

West Indian commentator Cozier remembers as a schoolboy waking up early to listen to Arlott. 'In the West Indies he is the voice of cricket. He is better known than most of the England players. Whenever a school cricket match is in progress, you'll always find young boys sitting under trees giving ball-by-ball commentaries – all imitating John Arlott.'

The man with the headache of finding a replacement for Arlott is TMS producer Peter Baxter. 'I doubt the system will throw up anyone like him again.

'We've had such plaudits from all sorts of areas over the past few years that you wonder if you could stand the loss of John Arlott. He is the greatest commentator in sport.'

So Arlott packs his bags and prepares to depart for the 'splendid quietness' of Alderney, leaving behind memories of summers past and a rich store of epigrams – like when Tufty Mann of South Africa had flummoxed England's George Mann with three successive googlies. 'Ah,' said Arlott in his rolling Hampshire voice, 'a clear case of Mann's inhumanity to Mann.' RADIO TIMES, JULY 1980

2 *The Voice of Cricket (by Henry Blofeld)*

John Arlott is adamant that cricket is not the major aspect of his life; and, indeed, his other interests, all approached with the same passionate enthusiasm, have always been many and varied. But, whatever his wishes may be, it will be for his commentaries and his contribution to the game of cricket that he will be longest remembered by most people.

The reason for this may simply be that of all his interests cricket is the one with the greatest mass appeal to his fellow human beings. For many thousands, John Arlott is the personification of cricket.

This is his 35th successive season doing ball-by-ball commentary on Test cricket in England. His inimitable Hampshire burr means cricket and instantly conjures up visions of a cricket ground and bat upon ball. No matter if he is appearing on, say, 'Any Questions?', the first sound of his voice will cause most listeners to switch their minds for a moment to the game of cricket.

In the year of his retirement he may understandably hope that his life will be looked at in the round, as he likes to see it himself. He had, of course, only himself to blame, though, that it is because of cricket that he is probably best known.

His genius lies with his ability to communicate both the game and its atmosphere and with the instinctive and skilful choice of words and phrases with which he does so. He is always a sympathetic and intensely human commentator who does not try to be clever or cruel or complicated, but likes to describe events as he sees them and in simple terms with which his listeners can easily relate.

I first joined the 'Test Match Special' team in 1974 at Old Trafford for the match against India. On the Saturday it was wet and cold and the only cluster of spectators in the ground was on the first-floor balcony which runs the length of the pavilion. Members huddled in raincoats were sitting behind the rather formidable iron railing which, half-way down, ballooned out in the shape of a considerable pot belly. Arlott described the bleak scene, told listeners about the knot of spectators on the balcony and described the balcony itself, 'with its portly iron railing'. Portly said it all.

I spoke with him in mid-May in the dining-room of his Hampshire house and he insisted that he put cricket into the overall perspective of his life. 'It rather offends me if anyone says that my whole life has been cricket. I have only enjoyed cricket so much because I enjoy so many other more important things that illuminate it, above all literature and art and the whole social history of England. Cricket is not the major part of my life and never has been. I've enjoyed cricket more and served it better for realising it was never the be-all and end-all of everything as, alas, so many cricketers think it is.'

Arlott has been a considerable collector all his life. A walk round his house reveals important collections of paintings, books (especially the works of Thomas Hardy, John Betjeman and Laurence Sterne), pottery, topographical water-colours, engraved glass, a major collection of aquatints, a considerable cellar of wine and, naturally, a remarkable cricket library.

He is, as he says, a man of many parts. He has decided at the age of 65 to call an end to active participation in cricket both as commentator and writer.

The man who began his life with the BBC as a poetry producer for the Eastern Service in September 1945 was given his first chance of cricket commentary because he happened to have the fixture list for the 1946 tour of England by the Indians in a drawer of his desk.

He needed only that one chance and in time became a national institution. Now he will broadcast his last Test Match, appropriately enough from Lord's, at the end of August when England play Australia, surely the most suitable of opponents for such an occasion, in a match which celebrates the centenary of Test cricket in England.

For most of three-and-a-half hours we talked about cricket and could have gone on for another three-and-a-half weeks. Arlott spoke of his life with the game, those things which have meant most to him and of the players he has enjoyed watching and meeting and describing the most down the years.

To Arlott, cricket has always reflected the society in which it is played. 'If you put the clock back in cricket you will kill it. The game couldn't survive as it was in the 1950s. The players today wouldn't want to play it as in the 1950s. My great happiness has always been the three-day county game. I've loved the intimate life of county cricket. The crowds are not too big, there's not too much noise and you're close to the players.'

He has always been a great friend of and to the players. 'It was the greatest compliment ever paid to me to be asked to be President of the Cricketers' Association when it was formed in 1967. I've seen it accepted by the Establishment, but we had a hard struggle. The Establishment hated us and a number of old players were against us. I've been touched to tears that the players have trusted me. I've seen the players become much more equitably paid, although I've been in a great minority in the cricket world as a radical.'

He talked of the player for whom he obviously has not only a greater affection than any other, but with whom he has also been a close friend and confidant for much of his life. Leo Harrison first played for Hampshire as a batsman in 1939 at the age of 17 when Charles Bray, the old Essex captain and cricket correspondent of the *Daily Herald*, wrote of him, 'I have seen the new Bradman.' After the war Harrison kept wicket for Hampshire, always fighting against failing eyesight. He played for the Players against the Gentlemen in 1951 although he never climbed to Test cricket. Arlott's great affection and admiration for him is easy to see.

'I've known Leo better than any other cricketer and it goes back to before the war. He was a good player, a bloody good philosopher and a great bloke. He's my closest cricketing friend; we've done many things together – golf, fishing, holidays, drinking – and our families have stayed in each other's houses. He was the model senior pro. He showed an utter dedication to the game. He never gave a quarter of an inch or spared himself and he was desperately interested in other people's cricket. This made him such a good senior pro. He was an old-fashioned professional who was on the Hampshire staff before the war under those old professionals who would give the young ones a murderous time. He grew up in the old school and was never frightened of competition or discipline. Later he was a good coach and a good builder of a house as well as an innings.'

Arlott, every inch a Hampshire man himself, wrote the story which perhaps sums up Harrison best in his recent 'Book of Cricketers'.

Harrison 'catches an opposing batsman behind the wicket and as his victim turns round disappointedly says, with dry sympathy, "Hard luck, mate: ain't half a bloody game, is it?"'

John Arlott had a great deal to do with the arrival of Basil D'Oliveira from South Africa and he was responsible for finding him his first job, as a pro with Middleton in the Lancashire League. 'I adopted him when I heard he wanted to play in England. I don't know why I thought I could do it or why I went on trying to find an opening for him.

'I thought I had done an ordinary human good turn. I didn't think I had done more than that and then, of course, he turned out to be an immensely dignified human being.

'I didn't even know what he looked like, but anyone who wrote to me as courteously and politely and persistently had to be all that he is. In 1960 Middleton had sacked Roy Gilchrist and they approached Wes Hall who would not give them an answer, and in the end, through John Kay, whom I had earlier approached unsuccessfully about Basil, they offered him £450 to play for them in 1960. I sent D'Oliveira a telegram which said, "This is your chance, take it, I don't think there will be another." They had a whip-round in the township and got him over here. His first port of call was my flat in London. At first he didn't know what to do in a white man's home with my wife and family. But if ever there's a natural gentleman, it's Basil.

'I think I was proudest of him at Headingley against the West Indians in 1966, when he faced the entire Charlie Griffith hatred and laughed at him. He and I simply agree about South Africa, too. Helping to bring him over was the greatest service I ever rendered to cricket, and more than that to the human race. I think it was the greatest thing I ever did in my life.'

We moved on to Botham. 'Botham is what I hoped Greig would be: a splendidly exciting extrovert. He is utterly open and he couldn't play as he does if he weren't. I hope he'll become a little more pragmatic and won't be saddled with the captaincy until he is. He is always combative, never shirks responsibilities, but plays it for fun as most of the old pros did. Botham plays to win prizes, but he is a natural competitor, not a spiteful competitor. I'm a little worried everything has happened to him so quickly. I don't want him to burn himself out. As an all-rounder, he's ahead of Greig and when he's become a more pragmatic batsman, he'll be a street ahead of Greig. He's a so much better bowler. Ian Botham is the most exciting English cricketer I have ever seen.'

He spoke of other players, some of whom have been famous and some who were more ordinary cricketers but characters who had left an impression with Arlott. 'I was in a quandary about Greig. I once saw him hit Brian Statham over mid-off for six. I wanted to like him, but desperately as I tried I could never do so. But I very much wanted to like such an exciting player. He thought I didn't like him because he was a South

African. I didn't think I could trust him; it was my instinct. But he was a wonderfully exciting cricketer.

'Greig set Packer up the wrong way. Anyone who knew the English market better would have done it in a more acceptable way. It was done with no understanding of British public opinion.

'Jack Hobbs was an exciting player. He used to hit leg-spinners to square leg and burst out laughing. It was out of sheer impudence. He was a colossal joker. You would have dinner with him and afterwards he'd say, "Do you recognise any of these?" and bring out your wallet and diary and watch and other things he had removed playfully and unnoticed during dinner. He was almost the perfect human being; modest, gentle, generous. He put on a knighthood and wore it as if he had been born to it. He had such grace and kindness.

'Garfield Sobers was the best all-rounder of them all. But he burnt himself out; the captaincy burnt him out. He couldn't relax as he liked between overs. He couldn't relax thinking about bowling changes.' Of Colin Milburn he said, 'He was such splendid fun.' And then sadly, 'I was with him the night he lost his eye. He and Dennis Breakwell had dropped me at the station.

'I get great pleasure from David Acfield, who is the happiest cricketer I've ever met. Then there was Bertie Buse who used to get good batsmen out, especially Len Hutton, with his medium-pace outswingers. Hutton would cover-drive him for four and then a little later play the stroke again to a ball which was slower and wider, and be caught at cover. Bertie would hug himself and Hutton would walk off fuming. Once, Bill Copson turned Bertie's cap round with a bouncer.'

Of some other West Indians: 'I admired Frank Worrell immensely, but Everton Weekes was the most explosive cricketer of all. I saw all his double centuries in 1950. He had incredible speed of footwork and strokemaking. He was like Bradman but more extravagant.

'I am very fond of Viv Richards. He is not only an exciting player who has done enough already, but as a human being and as a captain he could have an important effect on West Indian cricket.'

And finally of Bradman: 'He was the greatest destroying pragmatist I've ever seen. He had wonderful footwork and he was not only a player of strokes, he was a creator of strokes. I think he improved steadily as he lost the need to compete defensively. He was a typical Australian. If he didn't fight he reckoned somebody would walk on him. He was right too.'

I asked him what he thought he would miss the most after leading such a full life. He thought for a moment. 'I simply don't know. If I tell you I haven't had a summer holiday since 1939 and I've worked seven days a week since 1946, I'm telling the truth. I don't know what I'm going to do. I could easily do nothing at all. Or I might even play golf.'

Arlott the man comes through strongly in his conversation and each comment seems to bring flesh and blood to the player he is discussing.

Emotion, too, is seldom far from the surface. At the end of it all, he was certain about one thing: 'The most important aspect of my life has been my family relationships; they have made me happiest, and have hurt me most.'

It is all an intensely human story, and cricket and broadcasting are two fields which will be decidedly the poorer for John Arlott's retirement. But I doubt he will stay still, and other subjects will soon benefit from his attention, his interest and his enthusiasm. RADIO TIMES, JULY 1980

How About This Hutton?

A piece of Reuters tape message gave details of the latest England score in the Johannesburg Test with South Africa:

P. A. Gibb	*not out*	559
Paynter, E.	*not out*	1009
Extras		5

But it was the machine which had got the Christmas spirit: Paynter was finally out for 117 and Gibb 93.

REYNOLDS NEWS, 24 DECEMBER 1938

GILLIGAN AFTER DINNER

When I toured India in pre-War days I was so impressed by the cricket of S. Wazir Ali that I suggested the Indian should qualify for Sussex. And promptly forgot all about it.

Some weeks later the Sussex secretary, W. L. Knowles, was awakened at 1 am by the violent ringing of the doorbell at his Hove residence.

Looking out of the window he saw a dark, swarthy individual somewhat oddly clad, who, in no uncertain terms demanded hospitality. Mr Knowles was not amused.

Upon winning the toss at Edgbaston against the South Africans shortly after the First World War, I put them in on a wet wicket. While waiting for the opening batsmen to appear I said to my great Sussex compatriot, Maurice Tate, 'I think they're worried; look at the balcony.' And there, outside the window of their dressing-room sat seven South Africans, already padded up! Tate and I shot the South Africans out for 30!

A. E. R. GILLIGAN, FORMER ENGLAND AND SUSSEX CAPTAIN, IN AFTER-DINNER SPEECH

He Prayed in the Middle of a Test Match

RUSS EDGAR

Suddenly a breath of fresh air has swept through English cricket – and it could reach the proportions of a tornado in the third Test against Australia at Trent Bridge this week.

At last, after years of pushing and prodding, of dabbing and crabbing, we have another batsman with the same devil-may-care spirit of the great Denis Compton, who threw convention to the winds back in the 1950s.

Compton of the well-groomed hair and the flashing, cavalier bat; Compton of the cheeky run and the flowing boundaries. They used to call him Denis the Menace – and he *was* to bowlers all over the world.

Now, after 20 years, a chap called Derek Randall has thrown off the robot look of the 1970s English cricketer; has infused some life-saving red blood into a game that has often looked too anaemic to survive.

Randall has all the cheekiness and colour of a Compton – and he'll be determined to splash some bright paint on to the Trent Bridge canvas.

The first Test on your home ground is always something special, and Randall wants to make this match a really memorable occasion.

He carved his name with pride on the tour of India last winter – and then hit the real glory road in Melbourne's Centenary Test with a sparkling 174.

What a way to treat your first Aussie Test match! No wonder that even great fast bowlers such as Jeff Thomson and Dennis Lillee rate Randall one of the best.

There's an impish facet of his uncomplicated character that makes him one of the most endearing personalities to arrive on the Test scene for years.

And no amount of pressure or responsibility will persuade the 26-year-old Nottinghamshire product that the game is not to be played for enjoyment as much as winning.

Take the time in India when a critical crowd gave him the slow handclap because he was scratching nervously around for runs in the middle of a Test.

Most recent English batsmen would have got out to a panic shot – not Randall. He merely put his bat down, knelt to the ground and raised his hands in prayer.

'The crowd went wild with laughter,' he recalls. 'They appreciated the gesture and it took a lot of worry out of the situation for me.

'There are times when you can get yourself into a corner because you are not playing well and letting things bother you.

'But doing something different often provides an escape route. I know there's a time and place for joking about it, but it helps me at times.

'Acting the fool a bit and getting the crowd involved in the game was something Tony Greig used to encourage on tour, and I'll never forget an incident he had with Solkar, one of the Indian players.

'Solkar tried to hook three successive deliveries from Bob Willis but was a mile away from making contact on each occasion.

'So Greggy went up to him, took the bat out of his hand and showed him how it was done.

'It's that kind of humour that is good for the game and, within reason, I don't see any harm in having a bit of fun with crowds.'

Enthusiastic Indian fans are reckoned to be the most vehemently partisan in the world but they rapidly accepted Randall as a huge favourite.

His play-acting on the field – cartwheels and handstands are specialities – had them cheering and they also appreciated the brilliance of his fielding.

Adds Randall: 'They don't have many athletic fielders out in India and if someone makes a special effort to stop the ball they think it's marvellous.

'If the ball goes past a fielder out there it's as good as four, but that's not my idea of keeping runs down.

'I've always regarded fielding as a very important part of the game, even from a young age.

'When I first started playing local cricket for Retford, I got into the side on the strength of it and that was the case with Notts and England.

'It might help me stay there so I'll always pay as much attention to stopping runs as scoring them.

'Being skinny has helped my fielding and I've also got long arms, but I suppose it is something that comes natural.'

As a schoolboy in Retford, who honoured him with a civic reception earlier this year, the art of batsmanship also came readily to him.

His mother played a significant part in his development, but one day she must have doubted the wisdom of encouraging his extravagant stroke play.

Randall recalls: 'My mother used to bowl at me in the back garden at home, but on one occasion I got a bit carried away and drove the ball straight through a window.

'It took ages to put new glass in and even longer to persuade her to continue the session.

'The trouble was I smacked the first delivery of her second spell straight through the same window.'

Cricket has benefited from his mother's decision not to ban the game from that moment on, but it was Randall's own perseverance that first led to his introduction at competitive level. He was not even a teenager when he went along to the Retford Cricket Club and sat on the pavilion steps with cricket gear stuffed inside an old bag.

He waited long hours in the hope that one team or the other would turn up a man short. Occasionally he got his chance and his flair and enthusiasm were not wasted on the locals.

It was a proud moment for the club when they pointed him in the direction of Trent Bridge to make his name at county level.

He still does not regard himself as an England fixture despite his fine innings at Lord's in the second Test, and is out to get fully established in the current series against Australia.

That's why Derek Randall is determined to put his bold signature on the Trent Bridge match. Certainly Test cricket needs personalities like him. TITBITS, JUNE 1977

A Rose Amid Black Death

JAMES LAWTON

When Wes Hall and Charlie Griffith bowled in the English summer of 1966 the West Indian drums sounded not for carnival but for carnage.

There was the scent of blood in the air as a distinguished English captain, M. J. K. Smith, had his Test career swept away by a sheer and devilish pace.

Colin Cowdrey, Ken Barrington and Jim Parks swayed, ducked, and were diminished. Only Colin Milburn seemed relaxed in the battle.

Hall thundered to the wicket in great bounding strides, a gold chain swinging across his bared chest, and the red ball in his great fist seemed to carry the menace of a cutlass. It was hard to imagine that a more fearsome man had sailed the Caribbean.

The threat of Griffith came more subtly. His run was shorter but in the final explosion of effort he seemed to catch fire. And some said he threw the ball.

For English cricket the need was for a man of steel, a man to face the challenge squarely and without fear of the heat.

Astonishingly the call went out to the most gently persuasive of batsmen, Tom Graveney. No one was more surprised than the 39-year-old himself.

He had watched remotely the humiliating course of that first Test match at Old Trafford, when England crumbled to defeat by an innings and 40 runs in three days.

More than three years and 38 Tests had gone by since his last appearance for England. The man whose cricket had been moulded against the soft backcloth of the Cotswolds, who was about delicacy and whimsy rather than shot and shell, had been regretfully consigned to the shelf.

He was, they said, beautiful to watch. He was so marvellously reminiscent of Walter Hammond in his easiest moments. His stroke-play was the smoothest, rippling poetry.

One critic, the austere J. H. Kilburn, observed: 'An England team without Graveney is like a June garden without roses, a banquet without wine.'

But they also said that Tom Graveney was not the man for the crunch.

Today Graveney chuckles in the bar of his pub beside Cheltenham racecourse and recalls:

'A lot of the stern men of cricket were against me for various reasons. One of them, I'm sure, was that they suspected, correctly, that I actually enjoyed the game.'

In fact by 1966 Graveney had inserted a spine of iron into the velvet clothing of his game.

'Disputes at Gloucestershire, and registration problems with my new county Worcestershire, had left me with a blank summer in 1961,' he remembers.

'The experience had affected me. My play had become more determined.'

The gradual change had been noticed, Mike Smith was out for the Second Test at Lord's. Graveney was England's counter to what was being described mirthlessly, in the dressing-rooms, as the 'Black Death'.

The dramatic outline of that day at Lord's is etched vividly across Graveney's memory.

'Do you know,' he says, 'they cheered and clapped me all the way to the wicket.

'Seymour Nurse, who was fielding at first slip, brought me down to reality. He trotted all the way up to Wes Hall's starting mark and whispered in his ear.

'Nurse had played with me in a Commonwealth touring team the previous year. He was pointing out that I always played forward to my first ball.

'Hall delivered one short but it didn't get up too far. I knew then that I had a chance.'

It seemed that he had been at the wicket for a moment such was the easy passage of time. The truth was that he had been at the wicket four hours, 20 minutes and he stood at 90.

Graveney recalls: 'I felt fine, the ball was coming on to the bat nicely. I pulled Wes Hall for two, then I sent him for four, just beyond third man.

'Gary Sobers moved third man squarer and I decided I would "thin" the next one between slips and gully. Hall got it to bounce and I was out, caught behind.'

Graveney's bat was a constant source of comfort to English hearts that summer. Hall and Griffith were, in reality, too much of a challenge and we lost the series 3–1.

But England won the Lord's Test, where Graveney batted with deep courage with an injured hand in the second innings until victory was assured.

He finished the series with 459 runs from seven innings and an average of 76·50. DAILY EXPRESS, 28 OCTOBER 1977

My Greatest Innings

BILL EDRICH, RETOLD BY LAURIE MUMFORD

Bill Edrich made a habit of failure when it came to the big-time.

To complete 1,000 runs in May, as he did in 1938, made him an automatic choice for the Test team.

Yet in six innings against Australia his aggregate was a meagre 67, with 28 at Leeds his highest score.

That he was retained for the subsequent tour of South Africa was due, according to his detractors, to him being 'one of the favoured ones at Lord's'.

His captain Wally Hammond, had a different explanation. He pointed out that as a useful fast bowler and brilliant fielder Edrich was 'so good at the bits and pieces'.

Even Hammond's patience must have been near exhaustion when Edrich had consecutive Test innings of 4, 10, 0, 6 and 1.

That was the situation that March day in Durban where, in the final Test, England had been set the mammoth task of scoring 696 to win.

The previous evening Edrich had been out with H. G. (Tuppy) Owen-Smith, who played rugby both for England and the Springboks, as well as cricket for South Africa.

Edrich recalls: 'It was one of the few times in my life I had been really fed up.

'Tuppy must have sensed I was miserable and took me off to a country club for a beer or two.

'I enjoyed myself that night, or rather morning, and when I arrived at the ground I had never felt better.'

Then came the surprise. Edrich had been batting at No 6 but Hammond said: 'I think you had better go in first wicket down.'

Edrich says, 'I don't know what prompted his decision. Possibly he felt the situation was hopeless and nothing could be lost by the gamble, but it was certainly a turning point for me.'

Edrich marched out to the wicket with that determined stride of his to replace Len Hutton who had scored 55 of the first 78.

The first wayward delivery was cracked for four. And there were seven more crisp hits to the fence as Edrich stormed to 50 without a semblance of a chance.

On went Edrich with drives and pulls which sent the Springboks on frequent and often vain chases to the pickets.

His century was greeted with wild scenes of jubilation not only from the England players but by the sporting South Africans themselves.

The second wicket stand with Paul Gibb lasted nine hours and added 280.

But Edrich stayed to put on another 89 with Hammond before he was third out.

In seven hours 40 minutes he had so dominated the England effort that he had scored 219 with 25 fours out of 369.

The timeless Test – the longest in cricket history – dragged into its tenth day before it was mercifully halted by a thunderstorm, and the fact that the MCC had to catch a boat home!

LONDON EVENING NEWS, 2 AUGUST 1975

... and the Details of the Ten-Day Test Match

England's magnificent attempt to score the greatest-ever Test victory was foiled this afternoon by the bogey which had so often robbed cricket of a decisive victory – rain. They needed only 42 of the mammoth total (696) set by South Africa when their hopes were dashed – on the tenth day!

As soon as play was called off at the tea interval the South African Board of Control and the two captains went into a huddle to discuss whether it was possible to continue for another day. But at 5.45 pm the following statement was issued:

'The South African Cricket Association Control Board, in consultation with the captains, agreed that the match should be abandoned, the Board recognising that the MCC team would otherwise not have the requisite number of hours in Cape Town before sailing for home.'

So the match, which England so nearly won, was called off and South Africa lost the rubber gained in England four years ago. The match had gone into the *tenth* day, on one of which it was not possible to play owing to rain.

During the lunch interval England's captain, Walter Hammond, in a farewell message to South Africa, expressed the opinion that such games were not in the interests of cricket!

The Records: These records were set up in the Test:
Highest fourth-innings total, beating 572 by New South Wales against South Australia, Sydney 1907–08.
World aggregate for match of 1,981 runs, beating 1,919 by New South Wales *v* South Australia, Sydney 1925–26.

Longest first-class cricket match, ten days, beating nine days in England *v* West Indies, Kingston, 1930.
P. A. Gibb and W. J. Edrich, by adding 280, beat previous best for any wicket in Anglo–South African matches – 268 by Hobbs and Sutcliffe, Lord's, 1924

The Scores:
South Africa 530 (P. G. van der Byl 125, A. D. Nourse 103, A. Melville 78, R. E. Grieveson 75, E. J. Dalton 57; Perks 5 for 100) and 481 (A. Melville 103, van der Byl 97, Mitchell 98; Farnes 4 for 74)

England First Innings 316 (Ames 84, Paynter 62, Dalton 4 for 59)

SECOND INNINGS:

Hutton *b* Mitchell	55
P. A. Gibb *b* Dalton	120
Edrich *c* Gordon *b* Langton	219
W. R. Hammond *st* Grieveson *b* Dalton	140
Paynter *c* Grieveson *b* Gordon	75
Ames *not out*	17
B. H. Valentine *not out*	4
Extras	24
TOTAL (5 wickets)	654

REUTER, 15 MARCH 1939

Ray Illingworth: Conflict and Captaincy

MIKE STEVENSON

Raymond Illingworth's long and distinguished career contained a number of battles, none more fierce than those of the 1970–71 tour of Australia during which he helped to regain the Ashes for England.

The first problem that faced him on this tour was to win over the mercurial and unpredictable John Snow. If he had failed in this aim through poor man management or any other cause the success of the tour as a whole would have been jeopardised.

The first incident occurred during MCC's match against South Australia. The game was dead when South Australia's first innings reply to MCC's 451 for nine declared reached 646 for nine declared; but Snow, early in the innings, had fielded with a lassitude that had turned singles into twos and twos into threes to the obvious irritation of his colleagues, especially the bowlers!

Ray's answer was to summon him to the manager's room and, in

David Clark's presence, say to him, 'If you weren't an intelligent man, you'd be on the boat home. I'm perfectly happy for you to get fit in your own time. I don't want you to rush up to bowl at full pace until you're ready.

'I shall be needing you in the Tests but there's one thing I won't have and that is messing about in the field, so that the other bowlers say, "If he can mess about, so can we." If that happens it won't be long before the whole side has gone. I hope you can see some sense in this.'

If Snow had taken offence or refused to see Illy's point of view, a situation could easily have developed from which England would have suffered. Snow's bowling was the single most vital factor in winning the Ashes.

Thereafter Ray and John got on well on the tour and, after a marked improvement in Snow's fielding the following day, Illy made a point of thanking him for his co-operation.

During the same match a tail-ender called McCarthy hit Snow back over his head several times; at the team dinner in the evening Geoff Boycott and Ray charged him with a lack of pride in his own performance. 'Fred (Trueman) would have grabbed the ball and anyone who'd hit him over the top would have bloody well known about it!'

But Snow clearly did not share this view; he was always a man for the big occasion, a characteristic that cannot have escaped the attention of the Sussex members over the years!

It was during the second Test at Perth that the trouble started. There was some bounce in the wicket and Snow could, unlike any other bowler in the match or indeed the series, get the ball up chest high from just short of a length.

Umpire Lou Rowan at once appeared to presume that, every time this happened, Snow had bowled a bouncer and made his opinion known to bowler and captain in no uncertain terms.

Ray replied: 'They're not bouncers, Lou. He's got the ability to make it get up from just short of a length and you can't take that away from a fast bowler.'

Rowan was adamant that they were bouncers and there the matter rested until the next delivery, which Snow pitched on bouncer length; and as the ball fizzed high over the batsman's head, he said to Rowan: 'That's a bloody bouncer!' War had been declared.

It flared most dramatically in the seventh Test. The extra match had been arranged following the total loss of the third at Melbourne to continuous rain.

England were one up in the series and with their leading batsman, Boycott, absent through injury, were bowled out for 184, so that Australia, after one of the stormiest sessions in Test cricket led by 80 in the first innings.

The fuse was ignited when Terry Jenner ducked into a short delivery from Snow, who was then officially warned by umpire Rowan. Again the crucial definition of what constituted a bouncer was lurking behind the argument and ill-feeling.

Both Snow and Illingworth rounded on Rowan and Illy, admittedly incensed by what he regarded as gross injustice, was seen on countless television sets wagging an angry finger at Rowan, apparently rebuking him in the most forceful terms.

What he actually said, stressing the word 'one' was: 'He's only bowled one bouncer. You can't warn him for persistent short bowling.' Ray is still bitter that no one came to check what had actually occurred and that the incident was therefore incorrectly reported.

Illy was clearly at fault because he did not manage to conceal his anger and frustration, but he faced a desperately difficult situation from the cricketing angle alone; Ray knew Snow in his fury to be quite capable of bowling a real bouncer as he had done at Perth, and then of course he would not have been allowed to bowl again during the innings.

Illingworth freely admits now that he did not at the time consider the question of diplomacy. As an international cricketer he presumed that an umpire in an England *v* Australia Test match would be of international standard; Rowan's handling of a potentially explosive situation which had, in Ray's view, been created by Rowan's initial error in interpreting the law caused him to flare up in the heat of the moment.

Another cause of Illy's wrath was Rowan's claim that Snow had no right to bowl a bouncer to a tail-ender. Jenner had scored a century in a State match and was a competent bat; in the innings in question he was eventually fourth highest scorer for Australia with 30 at number ten. It was exceeding the legitimate powers of an umpire, he felt, for Rowan to make a pronouncement of this sort.

What followed must be viewed against a background of intense personal resentment between Illingworth and Rowan and the former's belief that Rowan's actual umpiring had deteriorated from initial competence to a point at which an official letter of complaint to the Australian Board was written by Illingworth which the manager, Clark, refused to hand to the Board before the final Test was concluded.

After the angry exchanges between the three principal actors, Snow retired to long leg and the bombardment of bottles and cans soon commenced. There have been differing accounts of what followed and Rowan's own version in his book 'The Umpire's Story' seems so transparently motivated by emotional involvement and personal prejudice that it is easier to trust, for example, the critical but generally fair and moderate description of events in E. W. Swanton's book 'Swanton in Australia'.

In one important particular, however, Illingworth is critical over an error of fact. 'Jim Swanton and one or two others got the incident wrong because they said that I took the side off the field the first time there was any trouble. That's completely wrong. It was the second time that there were cans and bottles thrown.

'After the first lot were thrown I called the players to the middle and we sat down for two or three minutes while some cops came on and cleared them off. Then we started to walk to our places and the throwing started again. If Brooks and Rowan had taken charge and had made the right announcement to the crowd, for example, "Behave yourselves or there won't be any cricket to watch," then I would never have been put in the position I was.'

As the bottle- and can-throwing intensified for the second time, Rowan's reaction was to say that it was both safe and proper to resume play; now Illy felt that he had no choice but to take his side off the field. Several former Australian captains, Richie Benaud and Bobbie Simpson among them, who had seen the whole sorry sequence of incidents from the Press-box or broadcasting point, were in full agreement with Illy's decision.

When the sides got back to playing cricket, Australia were eventually set 223 for victory on a wicket that was slightly sympathetic to spin. Even so Snow was the man the Aussies feared and, after yorking Ken Eastwood, he misjudged a hook by Stackpole off Lever and badly dislocated a finger in the boundary fence in almost the exact spot where earlier his confrontation with the crowd had precipitated the troubles. Australia, with the cutting edge of the England attack crucially blunted by Snow's departure, were clear favourites.

A captain and a team must be judged in adversity, and agreement is virtually universal that Illingworth's side, consistently frustrated by injury throughout the tour, responded superbly.

Lever and Underwood chipped away at the early batting while Stackpole suggested that he was perfectly capable of winning the match single-handed; but Illy embarked upon one of the most vital and excellent bowling stints of his career. He dismissed Redpath and schemed out Walters who, visibly vulnerable to speed, steered a delivery from Bob Willis with vertical bat to be caught by Basil D'Oliveira at third man.

Now Greg Chappell and Stackpole stood between England and the Ashes and Illy had them both, the former stumped and the latter bowled off his pads, sweeping. When the last wicket fell, Ray had earned figures of 3 for 39 off 20 eight-ball overs, England's best second-innings return.

Fulfilment and a sense of achievement, even triumph, were in abundance. England had regained the Ashes; but it was a tragedy for all concerned that such a wonderful match should have been marred by bitterness and controversy.

Illy, whose stock with his players could hardly have been higher, had demonstrated qualities during the series in general and the last Test in particular that had almost endeared him to the Australian cricketing public.

The sort of love–hate relationship that had developed was based on an understanding of his character and his attitudes to life and cricket. Illy was and is temperamentally far nearer to the average Australian than he is to the generations of amateur England captains who so often appeared to lack his fighting qualities.

Stubbornness is closely allied to courage: the former may have sometimes led him into error but the latter has prevented his flinching in a crisis. The heat had been intense but he had not wanted to leave the kitchen.

Extracted from 'Illy – A Biography of Ray Illingworth' by Mike Stevenson, published by Midas Books, and reviewed by THE SUNDAY TELEGRAPH, 26 MARCH 1978

Lord's of Cricket

PETER BROWNE

Sheltering in the pavilion at Lord's on an early spring day when sleet pelted the deserted Test match pitch, England batsman Bill Edrich saw a member of a newly arrived Indian touring team walk for the first time on to the world's most famous cricket ground. 'His teeth were chattering and his hair was plastered with snow,' Edrich recalls, 'yet he carried his hat in his hand. He saw my surprise and said: "I would have liked to take my shoes off, too. This place is holy to us."'

In the 20 countries round the world where the game is played, cricketers look on Lord's as their spiritual home. Addicts dream of pilgrimage to London's St John's Wood, and the green oasis of Lord's that is now one of the most valuable sites in the metropolis, covering more than 12 acres in an area where building land is so scarce that a third of an acre could fetch a six-figure sum.

Behind its high, prison-like walls, Lord's looks at first glance much like any other sports stadium, with tiered stands encircling a smooth expanse of grass. But to players, spectators and cricket writers alike this is 'sacred turf', its purpose made plain by the weather vane on top of the grandstand – a silhouette of Father Time, scythe shouldered, removing the bails from a set of stumps. Essayist Neville Cardus once described it as the Valhalla of cricketers: 'Countless days, famous for great deeds, have come to a resting place at Lord's.'

Such a day was that of the Gillette Cup Final in September 1971, when by late afternoon it seemed certain that Kent, with 197 runs for six wickets and only 28 more needed to win, must triumph over Lancashire. Confident of victory, Asif Iqbal, Kent's Pakistani star who had already scored 89, hit out so hard that every head in the stands turned towards the boundary. But Lancashire captain Jackie Bond catapulted himself through the air, desperately reaching for the catch, then fell backwards and rolled over and over. When he came to rest, one arm was stretched high, triumphantly holding the ball. It was so unexpected that there was sudden silence: then from 25,000 throats came a thunderous roar.

In that one electric moment, the entire course of the match changed. Only 14 more balls were needed to take the remaining three Kent wickets for a mere three runs, and ecstatic Lancastrians swarmed on to the pitch to chair Jackie Bond for one of the greatest catches ever seen in first-class cricket.

The hope of seeing such feats draws big crowds to Lord's, especially for the five-day Tests – England plays India this month and Pakistan in August. On such occasions up to 30,000 spectators pack the ground, 8,000 of them choosing to sprawl on the grass round the boundary, as though Lord's were some outsize village green; millions more watch at home on television. 'For an English cricketer,' says Test veteran Colin Cowdrey, 'there is no more dramatic moment than when there is a full house at Lord's, you are next man in, and a wicket falls.'

Lord's is much more than a cricket ground where some 40 important matches are played every season. It is also the world headquarters of the game that in Britain alone has 50,000 clubs and 500,000 players. The Marylebone Cricket Club, whose home Lord's has been since 1814, is internationally recognised as the custodian of cricket's traditions and the sole arbiter of its laws, besides playing a major role in its administration. Yet the MCC has no royal charter, and the club's powers are undefined by statute; its authority stands or falls by the goodwill of cricketers everywhere.

The MCC has been described as a private club with a public function. Membership, once aristocratic and exclusive, is today open to anyone sponsored by two members – though it still holds prestige enough for there to be a five-year waiting list.

Among the 16,000 men entitled to wear the coveted red and yellow tie, only about 2,000 are playing members. 'The vast majority,' says MCC secretary Billy Griffith, 'feel that by supporting the club they are supporting the game as a whole.' For their £12 a year subscription (£9 for members living outside London), they have free entry to Lord's at any time. To the public, Test match prices range from £2.10 for a grandstand seat to 85p. for standing room.

The heart of Lord's is the rambling, 84-year-old red brick pavilion dominating the ground. In its warren of offices work the staffs of the MCC, the National Cricket Association and the Test and County Cricket Board, administering between them every aspect of the game.

The pavilion gives MCC members the privilege of watching cricket from 3,000 seats in its front terrace, balcony and roof gallery – target in 1899 of the mightiest hit in Lord's history when Albert Trott drove a ball clean over the 66-foot roof. Even the wastepaper baskets are woven in MCC red and yellow in the pavilion, a male preserve where washroom doors are labelled OUT and NOT OUT, and where women are never admitted during a match – indeed, have only been allowed in at all since 1969. The MCC is firm about its priorities. 'We're delighted to see them,' explains Billy Griffith, 'but only after close of play.'

Every inch of the pavilion walls is covered with cricketing prints, portraits and photographs; there are bars, restaurants, a glass-fronted box for radio commentators and changing rooms at the top of the broad staircase down which players troop to walk the 100-foot Long Room and out on to the field.

The Long Room itself is lined with treasured relics, like a contemporary portrait of 'Lumpy' Stevens – who in the days of two-stump wickets so often bowled through the gap that in 1776 a middle stump was added – and probably the oldest cricket ball in captivity – the very one with which William Ward scored 278 for the MCC against Norfolk 154 years ago.

Displays of feeling in the pavilion are as unthinkable as the removal of a collar and tie in a heatwave. The story is still told at Lord's of the day the late C. Aubrey Smith, an eminent cricketer long before he became a Hollywood film star, was keeping up a forceful commentary on the play from his seat in the pavilion, and two crusty members became aware of the unaccustomed disturbance.

Asked one: 'Who's the fellow with the loud voice?' The other studied the world-famous actor for a while. 'Smith,' he said. 'Used to play for Sussex.'

Such single-minded devotion to cricket is characteristic of Lord's and of its 80 full-time staff members. Most often in the limelight are the groundsmen whose one aim in life is to produce perfect pitches on the 63-yard by 30-yard cricket 'table', despite problems unknown at Lord's until this turbulent decade. In 1970 the table had to be ringed with barbed wire and floodlights to counter anti-apartheid demonstrators protesting against a South African tour. Last August, when Test spectators were asked to leave following a bomb threat, thousands of them poured instead from the stands on to the ground, while the umpires stood firmly on the rain covers, hastily trundled out to protect the precious pitch from unauthorised boots.

For lesser games, head groundsman Jim Fairbrother rings the changes on the 18 other pitches laid out on the table, but the Test pitch is never used for any other purpose. Encouraged in autumn with fresh seed and top dressing, cosseted through winter and spring, its ten days of special pre-Test treatment include microscopic inspection for the slightest dent or fleck of weed, and up to 30 hours of rolling.

Despite generations of care, few pieces of ground so small have caused so much controversy as Lord's cricket table. Its pitches – waterlogged after heavy rain on the sloping, clay-bedded ground – were condemned as far back as the 1860s, because treacherously rebounding balls made them the most dangerous in the country. Now, for the first time since the table was laid down 160 years ago, it is being stripped, levelled, raised some seven inches and re-turfed so that by the 1976 season Lord's may at last have pitches more worthy of their setting.

The ghosts of cricket's past heroes will be watching, for they are immortalised in a unique museum which, unlike the pavilion, is open to the public. It houses some of the earliest pictorial records of the game, such as the painting of a 1760 match at Kenfield Hall, near Canterbury: two-stump wicket, bewigged umpires, under-arm bowling, curious curved bats. There is the ball off which W. G. Grace scored his hundredth century in first-class cricket in 1895, a rack of bats once used by England stalwarts like Sutcliffe, Hendren, Compton and Hutton, Don Bradman's boots, Jack Hobbs' cap. The Englishman's fondness for eccentric feats is epitomised by the stuffed bird perched on a ball labelled: 'This sparrow was killed at Lord's by a ball bowled by Jehangir Khan (Cambridge University) to T. N. Pearce (MCC) on 3 July 1936.'

But pride of place goes to a small red urn, less than six inches high, holding the Ashes for which England and Australia have fought symbolically since 1882, the year England was defeated for the first time on her own soil. The *Sporting Times* of the day published a mock obituary of English cricket, adding: 'The body will be cremated and the ashes taken to Australia.' When an English team visited Australia the following year and avenged the defeat, their captain was presented with the urn, filled with the ashes of a bail from the last match, to take back home – where it has remained, along with its embroidered velvet bag, since the urn itself is never competed for as a trophy.

The museum contains portraits of such past MCC dignitaries as Lord Harris, Lord Hawke and the Earl of Bessborough, lending colour to the common belief that Lord's was so called because of the MCC's aristocratic members. In fact it owes its name to a Yorkshireman of farming stock, cricket coach Thomas Lord, whose patrons founded the Marylebone Cricket Club in 1787 when he had a ground near the present Marylebone Station. Rapid development of central London twice forced him to pick up his turf and move before finally laying it at the rural St John's Wood, where the MCC played its first match in 1814, and in 1866 bought the freehold of the ground for £18,333. The pavilion was enlarged, stands were built, and the Middlesex County Cricket Club invited to use Lord's as their home ground, bringing with them a transfusion of first-class cricket.

From then on, Lord's was the No 1 ground. The first colonial cricketers to visit England had played there in 1868 – Aborigines from Australia who gave exhibitions of boomerang throwing in the intervals. When the first Australian touring side of non-Aborigines came ten years later, a powerful MCC side was shattered at being defeated in only four and a half hours. As Lord's historian Sir Pelham Warner has written: 'Modern cricket may be said to date from this Australian invasion, and that it did us no end of good cannot be doubted.'

It was the beginning of cricket's golden age, when the game was dominated by the mighty Dr W. G. Grace, 'a very big, powerful man, with a bristly black beard nearly to his waist, somewhat slanting eyes, great muscular arms and huge hands'.

Grace first played at Lord's in 1864, just after his sixteenth birthday. By the time he retired from cricket in 1908, at the age of 60, this formidable personality was reckoned to have done more than any other player to popularise the game. During his career he made 54,896 runs – 12,690 of them at Lord's, where he hit 19 centuries and took 654 wickets for the MCC.

In Grace's lifetime – commemorated at the members' entrance to Lord's by the Grace Gates inscribed 'The Great Cricketer, 1848–1915' – he saw the ground grow in stature from the preserve of a small, socially exclusive club to the acknowledged centre of international cricket. When he captained England against Australia in 1896, *The Times* thundered against 'the noisiness and rowdyism displayed as the crowds encroached on the ground' – fascinated, perhaps, by the spectacle of a ball bowled clean through Grace's beard.

The world of Test cricket has widened more than Grace could have imagined, the Australians being followed to Lord's by teams from South Africa, New Zealand, India, Pakistan and the West Indies. Many other great players have won reputations on the ground he knew so well, most notably Don Bradman and Jack Hobbs, and, recently, Gary Sobers.

But 'the Old Man' has always had a very special place in the affections of cricket enthusiasts, who love to tell of the two MCC members watching a match from the Long Room in the summer of 1939. Neither spoke a word until a workman walked in, took the bust of W. G. Grace from its pedestal, put it in a bag and carried it off. Then one member turned to the other and said: 'My God – that means war.'

Not that any such temporary upset was allowed to interrupt the proper business of Lord's. Although the RAF moved into the ground, cricket continued.

Like any other English institution, Lord's remains unruffled by the winds of change. MCC members survived the abolition of the 156-year-old distinction that as amateurs they were by definition Gentlemen, while professionals were merely Players, when in 1962 everyone playing the game became simply cricketers. Even the astonishing sight of guitar-playing calypso-singing West Indian supporters dancing across the ground in a carnival of celebration when their team won the Test last year caused no more than a twitching of moustaches in the pavilion.

Enjoyment, after all, is the sole and splendid purpose of the pleasant place which is the focus of England's national game. As Len Hutton, long the country's most famous batsman, once rhapsodised: 'Lord's – and cricket again! The very thought is magical. It brings us with one cheerful and enormous leap into a world for which we have been waiting all winter.'

And as a little man in a large crowd said to MCC secretary Billy Griffith, who asked sympathetically whether he could see anything of the game: 'Not much. But I'm happy just to be at Lord's.'

READERS DIGEST, 15 JUNE 1974

Cricket is Still the Safety Valve

ROBIN MARLAR

Oh! What a high summer drubbing the West Indian cricketers gave us there on the Oval, the Duke of Cornwall's cabbage patch at the end of the Lambeth Walk, in sight of the heart of old England, broken Big Ben. If we cannot play cricket, what can we do? But Lord's has survived the shock without needing a phlegm transfusion and if Parliament is recalled it will be because the green grass of the Oval is burned brown and not because West Indian fast bowlers scorched England's batting.

The prognostication is that England's cricket will survive and revive. The last such Test defeat was dished out by Sir Donald Bradman's Australians in 1948. Alec Bedser, now Chairman of Selectors, bagged a pair of spectacles in that match. And in his last Test, Bradman himself made nought, though that duck made more news than Bedser's. Five years later Sir Leonard Hutton, who made 30 of England's 52 at the Oval, won the Ashes on that same ground. So relax, folks: anyway, we are supposed to be good at losing.

Nevertheless, the demise deserves a post-mortem. The first finding must be confirmation that the instrument used is both unpredictable and deadly. Annihilated by Australia last winter, the West Indies are now yet again proved famous for their effervescent cricketing talent. So let us praise them. In the 1930s it made the front page of the evening papers if Bradman made either a double century or nought. Richards is beginning to look as if he, too, is a phenomenon among batsmen. Roberts is already a record breaker amongst fast bowlers; Holding surely the most graceful missile propeller in all world sport.

The background noises to England's defeat will be the wailing of those responsible for putting the team in the field and the gnashing of teeth by those after their blood. The cricketing public must now think that these teeth have already ripped off the selectors' trousers and that it is only a question of time before they pull Bedser's bottom off the chairman's seat.

Too many overseas players, the indiscipline of one-day cricket, the difficulty of reconciling budget-conscious comprehensive education and leisurely team games like cricket, the barrenness of the 1960s – these are Bedser's defences. He will hate to give up as a failure. Alas, no man in his position could have succeeded. At least this time he put batsmen in the field who didn't run away. But perhaps a tougher man is needed, a more ruthless approach to failure. A wag suggested Idi Amin, Brian Close or Raymond Illingworth would be better.

For me, the post-mortem is less interesting than the paradox that it is West Indian cricket that is in a much worse state than England's. Events at Montreal have confirmed fears that the Oval could be the last Test – as we have known them – between England and the West Indies. It will be unless the Governments of Guyana and Jamaica rescind their present instruction that no one who has played or coached in South Africa can enter their countries as a member of an international team. To these governments, this seems a logical extension of a resolute determination to cut out the racialist canker which is South Africa. My response to this is a cynical snort: and so would yours be if you had listened to the tales the Indians tell in Guyana, for they are not so different from those told by coloureds in Cape Town. To me, both regimes are odious: the question of degree, whilst interesting and relevant, is less real, less significant than the feelings of hopelessness about the future of these and many other areas in the world. Ulster, for example. Or Brixton, hard by Kennington Oval.

Set against such deeply divided backgrounds, the search must go on for any vehicle to encompass a sense of humour, harmony and unity of purpose, even for a few hours. International sport can be such a vehicle. Convinced of this truth, most sporting bodies want only to be allowed freedom to stage their own events – responsibly and without outside interference. Whereas governments see the Olympic movement as an ideal political pressure vessel, the majority view from within is one of helpless resentment.

Within sport, international cricket has usually been administered with decency and a healthy respect for change. The discussion about cricket's relationship with South Africa, known as the d'Oliveira affair, was one of the most impressive debates I have attended. As a result of it, South Africa was expelled from world cricket. Because of that, a real measure of racial integration has since been achieved in that unhappy country. There is little enough such progress in other spheres.

Descending quickly from moral stratosphere to parish pump: the existence in Britain of black ghettoes, the lack of uniformity of opportunity for black and white, unpleasant facts both today and tomorrow, demand the careful maintenance of pressure valves and ventilation holes. Cricket therefore needs to be carefully preserved and even more public praise given to its values and virtues: this time once again it is the West Indies who have drawn our attention to some of them.

As for the future, the day will surely come when the West Indians who cheered their men at the Oval return to cheer England to victory against Australia. And if we are sad that Gordon Greenidge, from 13 a boy of Berkshire and a man of Hampshire, chose to play for West Indies rather than England, his son may proudly wear the lions of England. In cricket and in sport there is always hope. Free and fair dealings as well. Perhaps that point will not be lost on the politicians of Guyana and Jamaica. SUNDAY TIMES, 22 AUGUST 1976

Compton's Temperament

GEORGE DUCKWORTH

Let's stay on the optimistic note for the moment. The 'Pat' Hendrens don't grow on every currant bush, but who will say that Middlesex aren't in process of producing another Pat Hendren, not for Middlesex only, but for England?

I am not referring to 'Bill' Edrich, who is very like Hendren physically, but to Denis Compton, who seems to me more of a Hendren in cricket qualities.

The careers of Hendren and Compton have run very much on the same lines: reading more like fiction than fact. They both went to Lord's as boys from school: spent their early days selling matchcards on the ground, watching the stars as they sold their wares, and eventually rising to first-class cricket.

It is my honest opinion that Denis Compton will go all the way in cricket: the ability is there, undoubtedly, and the temperament, which is equally important.

Here, by way of illustration of the Denis Compton temperament, I can interpose a story, told in dressing-rooms, connected with the Test match against the Australians at Leeds last season.

On the Sunday afternoon the players of both teams had to fulfil a social engagement. Everybody was ready, most of the players in the waiting motor-cars, when the discovery was made that one man was missing – Denis Compton. After an exhaustive search Denis was found in a corner of the hotel – fast asleep.

The postscript to that story was provided by young Joe Hardstaff. When somebody expressed surprise that Compton should be fast asleep, and keeping the whole party waiting, Joe remarked: 'It's just like him. Why, when he's the next man in he has to be reminded to get his pads on!'

In such a remark, whether wittingly or otherwise, there was paid a fine compliment to the temperament of Denis Compton. Not marching about the pavilion, like a cat on hot bricks, while waiting his turn to bat, but 'having to be reminded that it is time to put his pads on'.

SUNDAY EMPIRE NEWS, 28 MAY 1937

A Life in the Day of . . .

DAVID SHEPPARD TALKING TO GORDON BURN

Seven's my getting-up time, but I need an alarm to do it: I generally come to the surface from quite a long way away. I always dress first, then shave. I'm an electric shaver. I don't automatically wear a dog-collar, it depends on who I'm going to be seeing during the day, but most days I do and it does save a number of decisions in the morning.

We're very unsociable breakfasters in this house, we do it in shifts, mine first. In summer, the first thing I do is open the front door to wake up the house. Facing east, we get some marvellous sun-rises, and I like to stand and drink it in.

Then there's a cat to feed, which I do. I make a cup of tea for my wife, Grace, and take it up. I wake our daughter, Jenny, who's 15, at half-past seven, and then I have my breakfast. I'm on high-fibre breakfasts at the moment: grapefruit, cereal which I sprinkle this natural bran on, home-made bread toasted, some chunky marmalade. And – oh yes! I nearly forgot. I stand on the scales every morning, in the bedroom. That's the very first thing I do. I put weight on easily, so I like to keep an eye on that.

I listen to Radio 4 while I'm eating and look at the paper. We took *The Times* and the *Mirror* for some years, but we're on to *The Guardian* and the *Mail* at the moment. And the *Liverpool Post*.

I always used to start with the cricket page. As a boy, long before I ever dreamed of being selected to play for England, I used to devour the figures and facts. And now that I haven't played a game for five years – I got it down to about four games a year before I stopped, which I found altogether too tantalising – I've found I've become a follower again and the cricket page is a sort of bonus prize for having got through the rest of the paper. All in all, I'm a very erratic reader. An awful lot of religious magazines come on to my desk, as well as other periodicals, so I sometimes get other people to read things for me and then tell me of parts that would particularly interest me.

I've disappeared from the breakfast table by the time my daughter appears, and then my chaplain comes for morning prayers at half-past eight. We go into the Chapel – what used to be the billiards room until they curtained it off – and we use what's called Series 3, the modern worship the Church is using most at the moment. That will take us about

15 minutes, and then for 10 minutes more we take up other issues in prayer. There is a calendar of prayer in the diocese, covering the year, and other bodies and individuals to pray for. We take the newspaper and spread it on the floor as a reminder: usually there are very few subjects on the front page we wouldn't focus our minds on in prayer. There's more often than not a hurried consultation afterwards, but I'm wanting to get off to the office in Church House, at this point, not caring to arrive much after half-past nine.

I get a cup of coffee put on my desk mid-morning, but I never stop for it; I abandoned coffee-breaks in my first term at Cambridge, because the academic year is so short for a cricketer. I was playing cricket April to September. Lunchtime, either my secretary brings something into the office and I have a working lunch, or I come home and Grace puts on a soup-and-cheese lunch.

Our house is a fine one for parties which we enjoy very much. We're having one this evening, as a matter of fact. An 'informal buffet supper' we call it, which means we eat off our laps, in the drawing-room. One thing I love is juggling with names to make a list of people who might fit together. It's something my wife and I both love, actually, because it's something we promote and do together. She has a real gift for these evenings and cooks everything herself, though just recently Jenny has proved an accomplished cook, too.

Normally, evenings are the most crucial time to be available for work, so we feed together about 6.30 before I have to be off. We use a utility-cum-family room that we withdraw to at the back of the house.

I take one day a week off, usually Saturday. If Saturday gets clobbered, I write it in for Monday. I also take rather chunky holidays – eight weeks a year.

I'm a bit of a sucker for the box when it's on, which tends to be Saturday. We're very inclined to watch 'The Two Ronnies', and I would watch 'Match of the Day' if Liverpool, Everton or West Ham were on.

Mentally I want to switch off very often in the evenings, because it's usually quite late when I get in; and there are several evenings when we take time to share each other's happenings. So most evenings we'll talk a number of issues through, lying in bed.

Last thing, we'll read something from a book of Bible readings and pray together around the people and the issues we've met during the day as well as for our families. This is something we've always done. To look God in the eyes, so to speak, you've got to look each other in the eyes. It means that even though there might have been a snarl-up during the day, which does occasionally happen, we have never ever gone to sleep angry with each other. SUNDAY TIMES MAGAZINE, 1978

Quick Extras

Worcester opener Alan Ormrod scored his 20,000th first-class run yesterday, despite breaking his arm. Ormrod was one short of his target on 79 when Essex paceman Norbert Phillip struck him, but, with the help of a pain-killing spray, he continued before retiring on 84.

As the final Test drifted to another gloomy statistic in the records, England's new skipper, Geoff Boycott, gave three reasons for the failure to obtain conclusive results in Pakistan.

Only the first Test between the two countries in Lahore in 1961, when England won by five wickets, has finished. The past eleven have now been drawn, including all three in the easily-forgotten series ending yesterday.

Boycott, who took over from Mike Brearley when he broke an arm, blamed slow pitches, constant interruptions – even yesterday's play began eight minutes late for no logical reason – and Pakistan's attitude to defeat.

'Where I come from,' he said, 'A national disaster is when a pit roof collapses and 20 men die. Here defeat is regarded as a national disaster.'

On pitches, Boycott said they were not conducive to results, which was sad for cricket. He added: 'You find difficulty in scoring when a spongy ball hits the bottom three inches of the bat.'

IAN WOOLDRIDGE, DAILY MAIL, 24 JANUARY 1978

Several Pakistani men are driving round in new Sunbeam Alpines, thanks to a sponsorship loan from Chrysler.

And the tourists have not been without their problems. Skipper Wasim Bari got lost for more than an hour at Spaghetti Junction while travelling to the first Test at Edgbaston.

Scene, pavilion of famous club ground in South of England. Veteran Club Captain, watching last stages of First XI match. In staggers small shrimp, clutching bat and pads far too large.

'Where've you been, sonny?'

'With the Fifth XI, Sir.'

'How did you fare?'

'We had a wonderful game. They were all out for 21; we got 22 for 9.'

Came the interested reply: 'Who got all the runs?'

Australia's Mr Robert Menzies, a real cricket fanatic (he has a radio and TV set installed in his car while he is here, to keep tabs on the latest scores) told the Lord's Taverners yesterday of the time a British Prime Minister ignored the cricket season – and called a conference for January.

'I replied "No, what about June?"' he said. 'There was a little pause while other people were consulted, a little hesitation, and a little doubt.

'I sent a second wire because I knew this Prime Minister well, saying "is there nobody on your staff who keeps a list of the cricket fixtures?"

'They instantly fixed the conference for June – the day after the Lord's Test match.

'That,' said Mr Menzies, 'was civilisation at its best. It goes to show how important it is for a country like Great Britain to have a Prime Minister who understands about cricket.'

Who was this Prime Minister who forgot his cricketing manners, and then made amends?

It was Sir Anthony Eden. DAILY EXPRESS, 1960

Cricket lends itself to stories as much as, if not more than, any other game, and I liked that I heard the other day, which, like the rest, is absolutely true:

It concerned someone who apparently needed taking down a peg or two, and was, at the time, next man in. At the fall of the wicket that summoned him to the crease, the wicket-keeper kept the ball, the fast bowler rolled his sleeves another inch, pounded in breathing fire and brimstone and let fly with the empty hand.

The wicket-keeper promptly threw the ball in the air and the umpire gave him out. 'Good Lord,' said the bemused batsman, as he returned to the pavilion, 'he must be fast. I never even saw it.' ROY PESKETT

Some years ago when Fred Trueman captained a multi-racial side, he was asked for the batting order. He looked around the dressing-room and said: 'Black, white, black, black, white, black, white, white...'

The whole dressing-room, comprising some of the finest players of the world at the time, burst into laughter.

Rural England Department (to hell with the weather division): It was unfortunate that the torrential rain caused a late start in what was to have been a full day of cricket, but spectators who had braved the elements were rewarded by a brilliant display of bathing by the visitors' opening pair. MISPRINT FROM THE EVENING STANDARD

The Infidel who Brought His Golden Hoard to Cricket

DAVID LEITCH

For the ravening hordes of the Australian cricket public a five-year wait is over. On Friday they settled down – if that is the phrase – to relish the sight of a full-strength Aussie team unleashed for the first of three Test Matches against the 'Pommie bastards' (as the more polite of them call the English). In the last full-strength series Down-Under – the English débâcle of 1974–75 – their team won by four games to one. Now the crowd has once again got a whiff of their enemies and will be satisfied only when they have seen them battered, bruised, beaten and, ideally, torn limb from limb. For, as always, the colonials are aching to avenge a thousand snubs – some actual, some invented and many festering in the historical abysses of the collective Australian inferiority complex which Kerry Packer exemplifies and knows how to exploit for cash.

Fuel is added to the flames by the MCC's refusal to put the Ashes at stake, though all Australians will probably still take it for granted that they are being fought for psychologically and the only reason why the powers that be at Lord's have held them back is the certainty that England, despite a run of successes against teams bereft of Packer stars, is heading for humiliating defeat.

Under headlines of an amplitude appropriate to natural cataclysms, the Australian tabloids have excoriated this latest Anglo-Saxon outrage and used it as heaven-sent promotion for Packer's triumph, the success of his Blitzkrieg against what was once the Game's Establishment.

Game? Establishment? Such venerable concepts are no longer meaningful in an Australian context. The shotgun wedding between the cricketing Establishment and Kerry Packer's inexorable money-machine has spawned an unruly brat of a cricketing offspring, as yet unchristened: 'Punk cricket' might be apt – it reflects the new crudeness and needle and ill-concealed aggro generated by the Packer-inspired players' revolt.

The merry notion of having bunny-girls serve the players with drinks was tried in Packer's first World Series Cricket season and provoked derision. Bunnies, therefore, are out. But the theme song 'C'mon Aussie, Aussie C'mon' piped across grounds worked well enough as an advertising jingle to top the Australian hit parade. Naturally, it will be retained.

Instead of being a 'game' with its unassuming and civilised overtones implying diversion and leisure, Packer's cricket, like the programmes he pumps out between the ads on his Channel 9 TV station, or the text that complements the display advertising in his mass circulation magazines, has become simply 'the product'.

As for 'Establishment', the word may once have referred to neanderthal figures like Sir Donald Bradman, who batted like Menuhin plays the violin, or Sir Neville Cardus whose accounts of cricket were literate as well as lyrical. Now, despite the brave and hollow pronouncements of the Australian Cricket Board, whose chairman Bob Parish may not be quite neanderthal but is still, poor fellow, 62, Kerry Packer is the cricketing Establishment in the Southern Hemisphere. More unpalatable yet for those who wear club ties, Packer (who favours sports shirts featuring bilious cobras) has won his war, bought the game and has retired to the rear lines like a victorious field-marshal.

Individual battles, such as the current series, can now be left to gifted young brigadiers. And, as the crowning insult, Packer has chosen as executrix for this year's campaign a 29-year-old former secretary called Irene Cave. Not only is Ms Cave charming – more charming even than Mr Parish – she is sublimely unhampered by prejudice or even information concerning what she pleasantly calls 'the Classical Cricket'.

No one has so far heard Ms Cave call umpires referees but when challenged to name a member of Australia's 1948 team, having referred to it loftily as 'the golden age we want to, like, get back to,' she answers briskly: 'Don't get smart.' Despite claims that she played cricket as a girl and the sincere statement that she enjoyed last year's World Series Cricket 'Supertests' so much she even got contact lenses to see them better, she sometimes refers absent-mindedly to the tea-interval as 'half-time'.

Such fits of abstraction do not extend to her job, or role as she prefers to call it, as 'Series Co-ordinator'. Apart from getting on with Mr Parish, which she finds 'no hassle', this involves, in her own words, getting 'bums on seats'. This phrase, delicately bowdlerised to 'behinds' in most of the Australian papers who interviewed the new cricket supremo after her counterpart Mr Parish had announced last July that the ACD and Mr Packer were going up the aisle together, has now been dropped from Ms Cave's repertoire. Nor has any more been heard of the first promotional idea she was able to produce 'off the top of her head' – a contest for the best-dressed yobbo on Sydney Cricket Ground's 'Hill', where everyone is the best-dressed yobbo. Still, it is hard to believe that Mr Packer, even if he has now given orders to soft-pedal the outrage, didn't enjoy his protégée's remarks.

The Packer camp is now going through a period of statesmanlike discretion. But, happily for those who want to know more about the philosophy behind The Man, Andrew Caro, former general manager and executive head of the World Series Cricket organisation, has chronicled the cricket war in a book entitled 'With a Straight Bat', appropriately published by a Hong Kong company called The Sales Machine in association with Doubleday.

'If cricket is to grow and survive in competition with other forms of entertainment,' writes Caro, 'it has to appeal to people for whom Neville Cardus is unknown and Bradman is the name of a stand ... If there's a crowd of 30,000 most will be under 30. They remember little and care less about the good old days. For them cricket was not just a new game, it is a new scene.'

Fully to exploit cricket's business possibilities in Australia it was necessary to attract audiences from social groups who had not hitherto watched the game – women, children and the urban proletariat including Greeks and Italians. 'Traditional audiences were more mature and quieter than ours', observes Caro sagely.

Some thought was also given to the fact that the various elements of this new audience were not entirely mutually compatible. The denizens of the Hill, an unlovely mound of scrubby grass which makes the Kop at Liverpool look like a box at Covent Garden, could not really be allowed to spill over to mingle with Packer's new family audience. So the most effective possible 'cordon sanitaire' has been set up – drink has been prohibited at the other end of the ground.

The WSC logo of a ball and stumps became as ubiquitous as the anthem jingles which introduced the sides. The Australian board did their best to promote their Ashes series (which, unfortunately for them, England won). As their brand image they chose, of all things, medieval knights in armour.

Presumably they thought such a chivalrous and a feudal symbol singularly appropriate. But to the hawkers of Punk Cricket, who had turned the game's values upside down, it was nothing less than criminal. 'The Australian Board betrayed cricket in the eyes of the public,' Caro fumes. 'It was sold as being old-fashioned and respectable. What cricket needed to be was ... relevant to the society in which our children live and, in a teenage word, "unreal".'

Caro continues: 'Between 1977 and 1979 cricket was rushed into the second half of the 20th century. It was taken away from its middle-class guardians and resold to the masses. It is a popular sport again as it was in the 1890s and 1930s. The middle-class humbug about character building, fair play and respectability which is summed up in the words "it's not cricket", has been exposed for what it is. It is not cricket and in 1979, it's not promotable and it does not generate the cash.'

What Packer has done is, quite simply, treat cricket as sports are treated in America. He has packaged it for easy consumption and where it didn't fit the package, he has changed its shape. Predictably, such excesses have shocked and outraged the ancient regime of enthusiasts of this subtle and beautiful game. To Packer money was the bottom line but the outrage he has caused on the way must be food and drink to his rampaging ego.

The capacity to shock is after all his speciality. Many of his lieutenants – and even more ex-lieutenants – delight in giving examples of it. A classic is the tale of what greeted Rowan Ayers when he first visited Packer headquarters. Ayers, a veteran BBC man from London, had been hired by Channel 9 TV in Sydney to boost its prestige. He was taken aback to find the chairman of Consolidated Holdings cuddling an elephant gun aimed out of the window towards the busy throng in Castlereagh Street.

Kerry Packer pulled the trigger as Ayers entered and said: 'Bang.'

'Got the mug,' he continued. 'That's the 149th today.'

Although relieved to find that the weapon was not loaded – 'Kerry was only practising shooting people,' Ayers explained later – the BBC man remained somewhat overawed throughout the meeting.

'We ought to do something big,' Packer concluded pensively. Ayers was on his way out, pondering this matter of scale, when Packer's inimitably raucous and cheery voice added an inspiration: 'Let's do Africa. That's big, isn't it?'

A couple of years and a lot of trouble later, Channel 9 completed a mammoth film on Africa which was co-financed by Time-Life in the United States.

Kerry Francis Bullmore Packer had to wait for the middle 1970s and his own late thirties before he could make such bold strokes on an international canvas. For until his father, the legendary Sir Frank Packer, died in 1974, Kerry was very much in the paternal shadow. And even then it took him another two or three years to become known, first in his native Sydney, then abroad, as someone in his own right.

Previously, such limited celebrity as he enjoyed – largely among the Consolidated staff of 2,800 in Sydney – derived somewhat backhandedly from being his father's son. Worse, he was the younger son, and thanks to the cruel family nickname of 'Boofhead' with which Sir Frank had burdened him, he was widely thought to be 'the dumb one'. Elder brother Clyde, who had made a modest impact in New South Wales politics, was supposed to be the 'dauphin' of the Press and TV empire ruthlessly constructed by Sir Frank, an old-fashioned newspaper baron in every sense of the word.

Sir Frank's excesses were famous. For instance, he disposed of a Rolls-Royce with 44 miles on the clock because 'it was too small for someone to sit in the back with his hat on'. Such gestures convinced people that he was a barefoot boy who had clawed his way up from the gutter.

This was by no means the case. His own father (and Kerry's grandfather), Robert Clyde Packer, was editor of the now defunct Sydney *Sunday Times*, and Sir Frank's own battered appearance was the legacy of a career as an amateur heavy-weight, not early days fighting for boxing-booth purses, as many assumed. Having married Gretel Bullmore, said to be one of the most beautiful women of his time, Packer pere built up two tabloids, the *Daily Telegraph* and *Sunday Telegraph*, on a diet of extreme right-wing politics unimaginable anywhere except in Australia during the Menzies epoch.

Sir Frank's temper was famous, as were the occasions when he tried to sack people not on his staff, like a visiting postman who had used the wrong lift in the *Telegraph* building. He dominated the left-wing print unions, sometimes by personal physical intimidation.

Despite protests from his composing room, for instance, he forced through his own inimitable emendation to the bill reading STALIN DEAD OFFICIAL which the *Telegraph* printed to announce the latest news from Moscow in March 1953. The Packer-written version which stunned readers the next day proclaimed: STALIN DEAD OFFICIAL – HOORAY! Such extravagances, including the famous *Telegraph* leader advocating that black hostages be taken and shot if civil rights riots continued, became part of the folklore of Sydney's 'yellow' journalistic tradition.

By all accounts, including their own, Sir Frank employed a similarly brutal approach in bringing up his two sons. Clyde, who broke with his father in the end, is more reticent, and perhaps has more reservations, than his younger brother.

Kerry's on-the-record comments make the best of what was evidently a difficult childhood.

'I was scared of my father, sure,' he insists. 'But I never knew him to be unfair. I remember him as a strong man who believed in corporal punishment. I mean he used to belt me with, er, a riding whip. He once told me that if ever I believed I was being unfairly whipped, I should call upon him for a stay of execution and tell him why I thought so. He told me this may not stop the whipping, but that if I thought I did not deserve it, to tell him why not.'

When telling this story he always pauses at this point and adds rather portentously: 'I can never remember calling on that privilege.'

Kerry Packer is never lacking in filial duty – his intimates say he talks about his father a lot, and even has a special incantatory voice that he adopts when he mentions the old man.

There are indications that he was less philosophical at the time, particularly when one considers the full version of a 'Sir Frank' anecdote which is often repeated. The teenage Kerry transgressed by forgetting to bring his tennis racket home from school for the Easter holidays. He was commanded to go back to school and get it, a journey of 1,200 miles by train as the boy was attending Geelong Grammar School in Melbourne. Kerry tells the story nowadays to exemplify a lesson well learnt; never since that hellish weekend has he forgotten the value of his own property and the need to look after it. Here was Sir Frank being 'hard but fair'.

At the time, it seems, the unfortunate schoolboy saw it differently. With half the punishment journey completed, he sent an angry and sad telegram from Melbourne to his father's grand house in Sydney's elite

Bellevue Road, the same street where he now has his own family of a boy (Jamie) and a girl (Gretel).

'Arrived Melbourne safely,' the telegram read. 'No Love, Kerry.'

If Sir Frank was a difficult act to follow, he was an impossible one to live with. Although both sons were given important titles during his lifetime, neither was allowed real independence. When the senior Packer took the hardest decision of his life and sold his beloved newspapers to Rupert Murdoch in 1972, one reason advanced was that in their father's eyes neither son was worthy to take over the succession.

Clyde had been made joint managing director of Channel 9 TV, a post that turned out to be more honorific than real when in the same year it became clear that the Labour Party under Gough Whitlam was heading for electoral victory.

A dispute over whether or not the trades union leader, Bob Hawke, should be interviewed on the channel's main talk programme, 'A Current Affair', led to Clyde resigning. As usual the old man had his way. Not only was Channel 9 prevented from giving the Labour leader a hearing, the programme's presenter, Mike Willesee, was sacked shortly afterwards.

Since Clyde had walked out in disgust, the obedient Kerry was sent round to the studios with a letter from his father to say that the show was going out for the last time. Again obeying orders to the letter, he stood in the control room while Willesee conducted the live programme, ready to wipe the commentator off the air if he made any reference to Sir Frank's ultimatum.

This was all in the best Sir Frank tradition, for in the 1950s, enraged periodically by Channel 9's (admittedly rare) cultural offerings, the old man would ring the studios and order them to black out what they were showing immediately and screen some footage of one of his horses romping home instead. However, for Clyde this final act of autocracy was impossible to accept; there was a breach between father and son and Clyde did not speak freely or often to his father thereafter.

But relations with Kerry, who obeyed his father till the end, were not so deeply affected. 'I don't think Kerry and I ever had a real split,' Clyde says. 'We never had a blazing row. We weren't close enough for that.' Neither emotionally nor – after 1974 – even geographically; for when his father died, Clyde wound up his Australian affairs and went to live in Los Angeles.

Until his late twenties Clyde had been favourite son, heir apparent, the bright one whose speed was meant to make up for 'Boofhead's' dullness and lethargy. But mysteriously he abdicated before ascending the commercial throne. The matter is now not discussed. When people ask Clyde about Kerry he says 'I'm not my brother's wicket-keeper.'

The details of what occurred immediately before Clyde's departure have never been revealed. But the best information is that the younger brother bought out the elder for some £2½ million – in cash.

In 1979 the stock market valued the family holding, which Kerry has dominated ever since, at nearly £12 million; his family's annual income from it, probably around the £1 million mark, already made him one of the richest men in Australia.

On the face of it then, the deal between the two brothers seems markedly to have favoured Kerry. Clyde has never expressed any regrets and both men seem content to have gone their very different ways. Apart from the transaction with Clyde, Kerry Packer had already demonstrated that, whatever his father's reservations, 'Boofhead' knew what he was up to when it came to the publishing business. But since Sir Frank regarded his empire's women's magazines with derision, the fact that Kerry had made a success with a 'new product' called 'Cleo', a watered-down Antipodean version of the US 'Cosmopolitan', won him scant laurels.

Unlike his father, who is said to have worn a track along the carpet from his suite on the third floor to the composing room on the second, Kerry Packer believes in leaving both his editors and their publications in comparative tranquillity. Although his own political views are right-wing, and he is a firm supporter of Prime Minister Malcolm Fraser, his executives insist that the boss is more interested in impact – and commercial success – than ideology.

One of his closest associates, John Cornell, wears a comic life-saver's cap to play 'Strop' in 'Laugh In', a Channel 9 down-market comedy show. 'Strop' is the personification of the 'ocker', the beer-drinking, sports-mad, chauvinistic, moronic Australian male of caricature.

Packer can sound very like 'Strop' – the big-game head collection, the definition of hell as a night at the opera listening to Joan Sutherland, his preferred alternative (watching Starsky and Hutch or Charlie's Angels, both Channel 9 programmes).

However, since he can be subtle and ironic, there is more to Packer than this stereotype. (There is more to Cornell than 'Strop' for that matter. He acted as link man between discontented Australian cricketers and Packer. Almost blasphemously, some MCC members thought, Cornell used the Melbourne Centenary Test as 'cover' to get the first defecting players signed up provisionally – without, to take one example, a figure as knowledgeable as Richie Benaud hearing so much as a whisper.)

When it suits him Kerry Packer can be at least as devious as Cornell. Though he is certainly more interested in television than print, his much advertised disenchantment with newspapers – 'a second-class media nowadays compared with broadcasting,' he says ungrammatically – does not preclude shrewd manipulation of reporters, and particularly women, often it would appear for his own personal amusement.

He plays up to his role as chauvinist pig. One anecdote, much cited by local feminists, has the hallmark of a Packer invention he has floated into the media for a private laugh. It tells how he decided to extend his honeymoon from one day to three 'because it turned out that the wild pig shooting was so good'.

In the 'ocker' tradition, Packer is most at ease in male company. Since he likes talking, not writing memoranda, there is a ritual drinks session in his Castlereagh Street suite most evenings. Sir Frank believed in the virtues of shabbiness in newspaper offices. His son has had the place polished up and banned the tomato sauce bottles from the dining-room. When he thinks there has been enough chat, Kerry follows his father's tradition of ringing a bell to warn everyone to go home.

He himself consumes only what he calls 'softies' – cans of frozen low-calorie drinks. This is heinous in 'ocker' terms, but friends, most of whom are also employees, forgive him. 'Kerry's a good bloke,' they say.

George Negus, a former Left-wing journalist now working for Packer's TV, tried to explain what this ultimate male tribute means in the case of his boss. 'He's not tyrannical, as I expected; and he's put up with my politics, so far anyhow, and he's quite human, though of course he's tough and aggressive. Nobody called old Sir Frank 'a good bloke' in that way, and he probably wasn't. People were physically frightened of him, scared he might land them one. Nobody's scared of Kerry that way.'

Despite his games with guns, there is nothing on the record about Packer shooting anyone (animals are different); and only one account of his being in a fight. Predictably, this was in Sir Frank's day. The Packer and Murdoch interests fell into dispute in 1960 over the takeover of a small Sydney newspaper. There was an impressive punch-up in the streets outside its offices, and Kerry collected two black eyes and a torn shirt.

His great bulk, not far off 18 stone despite the 'no-cals', is usually directed at inanimate not human targets when it comes to physical violence. He has been known to kick his office door open, arriving early and finding it locked, and he once assaulted an Italian chair of David Frost's, which for some reason he disliked. It may be he has created a wrong impression, deliberately even, by telling people so often how much he admires Genghis Khan.

'Not exactly lovable, I suppose, but my favourite historical character because he was so damned efficient.'

Despite an expensive education at schools modelled on English originals, he will never be loved by the kind of people who wear club ties; in Melbourne this is as true as in Marylebone. 'You can't polish Kerry,' commented Elizabeth Fell, a friend of his wife's since school. 'It's like putting nail varnish on a Wellington boot.'

His father, who paid all those school fees, would be neither surprised nor disappointed, very likely. When the brothers were in their early twenties he enrolled them in various clubs, including the Athenaeum (the Melbourne Athenaeum that is). 'By your thirties you'll have trodden on so many bloody corns no good club will have you,' he explained.

Sir Frank may have been a figure as worthy of respect as Kerry Packer claims him to be. But, very likely the son has more imagination, not to say more unholy and heretical impertinence, than even his outrageous sire. When Packer 'fils' wants to join a club that doesn't want him, he is likely to be of a mind to go out and buy it.

The 'club' that ran Australian cricket did not want Packer. So he bought it. But for how much? Was it, as his enemies at Lord's and elsewhere dearly hope, too much? Could it, perchance, turn out that his combination of greed and egotism will cause a nasty bruise where his heart is reputed to be – in his hip pocket?

Simply stated, the deal he made with a demoralised and beaten Australian Cricket Board last July rendered him a great deal for relatively little. In exchange for £2 million sterling Packer gained exclusive TV and promotional rights to cricket in the next three years and the option to extend the contract to cover the next 10. This includes the rights to produce and reap the profits from whatever related merchandise his ever-inventive organisation can dream up.

But, of course, this final outlay is only a drop in the bucket of money that Packer has poured out to win his war against official cricket.

Although the definitive statistics will probably remain a secret, a reasonable estimate suggests that he spent four million pounds on his crucial early campaigns.

The Department of Economics at Melbourne University have found the subject interesting enough for them to have made it a subject for research. Their figures are as follows: Packer's deficits in staging the World Series 'Supertests' in 1977–78 and 1978–79 were respectively £1·05 million and £1·35 million.

The cost of paying salaries to some 60 world star players in 1978–79 ran to approximately £750,000. During its two Australian seasons World Series Cricket spent an additional 'several millions' – a splendidly vague Packeresque assessment – promoting and packaging the Supertests.

This grandiose investment, covering everything from fancy clothes for the players to the installation of specially laid pitches on football grounds and baseball-style floodlights for night cricket, failed to achieve impressive short-term results. In the first season the crowds, despite all the ballyhoo, were notably reluctant to fight their way through the turnstiles. Although some of the 1978–79 night matches in Sydney brought in as many as 40,000 spectators, Andrew Caro's sanguine assertion that in Melbourne as well as Sydney Packer had tapped 'a vast reservoir of new spectators' is no doubt tinged with PR-man's hyperbole.

The TV ratings, however, which are said to be very reliable, give a clear picture of Packer's position before the so-called 'compromise' was negotiated in the summer of 1979.

Take the figures for Saturday, 3 December 1978, a day when Packer was staging a Supertest, a conventional or 'traditional' Test match during the Australia–England Ashes series was in progress and, by way of competition to both, the other channels were running top-class tennis. According to the Australian ratings scale, tennis attracted an index of 18·1, the conventional Test match 5·6 and the WSC Supertest 5·3.

This is a fair average result – tennis always had more daytime viewers than both forms of cricket combined.

Packer is gambling that he can revolutionise Australian tastes to the point where cricket can command at least as impassioned a TV audience as tennis. Ideally, from his point of view, his cricket should become a powerful enough magnet to outdraw all the other sports too. This month he is screening his 'victory' tests in opposition to the Victorian Open Golf Championship, national rowing regattas and the Olympic swimming trials, all of which have strong local appeal.

The current season (Australia *v* England and Australia *v* West Indies) is a promoter's dream; the world's best teams playing Packer's new brutalist cricket as if empires were at stake. And under the reluctant imprimatur of the game's traditional authorities.

Another bonus from Packer's acquisition is that it saves him a great deal of money which he would otherwise have to spend on making or buying programmes for his television channel.

In the costly experimental season of 1977–78 cricket provided him with no less than 315 hours of buckshee TV product.

Cricket is the platonic ideal of a time-filler in the commercial TV sandwich. So with the Australian audience becoming increasingly keen on 'local' product and a good chance that new regulations will dictate that 'local content' must fill more TV time (some experts predict as much as 50 per cent), Packer's purchase should turn out to be a sensational bargain. Particularly if Brearley and his elitist, lily-white exponents of 'the Classical Cricket' take a hammering, literally if possible, from the vengeful Aussies. If we're losers, Kerry's surely on to a winner.

Like all Australians who make a point of being 'one of the boys', Packer likes to gamble. On the eve of his victory, or compromise, last summer he was in London at Aspinall's and reports filtered back that he had won a variety of sums, the consensus being £40,000. When the local Sydney gossip columnists rang Castlereagh Street for confirmation of this latest Anti-Pom coup, no one was prepared to confirm the amount. Packer himself, however, had no hesitation when one enterprising reporter inquired what his biggest ever win had been. 'Cricket,' Packer replied. There is every reason to believe he was telling the truth.

SUNDAY TIMES MAGAZINE, 16 DECEMBER 1979

Boycott: the Hero They All Love to Hate

JOHN MORGAN

Geoffrey Boycott is very much like Lester Piggott. But like Piggott, who rides race horses better than anyone else in the world, he has no peer. Boycott, the enigmatic figure who returns to the England side against New Zealand today, is the best opening bat in the world.

He also engenders more arguments, more fury, more passion among cricket followers than W. G. Grace who, reputedly, needed to see all three stumps knocked out of the ground before he would agree that he might be out!

Boycott is no middle liner. You love him or you hate him.

Former England captain Tony Greig put into words in a Sydney newspaper the thought of many Boycott critics.

Greig wrote: 'His ability to be where fast bowlers aren't has long been a talking point among cricketers. By some stroke of good fortune he has steered clear of the game's fast bowlers for the past five years.'

Yet in 1977, on the same Trent Bridge wicket where today he reappears for England, Boycott scored his 100th century to win back the Ashes from Australia.

Then he became a national hero and a grateful country unanimously elected him *Daily Express* Sportsman of the Year.

But even in that Ashes-winning return there had to be controversy. Boycott ran out local hero Derek Randall.

If the Boycott form book runs true he will hit a come-back century. He always does.

Yet still it will be said of the 37-year-old bachelor from the village of Fitzwilliam, that he only plays for himself.

Perhaps the accusation dates back to an innings at Lord's during his first full season for Yorkshire back in 1963.

On a rain-affected wicket Yorkshire were bowled out for 144 of which Boycott scored a brilliant 90.

As he came up the stairs, tears streaming down his cheeks, he brushed past a man who said, 'Well played, son.'

Geoff never heard that rare tribute from his hero, Sir Len Hutton. He so badly wanted a hundred on his first appearance at Lord's that to him that superb 90 was failure. DAILY EXPRESS, 10 AUGUST 1978

RIBBONED COAT

Did You Know? The first time a blazer was used as official uniform for a sports club, was in 1836 by the Mexican Cricket Union.

Brearley v *Thomson*

MIKE BREARLEY

Jeff Thomson of Australia is one of the fastest and most hostile bowlers in the world. Facing his 90-mile-an-hour deliveries last summer, Mike Brearley, the philosophy Don chosen to captain England after Greig's dramatic sacking, would hum a cello passage from a favourite Beethoven quartet to himself to ease the tension. Batting is for him a concentrated pleasure akin to an art form. His thoughtful and sensitive style of captaincy was to bring England a triumphant victory in the Test series.

The first thing most cricket followers ask me is what it is like to bat against such out-and-out fast bowlers as Holding, Roberts, Daniel, Lillee, Pascoe and Thomson. My short answer is 'exciting'. The adrenalin is pumping, you are alert and, as Dr Johnson said about the man who faces hanging 'it concentrates his mind wonderfully'.

Thomson was bowling with more hostility that second innings at Old Trafford then he did all summer – angrily, as if expressing all the frustration of a side about to lose in England for the first time in fourteen Tests.

He looked hostile, too. He's known as 'Two-Up' among the Australian players, because at times he has given two fingers to the crowd.

Coming in only a few minutes before close of play both hinders and helps a batsman. The most dangerous part of an innings is when you start and, over two days, you obviously start twice. On the other hand, you can see the end, you know how long you have to stick out. I don't mind going to the crease after a long time in the field, however, because I'm relaxed and play a bit more freely because of it. If I could trust my body more, let it go more, I often think, I might do better.

I took middle-stump guard, as I do every innings. I then looked round the field. Thomson, whom I didn't face until the last five balls of the evening, had brought up everybody except fine leg. With that attacking field, if he did pitch it up, which he would have to do every now and again, I knew if I came into the ball firmly there would be some ones and twos to be had.

I looked especially for the short leg because for a certain ball, one about middle-and-leg that bounces high, there is a danger of being caught at short leg. It is important to know that if short leg is just in front of square, you can get out of trouble at the last moment by turning the ball behind square, which I had just done to a delivery from Max Walker.

I then tick off a few check-points of my stance, though rather less meticulously than some golfers such as Jack Nicklaus or, I'm told, Graham Marsh, whose brother, incidentally, was a full sixty feet behind me. Is my head upright? 'Keep your head still.' Are my hands holding the bat easily?

I hum to ease the tension. I like to let musical themes run through my head and my favourite is the cello passage from the opening of the first Rasoumoffsky Quartet. I use the music like a talisman: how can I ever be out with this tune running through my head? I was comfortable. It was cool that evening and my helmet wasn't sweaty and my chest-protector, a pad nine inches square, felt snug.

Thomson reached his mark: he glared. I stopped humming. I replaced it with a different theme – 'take it easy, you'll see him soon enough' – and he started in. I have never seen him come in from such a long run-up, about fifty yards. I don't like to concentrate on a fast bowler until he is well into his run-up, perhaps half-way, because you get over-impressed by his power and speed and become mesmerised. As he approaches the wicket, I stand up and lift my bat high.

Thomson's unusual catapult-like action makes it sometimes hard to pick up the ball early. At Old Trafford the screens are better than on any other Test ground, and I cannot remember having difficulty seeing the ball. As he delivers the ball, I move a little on to the back foot. This movement gives me a fraction of a second longer to react, and it does not prevent me from coming forward into the ball if it is pitched up.

One thing that gives me pleasure is playing a fast bowler straight back down the pitch. Thomson bowled one to me that was just slightly leg-side, fairly well up, and I played it perfectly balanced, coming into the ball and it went to mid-on for two. I hit another ball to cover for two. When play ended that day I had six runs on the board. I was satisfied.

Adapted from 'The Return of the Ashes' by Mike Brearley and Dudley Doust, published by Pelham Books, 1979 and highlighted in THE SUNDAY TIMES, 3 JUNE 1978

The Day Freddie Trueman Was Crowned King

Aircraftman Frederick Sewards Trueman, celebrated his 21st birthday on 6 February 1952 – the day that Princess Elizabeth became Queen.

Celebration, though, is perhaps an extravagant way of putting it.

For a young cricketer of startling talent, and an already turbulent spirit, mooching about a storehouse of an RAF camp seemed a dark affront.

But if these were momentous days for the young Princess, the restless Yorkshireman too was soon to know the sudden thrust of fame.

It came to him like a crack of thunder when the Indian tourists arrived for a series of four Test matches.

Wisden, the cricketers' almanac, records that Trueman swept into

Test cricket like a wild wind, claiming 29 Indian wickets, his bowling so filled with life and venom that the Indian batsmen visibly retreated.

But the dusty pages scarcely translate fully the drama of 7 June 1952 – exactly 25 years ago from Jubilee Day.

A news agency reporter filed a 'rush' score from the Headingley Press box on the Indian second innings. India nought for four. He was rung back immediately. 'You mean, surely, old chap, four for nought.'

'No, I mean nought for four.'

It might be said to be the moment F. S. Trueman arrived.

Trueman's contribution to the most dramatic burst of opening bowling in the history of Test cricket was three wickets for no runs.

He recalls: 'Len Hutton let me bowl down the hill in the second innings and all Pankaj Roy could do with my second ball was scoop it into Denis Compton's hands. Alec Bedser had Gaekwad caught in the gully in his first over, and then I got among 'em.

'They sent in wicket-keeper Mantri early and I decided to give him my slower ball. I'll not forget it. It pitched on the middle stump, straightened out and took the off stump.'

Manjrekar went next ball and it fell to skipper Vijay Hazare to avert the hat-trick. Headingley might have been a plaza de toros and young Trueman a black bull from Andalusia.

He roared to the wicket, the ball sped like a bullet, Hazare waited for the crash of splintered wood or flesh and bone but heard only the rush of air and the smack of collision with Godfrey Evans's gloves.

Says Trueman: 'The first he saw of it was when Godfrey tossed it back to me.'

Hazare, like a blind man in a minefield, negotiated 56 runs. But Trueman got him in the end, clean bowled, and England won comfortably.

His figures for his first Test match were three for 89 and four for 27. His reward: a telegram from the RAF which said that as the Test had finished early he was expected back at camp on Sunday, 8 am.

Trueman's bowling in that Test series earned rich praise. Wisden, a conservative organ, said that it could be compared to the best of Larwood.

But young, raw Yorkshiremen with a reluctance to doff their caps had to be kept in their place, didn't you know.

One England selector offered the thought: 'I hope he takes one for a hundred in the next Test. It will give him some idea of balance.' It was a hope as forlorn as it was putrid. At Lord's he took four for 72 in the first innings and four for 110 in the second.

Trueman was suitably impressed with his own form. By the third Test – at Old Trafford, he was telling the doyen of English seam bowling, Alec Bedser: 'You keep 'em quiet. I'll get 'em out.'

It is a mood that has rarely left Trueman. Still he will reinforce a point in argument by announcing: 'Tha' knows, I was reckoned to have the most perfect bowling action of all time.' And that initial impact against the Indians did much to mould his extrovert nature.

Some 20 years later he met one of his victims, the batsman Adhikari, who was now a colonel in the Indian Army and managing a new Indian touring party.

'Glad to see you've got your colour back, colonel,' said Freddie Trueman   DAILY EXPRESS, 7 JUNE 1977

AUSSIE STORIES

Jack Fingleton recalls the 1932 'Bodyline' tour: There was the day when Warner and Palairet, his assistant manager, came into our Adelaide dressing-room to commiserate with the stricken Woodfull. Woodfull, under medical attention, said to the two Englishmen: 'I don't want to discuss it. There are two sides out there. One is playing cricket, the other isn't.' Warner and Palairet left the room in acute distress. Warner wrote in a book later: 'Unfortunately, there was a member of the Australian team who was a journalist and next day the story was blazoned all over the front pages of their newspapers.' That was a hard one at me. I was the only journalist in the two teams and I knew stories of that tour to make a newspaperman's pen drip with ink. But I kept quiet. The reporter who got the story told me years afterwards of how he made a rendezvous with one of our team the night of the incident and he was told all. The stigma stayed with me. I told Woodfull years later who the 'culprit' was.

'A pity,' said Woodfull, 'that cost you the 1934 tour in England.'
SUNDAY TIMES, 28 JULY 1968

Jack Fingleton on Stan McCabe's innings at Trent Bridge in 1938:

I was standing next to Don Bradman on the dressing-room balcony that day when he called inside to some of our fellows engaged on various dressing-room activities: 'Come and see this. Don't miss a moment of it. You will never see the like of it again.'
'FINGLETON ON CRICKET', COLLINS, 1972

Bowler in an Australian cricket match had taken two wickets with successive balls. Next ball missed stumps, hit wicket-keeper, bounced back, hit batsman (out of his crease), rebounded into stumps. Victorian Cricket Association has ruled 'run-out'. Another hat-trick missed.
LONDON STAR, 19 NOVEMBER 1942

The Old Lady Who Moulded a Man for England

IAN WOOLDRIDGE

Far from the fashionable beaches, on a headland with a toy-town lighthouse and a pink evangelical chapel and cottonwood trees that lean on their elbows under the Trade winds and occasional hurricane, Mrs Marie Stuart heard the news on a crackling bulletin from the BBC World Service in London.

'I was joyous and I did cry and laugh at the same time and I thanked the kind Lord for being so good to an old lady' she recalled in precisely those arresting, half-Biblical phrases.

The idiom, part Devon-burred, part missionary-inspired, part Deep South in its syncopation, is pure plantation Barbadian and impossible to sustain in an English newspaper column.

But here, before I abandon it for good, is exactly what Marie Stuart went on to say about the one of her 19 grandchildren, a descendant as she herself is of the 20,000 African slaves shipped in during the 17th century to work the cane fields, who at last has brought celebrity to her family and the 184-soul East Point community where most ladies still carry the shopping on their heads:

'I taught he right,' said Mrs Stuart. 'I taught he that we'm all God's children, black and white. I taught he never to be disrespectful to nobody and then the Good Lord's blessings will shine on you.'

Last September they shone on her grandson, Roland Orlando Butcher, who was born 27 years ago in Mrs Stuart's Wendy House-sized cottage in the sloping pasture just down from the lighthouse. The fulfilment comes on Thursday when he flies back to the Caribbean with the unique status of being the first West Indian-born cricketer ever to be chosen to tour with an England team.

Roland Butcher himself is apprehensive. 'I am sure some of the crowds will give me a bad time since they regard me as a traitor playing for England and not the West Indies,' he admits. That may well be so in the more militant, emergent-black atmospheres of Trinidad and Jamaica. It will not be so in Barbados. Barbados, the gentle Little England of the Caribbean chain, shares Marie Stuart's pride in the local boy who made good far away.

And Mrs Stuart's pride, understandably, is sheer joy to witness.

If Butcher's success owes much to a hard six-year apprenticeship with Middlesex County Cricket Club, the strength of character that forced him on owes even more to the grandmother who alone schooled him in the simple humanities, table manners and the Ten Commandments between the ages of two and thirteen.

When Butcher was two his carpenter father carpet-bagged it to London in search of work. When he was four his housemaid mother joined her husband in England. It left Grandma Marie Stuart in sole charge of the tiny boy who has grown into England's newest batsman.

During those critical, formative years Butcher was, according to his gently prejudiced grandmother, 'a sweet, sweet boy who only came home from school in tears once. That was when they left him out of the school cricket team. Well, I went down to his master and said: "Why am you leaving our little boy out when you know he loves cricket?" so they picked him and he done real well.'

A determined sporting matriarch, Mrs Marie Stuart, and a gracious, ebullient, affectionate lady as well who greets totally unknown reporters from London not with a boring sterile old handshake but a huge enveloping embrace and warm involuntary kisses on both cheeks.

East Point, in the parish of St Philip, does not have much to contribute to the Barbadian gross national product but such as it has is there for the visitor.

Marie Stuart instantly flew out of her back door and returned with a whole harvest festival of gifts: a huge pumpkin, tropical vegetables, a bowlful of eggs snatched from a flurry of indignant hens.

She dismissed our protests. 'You must,' she cried. 'Everybody was so kind to me when I was in London. White people and black people was all friendly and nice and nobody shouted at me in the streets like I'd been told they would. You are such good people for all that cold weather.' Mrs Stuart's brief visit had been to attend Roland's marriage to a West Indian girl in Stevenage.

She rushed into the tiny living-room to produce the wedding pictures. They looked less like a nuptial group than some Martin Luther King memorial rally, but Mrs Stuart named nearly everyone, pointing them out with a gnarled, prominently-veined hand that still tends 13 sheep, nine black-belly goats, several squadrons of chicken, a large vegetable patch and profusions of tropical flowers.

She is 74 and doesn't have a single grey hair on her head. She looked gorgeous in the slim blue dress specially bought to be photographed in for the Barbadian newspaper that has just nominated her the island's Woman of the Week.

Alongside the shining, tiny living-room with its murals of Buckingham Palace, Piccadilly Circus and a particularly harrowing Crucifixion, was the even tinier bedroom in which Roland Butcher had grown strong on the way to the age of 13 and his eventual departure to join his parents in London.

Outside was the pink telephone on which Roland had rung from Britain to confirm the news she had heard of his selection for England on the BBC. 'He telephoned me right away because he's a good boy and he's never changed even though he's now got famous in England', she said. 'When he came back to Barbados last year he came out on the bus from Bridgetown and stayed in his old bedroom.'

Across two canefields there were goats tethered at backward short-leg and in the covers of the St Catherine ground where Butcher really came to prominence. It is a million miles from the piercing cacophony in which England are shortly to meet the ferocity of a West Indies pace attack powered by huge physical strength and fuelled by intense patriotism.

It is a patriotism Roland Butcher can no longer share. His allegiance is now to an England where he has a home, wife and son in Fulham. It is a patriotism, too, which has put his grandmother into something of a quandary.

She will catch the half-hourly bus on the 7p. journey down the coast to Bridgetown's towering Test match ground and there watch her grandson playing for England. Well versed in the knowledge that the meek shall inherit the earth she will, she says, 'sit there just watchin' Roland make all them runs without cheerin' nor clappin' for no one'.

There is neither road nor even path to her cottage. She stood there, nuzzled by goats and sheep, in her field and waved until we disappeared over the horizon. The kind Lord had done a fine job.

DAILY MAIL, 13 JANUARY 1981

Mervyn Who?
He Took One Test Wicket – Mine!

DENIS COMPTON

When the 80-odd former Australian Test players fly into London on Thursday to join us all in the celebrations that are part of the Cornhill Insurance Centenary Test, beginning at Lord's on Thursday week, memories will flood back. Especially for me.

I just wish I could have a tape recorder with me as I meet all my old buddies so that I could share with you the nostalgia that will pour out.

For this will be an occasion for talking as well as playing, for remembering and reliving, part at least, of 100 years of cricket history.

How else could it be when I know for instance that Keith Miller, Ray Lindwall, Lindsay Hassett, Arthur Morris, Neil Harvey, Bill Johnston, Don Tallon and Ernie Toshack of the 1948 Aussie side alone will be here?

So will Bill Ponsford and Bill ('Tiger') O'Reilly . . . two of the greatest names in any history of the game. So, too, will Mervyn Waite. Mervyn who, you will echo.

Although only a few might remember him, Mervyn opened Australia's bowling in the famous Oval Test of 1938. That was when Len

Hutton made his record 364 and England, after declaring at 903 for seven, won by an innings and 579 runs!

It was when we were well past 500 for three with runs pouring all over the ground and Eddie Paynter and I had been sitting with our pads on for two days waiting to go in that Eddie said 'I'll bet you a quid we don't make 10 between us – if we ever get in at all.'

'Right,' I replied. 'You're on.'

Sure enough, Eddie was leg-before to O'Reilly for a duck and, although I managed a single from the great man, I was immediately clean bowled with a straight half-volley from the said Mervyn Waite.

The point is that Mervyn finished with one for 150 and I was the only Test victim he ever claimed. He never forgot it and every time I hit Adelaide afterwards he would be there to greet me with: 'Compo, my one and only Test victim, come and have a drink.' It will be the same this week, except that I'll be buying.

You might ask what the golden oldies of the game talk about when they get together with the beer and wine flowing. It is about people and players rather than matches, although the odd Test that got away comes into it, and about fun rather than bitchery.

I suspect the modern zombie-like mode of helmet-wearing will get a fair thrashing, as well as the 'new' idea that fast bowling and the bouncer have just been invented. Shades of Frank Tyson, Lindwall and Miller when they were needled!

Clearly, we all have our own ideas of the 'best' or the 'greatest' of our time and talking now of England and Australia, I will argue through mine with anybody.

I rate Don Bradman the No 1 Aussie captain, with Freddie Brown the best England skipper I played under.

The fastest bowler? Without a doubt, in his two prime years, it has to be 'Typhoon' Tyson. For sheer pace I would back him against any of the likely lads of today.

But for consistent quality over a career I pick Lindwall, with Miller the most awkward, match-winning bowler when the mood took him.

Although he does not come into the fast bowler category, the quality man for England has to be Alec Bedser. After all, 104 of his 236 Test wickets were Aussies – and he got Bradman more than most.

The best batsman of my time – or since – has to be that man, Bradman, again. And, on the England side, I choose Len Hutton. As for the outstanding post-war batsman in England, I take Peter May.

Spin bowlers? O'Reilly, with his leg-breaks, high bouncy googly and lethal straight quickie, has to be top man. With Jim Laker, Bob Appleyard and the fastest leg-spinner of all time, Doug Wright, leading my 'home' list.

The best Test innings I have ever seen? I can still see it! It was the magnificent 232 Stan McCabe hit against us at Trent Bridge in 1938.

He made the runs out of 300 scored in less than four hours and produced such a spectacular explosion of glorious graceful strokes that even Bradman called his men to the balcony with the comment: 'Watch this ... you may never see the like in Test cricket again.'

My own best innings against Australia? Apart from the 102 in my first Test appearance, I would say the 184 at Trent Bridge in 1948, when I finally fell on my wicket, and the 145 not out at Old Trafford after I had played a Lindwall bouncer into my face and had to play most of the innings with a stitched and aching head decorated with plaster.

Which bowlers gave me most trouble? Who else but that terrible but magnificent pair, Lindwall and Miller? If one did not get you out, the other did.

I do not expect everyone will agree with my assessments – but it is the lighter side that will dominate the next couple of weeks ...

The Aussies are bound to recall the time at the Oval when Sid Barnes presented umpire Alec Skelding with a white stick and a little 'guide' dog! Skelding, a great character who always ended a day's cricket by lifting the bails and saying: 'And that, gentlemen, ends the entertainment for the day', took Sid's joke in his stride.

They will also recall the occasion when Miller, having had two lbw shouts turned down, halted in his walk back to tower over umpire Harry Baldwin and, using both hands, calmly turned up the brim of his trilby hat! Again, realising that it was fun and not dissent, Harry roared with the rest.

And I will come in for a full share of leg-pulling. I do not suppose Bill O'Reilly will let me forget that I was dropped off his bowling before I had scored in my first Test. By Bradman, no less. I won't tell you what Bill said.

The Test that got away will also come up for replay. I mean Headingley in 1948, when we should have romped away with a game the Aussies won by seven wickets. We set them to get 404 in 345 minutes on the last day and, because we could not hold a catch, shamefully, we let them score them.

I took opener Hassett's wicket and then had Bradman dropped twice off me before he had reached 20. He went on to make 173. When Arthur Morris had made 32, he was so far out of his crease that he started to walk back to the pavilion before realising that Godfrey Evans had not gathered the ball for the stumping and he got back. Arthur went on to make 182. And that, in a nutshell, was how a famous Test got away.

I reckon my mate, Godfrey Evans, was the best 'keeper of my time – he was superb standing up to Bedser. He insists that the Leeds match was the worst of his life. He went to bed early on the fourth night – and later swore that he would never do anything as foolish again. Going to bed early, I mean.

I could go on and on.

Now all we can do is hope for fine weather for the centenary Test and to pay a tribute to Cornhill for putting down an extra £90,000 to help the Test and County Cricket Board stage such an historic event.
SUNDAY EXPRESS, 17 AUGUST 1980

Gower – Grafting for a Living

PAUL WEAVER

The man called 'Lulu' by his fellow England cricketers because of his golden locks is back in the hit parade.

For not even Geoff Boycott has been able to match the consistency of the remodelled David Gower in the West Indies this winter.

Gower was leading England's batting averages at the start of the current Test with 401 first-class runs from six innings for an average of 66·83. Boycott has scored 434 runs in seven innings at 62·00, and the rest are nowhere in sight.

England's most gifted batsman told me: 'We were all pleased 10 days ago when the tour was given the go-ahead after the so-called Robin Jackman affair, but I reckon I was happier than most.

'I came out here with a point to prove, and if we had all gone home early it would only have been partly proved.

'I've taken a bit of stick in the past year or so. And when I think about it, I realise I could have played more for England last summer but no one can say I haven't worked hard and applied myself on this trip.

'I like to go for my shots and waft a few, but I've realised that you just can't carve these West Indian fast bowlers about. No one can cut and drive these men at will.

'I've grafted and played a few grinders. I want to be thought of as a good player, and that means more than being able to play attacking shots.

'If you score 40 or 50 against these West Indian fast bowlers you have to bat for something like two-and-a-half hours, and that means a lot of concentration. I've improved that part of my game.

'I'm only sorry we didn't play in Guyana because Timur Mohamed tells me that the Bourda at Georgetown is one of the best batting wickets in the world.'

In the two months England have been in the West Indies, Gower has made almost serene progress towards the ranks of the great batsmen.

His scores of 187, 77, 48, 27, 18 and 44 have each reflected a determination and self-discipline which the Leicestershire left-hander has been alarmingly short of in the past.

He will be 24 on April 1, and this will surely go down as his coming of age tour.

His nonchalance, often and wrongly interpreted as uncaring self-destructiveness, has only been upset once – by his controversial run-out against Barbados last Saturday.

He had scored a painstaking 18 when assuming the ball was 'dead' he left his crease to pat down the wicket at the end of an Albert Padmore over.

But he was given out when Collis King fielded swiftly and wicket-keeper David Murray broke the wicket.

Speaking about the incident for the first time, Gower said: 'It was a bad experience and I still feel sick and angry about it. Immediately afterwards I told myself to ride the thing and put it to the back of my mind. But the more I've thought about it since, the more it has annoyed me.

'I had played well – as well as I had on the whole of the tour – and was looking forward to getting some more runs under my belt on a good wicket and with the Third Test just round the corner. After that, to get out the way I did, was a bad show.

'I don't blame the square-leg umpire David Archer for giving me out. After all, if the ball wasn't "dead" I was out. But the other umpire, Stanton Parris at the bowler's end, was the one who surprised me, because I thought he had called "over" and was even moving towards square leg for the next over.

'I saw a few of the Barbados players afterwards and their batsman Emmerson Trotman said: "You weren't out, man. No way. The umpire had called 'over'." And Collis told me that he didn't deliberately try to run me out when he threw the ball back.

'I suppose it was a lesson for me, a real case of over and out. But I find the whole thing unforgettable. And I'm sure there would have been crowd trouble if the same thing had happened to a Barbados player.'

Looking back on the series of disasters that have befallen the England cricketers on this tour, Gower now reckons that things are looking brighter.

'We've had a lot of rain and setbacks, but now it's like starting all over again,' he says.

'We've had a very warm welcome in Barbados and the weather has been good. Some wives and girl friends are out here and the players feel more at home and relaxed. We're playing cricket and the morale is good.

'As far as the series is concerned, we're really up against it. Somewhere, we need a good day with the bat and a good day with the ball, bowling them out cheaply. They're a very good side.'

NEWS OF THE WORLD, JANUARY 1981

Short Runs

David Steele put on a pair of gloves at chilly Edgbaston yesterday . . . and gave Rohan Kanhai five runs towards his century.

Kanhai, of Warwickshire, had taken three runs off Mushtaq and Northants wicket-keeper, George Sharp, had thrown off his gloves to chase the ball, Steele promptly put them on to take John Dye's throw to the wicket.

But Australian umpire Tom Brooks decided that was illegal and awarded Kanhai five extra runs.

Editor's Note: This decision is covered in The Laws of Cricket. No 44, The Fieldsman . . . 'The fieldsman may stop the ball with any part of his person, but if he wilfully stop it otherwise five runs shall be added to the run or runs already made; if no run has been made, five shall be scored. The penalty shall be added to the score of the striker if the ball has been struck, but otherwise to the score of byes, leg-byes, no balls or wides as the case may be.

It is explained in 'Notes': A fieldsman may not use his cap, etc, for the purpose of fielding a ball; the five runs are a penalty and the batsmen do not change ends . . .

Tuesday, 15 September 1981, during BBC 1 Review of 1981 Test series, Richie Benaud asked Ian Botham:

'What caused you to give up the captaincy? Was it the long walk back to the pavilion at Lord's after your low score, and the silence of the crowd?'

'Not entirely. I had already felt that the selectors' decision to choose the captain on a match-to-match basis was not helping me, the team or my family. Kath was in the crowd that day, and I know she was upset at the way things were not working out. When I reached the dressing-room half the team were in various other parts of the pavilion. I told the rest I had decided to give up the captaincy. There was a frozen silence, which I appreciated in a sort of way. From that moment all I wanted to do was to collect Kath, get in the car and drive off. But first, I met Alec Bedser who heard my decision, and said that it was the selectors' wish that I was to take a rest from captaining the side.'

'Gentlemen queue here for Players'

WARTIME NOTICE INDICATING RATIONED CIGARETTES AVAILABLE AT SERVICES CANTEEN ON LORD'S CRICKET GROUND

From the Stock Exchange, where it is positively affirmed all the 'new' jokes come from, a cricket score:

Germany v *The Rest*

A. U. Stria	*run out*	0
C. Slovakia	*c* and *b* Hitler	0
P. O. Land	*c* Stalin *b* Hitler	10
D. Enmark	*run out*	0
N. Orway	*c* Quisling *b* Hitler	1
H. Olland	*retired hurt*	2
B. Elgium	*st* Leopold *b* Hitler	3
Luxe M. Bourg	*b* Hitler	0
F. R. Ance	*c* Mussolini *b* Hitler	20
G. B. Ritain	*not out*	20
A. Merica	*to bat*	
CLOSE OF PLAY		56 for 9

The *Daily Express* story (13 July 1940) forgot the twelfth man on each side, Russia and Japan.

The sentiment of the cricket association came more alive later, when, before Alamein, Montgomery told his troops to hit Hitler for 'six'.

Flying Officer Keith Carmody, who it has been said will probably captain Australia in the first peace-time Test matches, is a prisoner of war in German hands, it was announced last night.

A few hours before he went out on his last sortie, Carmody, captain of the RAAF cricket team which has proved almost invincible this season, complained to the Australian Prime Minister, Mr Curtin, that he and his fellow players, many of whom had been on operational duties, were being classed in Australia as 'Jap Dodgers'.

DAILY SKETCH, 1 AUGUST 1944

Editor's Note: Mr Curtin, who at the time was watching the match at Lord's between England and Australia, promised that he would see that the lie was nailed when he got back to Australia, which he did. I had a particularly close interest in this story because Keith asked me to be with him when we saw Mr Curtin. I got an exclusive interview, but unfortunately the Censor killed the story stone dead!

Heard during a speech at the Lord's Taverners spring luncheon, Cafe Royal, 22 April 1969:

Sir Learie Constantine was determined in one match to get the great Don Bradman. So, by using all his skill and cunning, 'I saved up my best ball and finally used it.

'And bowled The Don for 265!'

1,000 Days of Non-stop Cricket

J. L. MANNING

Frequently we read in newspapers and hear on television and radio that 'this was a boring match'. Boring to whom? To players, spectators or just a few reporters?

One man who should be more bored than most is Jimmy Binks, the Yorkshire wicket-keeper.

It is exhausting even to think what he has done. If he were asked what he did in his youth he would have to say: 'Well, I played in 335 consecutive county championship cricket matches.'

Can you imagine that? Three hundred and thirty-five matches: a commitment to 1,005 days of six hours each, week after week, month after month, summer after summer.

And he never missed one game. Not a single absence on account of fatigue, weariness, cramp, self-inflicted injury, depression, misery, melancholia, a grandmother's funeral, a race meeting, the State opening of Parliament, 'Coronation Street' or just plain fedupness.

Squatting behind the wickets, changing ends, slumping in the pavilion, patting his bat at the wicket, waiting for rain to stop, glancing at the sky, packing his bag and putting on his flannels, for ever and ever and a thousand days since 1955.

The imagination is stifled. But it is not a record. Ken Suttle, the Sussex opening batsman, has played 351 championship games in a row. His marathon began in 1954.

But a wicket-keeper's task is greater. He is bending to it all the time. Every ball is a spinning world of its own. He has to watch it, consider it, judge it and time it, even if no one else does.

I asked Binks if he ever got bored.

'I can stand it, but I don't think the spectators can,' he said.

But surely you must have fleeting moments when you say 'I've just about had enough?'

'To be honest, I suppose that does happen,' he said, 'but not often. It happens towards the end of a season when Yorkshire have no chance of winning the championship. That's not often, so it's not often I'm bored.'

Don't you ever get tired keeping wicket all day?

'Of course. But I'll tell you what: it's more tiring out in the field.'

I never thought of it that way. Binks says a wicket-keeper hears all the chat, sees all the play and is in almost every bit of the action.

'It's worst of all, though, in midweek. So few come to watch. It's not their fault and it's not ours. The players can take it, but sometimes the spectators can't. I feel sorry for them.'

I never thought of that, either. I wonder if the Clark Committee on county cricket did?

In 1966, they said, players were as negative and unenterprising as they were the year before. Yet only seven of 125 cricketers said they did not enjoy playing.

To men like Binks this was treason. And I begin to catch some understanding of what is going wrong. Words such as 'negative', 'unenterprising' and 'pointless' come too readily to our language of cricket. Some of its boredom is the tiresome frequency with which we use the word.

There is one point, however. Binks has lost count of how many wickets he has taken. After nearly 900, it gets a bit tedious.

DAILY MAIL, 13 JANUARY 1967

West Indian Summer

MICHAEL PARKINSON

There have been better teams (not many, and not much better) but there has been no more significant and influential team in the recent history of the game than Worrell's West Indians.

In 1960–61 they gave a live-saving boost to Australian cricket in a series which included possibly the greatest Test match ever played – the Brisbane Test which ended in a tie. For countless Australians Frank Worrell became their first non-white hero. He and his team were the saviours of Australian cricket: when they arrived the local game was in a pitiful state. The preceding tour by England had been catastrophically dull; another tour like that and Australian cricket might have perished. Worrell's team set the game alight. They lost the series but started the renaissance.

They came like crusaders to this country to find the English game in a coma. It was over-polite, over-coached, dying on its well-bred feet. The attempts at remedies contained a classic series of wrong diagnoses. We introduced knock-out cricket ('comic cricket' as the players know it), altered the rules, messed about with four stumps. Generally we tampered with the body of the game when it was suffering from a disease of the soul. It was like putting splints on a man suffering from a nervous breakdown.

English cricket at the start of the West Indian tour had reached the stage which British soccer found itself in in 1953 when the Hungarians came to Wembley and demonstrated a new and more effective way of playing the game.

For English cricket the West Indians were a necessary and long over-due purgative. They gave a new dimension to the game, put a bomb in the Long Room, peeled the skin from the eyes of an audience long blinded by boredom.

Those administrators and Long-Room lawyers who measure brighter cricket by the number of sixes hit in an innings will find cold comfort for their theories in the success of the tourists. The team is indisputably an attractive one, playing attractive cricket, and yet throughout the present Test series it scored no faster than England (most certainly not an attractive side) and bowled at a much slower rate. Their secret, and one which they have shared with two countries, is a new psychological approach to the game. And this is their strength and their importance.

They appeal to all levels and to all the senses. The connoisseur savours the silken techniques of Sobers and Worrell, just as the layman thrills to the menace and savagery of Kanhai's hitting or Hall's bowling. Suddenly this season people wanted to go and see Test cricket again. The only time UMP had more inquiries was when the West Indies came here in 1957. More people listened to it on the radio and watched it on television this year – and it is a near certainty that more people enjoyed the series.

More people also made a greater noise than they had done at a Test match before. For whatever Worrell and his team did for our game on the field of play, their brothers repeated in the stands for our spectators.

It would be a gross libel on Yorkshire cricket grounds generally, and Bramall Lane, Sheffield in particular, to say that the West Indians invented audience participation. But it is undeniable that they persuaded spectators in our more inhibited counties to stop sitting on their hands. Until this season spectators shared the general condition of the game. They were part of the same dreary, middle-class ritual, and were as noisy as falling snow.

My old man once went to Lord's to see the Australians on their last tour. They were batting against the MCC and Larter was bowling to McDonald. The Australian flashed at one ball, got a thick edge and snicked it to the boundary. It was a scruffy shot but everyone on the ground, including the red-faced man in front of us but excluding my old man, politely clapped the boundary. This was too much for a man reared at Bramall Lane. 'Get 'em t' middle or else get thissen back in t'hutch,' he bellowed, whereupon this red-faced man turned round and said: 'Do you mind – you're not at a bloody soccer match now, you know.'

One wonders what he would have made of the rapier-thin West Indian who ran on to the field at Old Trafford after Sobers had taken Dexter's wicket. He was wearing leather knee-breeches, yellow braces, knee socks, black plimsolls and a straw hat. As he ran to the middle he shouted: 'Dexter is a lord, but Sobers is de king.'

What the West Indian spectators brought to English cricket grounds was an uninhibited and total involvement with the game. They seek gods and not paragons. They are knowledgeable and generous with their praise and criticism of players on both sides.

During the Old Trafford Test Hunte was batting with Kanhai when a mix-up led to Kanhai being run out. Immediately poor Hunte was subjected to the kind of abuse that one only hears at Goodison Park on a Saturday afternoon. 'You silly nut-head,' shouted the man in front of me, waving a fistful of notes he had accumulated during a mammoth gambling session on the game. He exhorted Butcher, the incoming batsman, to 'run the silly nut-head out'. Trueman was implored to 'hit him on the head'.

They gamble wildly on a game and will bet on anything, from how many runs a player will get to what time drinks will be brought on to the field. They love outsize characters in the way children love comic papers. Trueman on the English side was their favourite. At Old Trafford he tried a few mischievous bumpers in a failing light. 'Better put de light on when Wes bowls, Freddie man,' he was told. He stuck two fingers up at them and grinned and they loved him.

The West Indians who live in this country have gained confidence and status from the performance of their team in the middle. Their confidence is apparent and a blessing. At Manchester, as an English player stopped the ball with his boot, a man in the posh seats shouted: 'Only bloody black men do that – it doesn't hurt them. They're not used to wearing boots.' But the West Indians within earshot only laughed. 'Nut-head', said the gambling man sadly.

They have every reason for confidence and joy. For during this tour West Indian cricket arrived finally and indisputably at maturity. It has taken three generations to achieve their present state, where they are not only a fine team but good enough to shape the destiny of the game. It is worth repeating, just to hammer the fact home to the blimps in the Long Room, that they beat England not because they scored faster or bowled quicker but because strategically and technically their game was superior to ours. They won, not with the improvised flair which has always been their natural and sometimes only ally, but with a toughness and hardness which made even Yorkshire look like a gang of cream puffs.

Their cricket has steel in it. It is hardened and disciplined. They are no longer the black and white minstrels of the cricket field but a team capable of beating anyone in the world at any level of this difficult and complex game.

They were beaten on this tour only in conditions peculiarly English. Whenever the sun was on them and the wicket true they appeared to be playing a different game from us. Like all great teams they have the ability to play hardest when it matters most. At Bramall Lane against Yorkshire they frisked along until the game reached a decisive point. And then the tempo of their play changed and they won with a ruthlessness which is essential to all great teams. Ellis Robinson once remarked (and we must never tire of quoting the classics): 'Cricket is made of them as knows and them as only thinks they know.' The West Indies now know.

The fulcrum of the team is the captain, Frank Worrell. In his youth he was one of the world's great all-rounders: a lyrical batsman, a useful bowler. Today, at 39 one of the oldest international sportsmen, he is undeniably the finest captain in the world, and one of the great captains of all times. He is the quintessence of the change and quality of the team. If you believe the old wives' tale about West Indians, then he ought to be volatile and excitable. Instead, he is placid to the point of appearing perpetually weary. Yet in reality he is shrewd, tough and has never been known to miss a trick. His ability for relaxation and complete detachment from everything has led him to be called 'conceited' and 'big-headed'. It started in Barbados, where he was born, and even today when he returns there he is likely to be barracked.

He has, of course, no conceit. The source of his calm stems from his belief that everything, even the result of a cricket match, is pre-ordained and no amount of worry will alter it. He often sleeps in the pavilion during a Test match.

He is revered by his players, and this in itself makes him unique among post-war West Indian captains. 'Frank knows everything you know about the game and then some more,' said the magnificent Garfield Sobers. Worrell acquired most of that extra knowledge in the Lancashire League where he played for many years.

Like all great captains he is given to intuitive inspiration. At Leeds, with Hall, the world's fastest bowler, unsweated and pawing the ground, he gave the ball to Sobers who immediately took a wicket. Ask him why he did it and the lids droop lower over the almond-shaped eyes and he says, 'Oh, it seemed a good idea at the time.' He is very much the father figure of this West Indian side.

It embarrasses him when you suggest this, but he is one of the few men in the world who can advise Kanhai that his technique is faulty, or calm the excitable Hall. In the Lord's Test, in a situation where the West Indian cricket could have fallen apart at the seams, Worrell calmed and inspired his team in a manner not witnessed on our cricket fields for generations. When Close made Hall angry with his impertinence, Worrell stopped the bowler, talked to him, patted his back, altered his field, even made him laugh. And Hall was calm where he could have lost his head.

Apart from his great captaincy, Worrell gave us one other treasure this summer, and that was his innings at Old Trafford in the Test. He batted with a serenity and beauty long missing from the game. Watching him you had the impression he didn't care whether he scored nought or 1,000. And you would have been right. Frank Worrell set aside personal ambition a long time ago; his only concern nowadays is whether the crowd is getting or not getting its money's worth.

Worrell apart, there were five other West Indians who enhanced our summer: Sobers, Hall, Griffith, Kanhai and Gibbs. Of these, Sobers is the most fascinating. He is one of the game's greatest all-rounders, one of the few men who can be mentioned in the same sentence as Keith Miller. An instinctive player who, like Worrell, is in the great tradition of West Indian stylists, Sobers is an exciting mixture of the primaeval and the beautiful. When he hooks his lips curl, his teeth glint, his body whirls and he strikes the ball with a savagery quite beyond the mental and physical capabilities of any white cricketer. And then he cover-drives and the poise and feeling for the shot are such that he might have been reared on the soft and silken fields of Charterhouse. His versatility is almost absurd. He is a dangerous left-arm seam bowler, with an action like polished glass, and a left-arm slow bowler of variety and imagination, who delights in exploding his Chinaman like a firecracker. Before the Leeds Test, when it seemed doubtful whether Sobers would play because of injury, Worrell was asked whether he would miss Sobers the batsman or Sobers the bowler. 'Neither,' he said. 'But I shall certainly miss Sobers the fielder.'

Kanhai bats as if he invented the art. At Old Trafford there was a remarkable instance of his genius. Allen was bowling tight at him. Obviously concerned with keeping him quiet. He did so for three overs until Kanhai, tiring of the game, dropped on one knee and pulled a ball pitched at least 18 inches outside his off stump to the square-leg boundary. It was a stroke of instinct, remarkable and demoralising. It was also, and perhaps this is the significant point, the kind of a shot you would never find described in any English cricket coaching manual.

Hall and Griffith became on this tour one of the great pairs of fast bowlers. They join Lindwall and Miller, Trueman and Statham. And, like all such combinations, each had his separate function. Hall was the big gun, the softener. Griffith was the destroyer. Maurice Leyland once said about fast bowling: 'None of us likes it, but we don't all let on.' One of the problems England had this summer was that too many of her batsmen made it only too obvious they didn't relish facing Hall's kind of pace.

Hall is one of the fastest bowlers the game has ever seen, and has an uninhibited delight in bowling bumpers: an honest bowler. Griffith is foxier. He uses his bumper not as a means of self-expression as does Hall but as a weapon to get rid of the batsmen. When it comes it is one of the most frightening balls in the game's history, a fearsome, leaping thing which climbs straight at the batsman from only just short of a length.

Lance Gibbs, like Griffith, displayed all his talents on the tour. A slim, handsome man, he is probably the finest off-spin bowler in the game today. Not once on the tour was he absolutely mastered by an English batsman, and in one Test at least – at Old Trafford – he bowled his team to victory. On the evening of the first day of this Test, when the West Indians were scoring runs with ease and building a match-winning total, someone said to Gibbs: 'Wicket looks dead, Lance.' Gibbs smiled and replied: 'Not dead, man, just sleeping.' He went on to take 11 wickets in the match.

The West Indians brought a new sun to our summer, weaved their brilliance through the fabric of our game, spun the gold of their talents generously. They like English crowds ('friendly,' says Worrell), hate the weather ('disgusting'). But many of them have grown used to the conditions, having played League cricket in the North Country for many seasons. Next year Kanhai and Gibbs are playing in the North East, Hall and King in the Lancashire League and Sobers in the Staffordshire League. They can earn more than £1,500 in a season, and often acquire a distinct Lancashire accent.

No one is quite sure how many miles they have travelled on the tour. Their own unique method of passing the time is to re-enact the latest Perry Mason drama they have seen on television. They adore Mason because he never loses. They adlib the plot for hours in an often riotous parody. Wesley Hall loves to play Mason (no one will say who plays Della Street).

The West Indians have shown us that the game of cricket can be beautiful and exciting without altering its structure. They have revealed the flaw in English cricket as being with the players and not the game.

They are not unaware of themselves as the greatest single influence on the game today, but generally are too charming and modest to talk about it. Ask Worrell to sum up his team and he says: 'It's quite a good one.' But surely, you say to him, it is more than that. Look what it did for Australian cricket. Look how it restored English cricket. Come now, surely this team is significant. And the eyelids droop even more, the smile becomes even more weary, and Frank Worrell says softly: 'They are a nice gang of chaps. A bunch of comedians really.'

SUNDAY TIMES MAGAZINE, 8 SEPTEMBER 1963

WORDS OF WISDOM

How to cure a cricketer's red nose – drink till it's purple."

BEACHCOMBER, DAILY EXPRESS

True story told by R. C. Robertson-Glasgow, on how he got his nickname: Playing for Oxford University against Essex I bowled old Charlie McGahey with a fanciful full toss, much to Charlie's disgust. When he got back to the pavilion, Essex captain Johnny Douglas asked what happened.

'Bowled out by a blighter I thought was dead two thousand years ago.'

'What's his name?' asked Johnny.

'Chap called Robinson Crusoe,' McGahey grunted.

Jim Laker and I Take 19 Wickets!

ROY PESKETT

Cricket makes great television. It comes over well on the little screen, and provides great entertainment for those who cannot get to the actual match.

And they, during an exciting Australian or West Indies series, are many.

I remember sitting through every ball bowled by Jim Laker when he took all ten wickets against Australia at Manchester.

I was watching the set in the Sports Editor's room at the *Daily Mail*. Being the middle of the summer, I did not have a great deal to do that afternoon, so sat on, and on.

Others with more urgent duties came and went. A head would pop in and say, 'How's it going?' To be told 'Laker's taken 6 for 40, fifteen in the match so far.'

Until only two wickets were left. Everybody, sensing that history was being made, the impossible feat of taking nine wickets in one innings of a Test against the Australians, and all ten in the next, was 'on'.

Nobody thought that he wouldn't have believed it in a boys' comic. The roar that went up in that room for the ninth wicket could have been heard at Old Trafford.

Then in came the luckless Gil Langley. He just didn't have a chance. Up ambled Jim Laker, that tireless, effortless run which had stamped itself into a stroll of victory.

Over went his arm, Langley moved across to pad up, and everybody in the Sports Editor's room appealed for lbw. And then slapped the back of the nearest neighbour as the umpire's finger went up.

Another great session on the goggle box came at the end of the Lord's Test with the West Indies in June 1963. It was almost unbearable as the tension mounted during that grey, tense afternoon.

At one stage, while Ted Dexter was batting, it looked long odds on England winning. Then the tide turned, turned again, ebbed backwards and forwards. Until there remained only time for one more over.

Frank Worrell, the West Indies skipper, still the calmest man on and off the television screen when all the world round him was going crazy, walked over to great lion-hearted Wesley Hall, coming up for his last, and perhaps, his most fateful over.

Worrell said something quietly to Hall, then turned to take his place in the field. Long after the excitement had died, Worrell revealed that after asking Hall whether he was strong enough to bowl that last over after his long, gruelling spell – Hall said, 'Try and stop me, man' – the captain said 'Wes, whatever you do, don't bowl a no-ball!'

That's how close the match stood. But let the brilliant on-the-spot report from Ian Wooldridge, which appeared in next morning's *Daily Mail*, tell the story:

'The most fantastic over Lord's has ever seen – stop pounding, pulse, while I tell the story of cricket's greatest last over. It began at Lord's last night at 5.55. It ended just after six.

'In those few minutes blue-bloods cavorted like children on the pavilion balconies, newspapermen stood and roared.

'So ended the Second Test between England and West Indies in a draw.

'After 29 hours and 55 minutes, England needed eight runs to win when the last over began.

'Wesley Hall, the world's fastest bowler, was turning at the end of his 22-yard run. Derek Shackleton, greying 38-year-old veteran from Hampshire, had to face him.

'He was last but one man in. For England's last hope, Colin Cowdrey, was still in the dressing room, with his fractured left arm in plaster.

'BALL ONE: Hall unleashed it like a bullet. At 90 mph, it swung viciously away. Shackleton lashed out and missed.

'BALL TWO: It was just as fast, but straighter. Shackleton dropped his bat on it and ran. Hall flung himself down the wicket to try and run out David Allen, racing from the other end. Hall stumbled. England – seven to win.

'BALL THREE: Allen turned it down the leg side for a single. Six to win.

'BALL FOUR: Shackleton lashed out, missed and stumbled. He looked up to find Allen racing at him. He ran. But Murray, West Indies' 19-year-old wicket-keeper, coolly tossed the ball to captain Frank Worrell.

'Worrell could not trust himself to throw. He had a two yard start on Shackleton and ran like an Olympic sprinter to the other end. Shackleton was run out.

'England six to win, two balls to go. And in came Colin Cowdrey. For 30 minutes he had been practising batting one-handed in the dressing-room for this moment. (Long afterwards he said that, had he been forced to use the bat, he would have batted left-handed.)

'Cowdrey, said many, was showing fool's courage to bat at all. It will already probably be twelve weeks before he can return to cricket. Another blow could finish his career. But, mercifully, it was Allen facing the bowling.

'BALL FIVE: Allen pushed it back.

'BALL SIX: Hall, in utter silence, tossed it from hand to hand and looked imploringly to the sky. He began to run, gold crucifix flying out behind him.

'England could win with a six. West Indies would win with a wicket.

'It was probably the fastest ball of Hall's life. It seered straight for Allen's middle stump. But Allen leant forward like a master and met it with a bold British bat.

'Cricket's great last over was done.

'The greatest cricketing contest on English soil ended without a victor or vanquished. The only winner was cricket itself.'

DAILY MAIL, 26 JUNE 1963

I Saw the Brisbane Tie

JACK FINGLETON

Let agnostics scoff if they wish, but do not disbelieve that Divine providence, with Dr Grace the likely chairman of the advisory committee, did ordain and control those tumultuous last minutes of play at Brisbane last Wednesday. No earthly cricket mind could have thought up such a fantastic finish. If presented in fiction, publishers would have spurned it beyond human credibility.

Wesley Hall had to win or lose the Test in that last over he started at six minutes to six. I saw him walk back slowly to his mark, fingering a cross on a chain he wears around his neck, and I could well imagine him saying a prayer: 'Lord, please, a miracle. Yet not one, but at least three. Please, O Lord.' He stood poised on his mark, giving his sleeve its last roll and taking huge gulps of air into his lungs for the final fling. Hall, with the new ball, was Worrell's final gamble, and what a hopeless one it seems at the last over. Australia three wickets in hand: six runs to win.

With 12 overs straight for four wickets for 38 runs earlier in the day, Hall had broken the Australian batting. Surely spinners on this fifth day could give the *coup-de-grâce*. But they could not, and Worrell sought more of Hall after they had failed. Hall, however, was tired, and Worrell, most wisely, took him off quickly. He kept him for the final gamble with the new ball when Australia would need some 30 or so to win.

Hall came on at 206. His first over did not suggest he could do the job. He bounced one at Davidson, which that noble hero pulled ferociously for four. The game looked over.

Diminutive Joe Solomon who, like Ramadhin, plays with his sleeves down, set the scene for the final over when he threw Davidson out from 12 yards away and side-on. Grout blundered when he scurried for a single from Sobers' seventh ball, because this left him ripe for execution at Hall's end in the final over of the day and match.

That was provided Benaud did not get a single from the final ball of

Sobers' over. Benaud meant to: Sobers never pounded a ball harder on a length than he did and some seven fielders galloped in on Benaud to cut off the single. It is history now how Hall hit Grout in the midriff and doubled him up, and how Benaud, without calling, charged to take a single from the unsuspecting West Indies with the ball in the very block-hole. And how Benaud got the strike. And how Hall got him very next ball with a thunderbolt that shot from the pitch and tempted Benaud's bat up with it for the tickle to Alexander. And how Grout, with a dazzling flash of genius, called Meckiff for a run when the ball went through to the keeper.

And how Grout, attempting the winning boundary, spooned it some 50 yards into the air and how Kanhai, with his all under the catch, saw Hall go over his head in Australian Rules football fashion, and muff the catch.

Negligently, the grass in Brisbane had not been cut for some days. An important point, because Meckiff's soaring hit to leg – Grout got a single from the missed catch – would have gone into the fence. As it was Hunte gained on it like an Olympic sprinter. From a full 100 yards away he wheeled and sent a low throw – a superlative throw – straight to Alexander who took it and hurled himself at the stumps as Grout dived for the line like a wing-threequarter at Twickenham.

This would have been the winning run. The two tied the game.

With a tremulous Kline to bat, Hall poised himself again, gulping and gulping in the air before he began his flying intimidatory run. Meckiff ran full tilt and Solomon, with only the one stump showing from square-leg, hit it from 10 yards. Nobody could get up for the throw-in. Solomon had to hit the stumps.

Worrell was the ideal skipper. He kept his men cool when some looked like boiling under the pressure. This game, of course, has set an impossible standard. It has created, too, some insufferable bores – I am one – who will prate as long as they live 'I saw the Brisbane tie.'

SUNDAY TIMES, 15 DECEMBER 1960

Tailpiece: The niece of the Queensland Prime Minister, unable to attend the match, was returning to her home 300 yards from the ground.

The stadium was so silent that she thought the game was over long since. In actual fact three balls were bowled while she walked nearly 300 yards. Then, as she turned to enter her front gate a thunderclap of noise told her what the world was soon to know, that Joe Solomon's accurate shy at the stumps had made the tie possible.

Overthrows

Until Ken Farnes' cricket bag dropped off the back of a car on the North Circular Road and the horrid secret that he took size 12 in boots was revealed, most of us thought Maurice Tate had the biggest feet in the game.

Tate's cricket boots no more than matched those of Farnes. Even then the Sussex attacker used to wear a couple of pairs of socks to pad 'em out!

Cheery 'Chub' Tate once told with a grin that he saw lollipops made in the shape of cricket boots in a Sydney sweetshop. 'Tate's two a penny' read the notice.

He told me, too, that on one Test tour Down Under the train carrying the English party stopped at a one-shack station in the back-blocks. It was midnight.

Up came a sunbitten farmer. 'Who's Tate?' he asked. Maurice was pointed out and, very deliberately, he reined his horse to the coach window. He peered in, said 'Why, I've got bigger feet,' then rode silently into the night." SUNDAY EMPIRE NEWS, 15 SEPTEMBER 1940

Barrage Balloon takes Time by the Forelock: Time is standing still at Lord's. Or rather lying down. The old ground looks almost undressed without the beloved bearded and bent figure over the score-box roof.

I'll risk saying now that the old gentleman with the scythe was hooked from his moorings by a cable of a barrage balloon. He escaped without serious hurt and is now putting bails on (or is he taking them off?) in a place of safety with the game's other heirlooms.
L. V. MANNING, DAILY SKETCH, 16 JULY 1942

Andrew Sandham, England and Surrey cricketer, hit a century yesterday on his 51st birthday. Sandham was playing for the Ferrets against Westminster Bank at Norbury. THE STAR, 7 SEPTEMBER 1941

I once captained a concert artistes' cricket team, consisting of myself, seven baritones, two tenors, and a child impersonator in plimsolls. DENNIS CASTLE AT LONDON PRESS CLUB

Item of cricket information carefully filed away: between June 3 and June 11 George Geary and Haydn Smith bowled unchanged for Leicestershire through four complete innings.

From Lord's score card, 19 August 1942: In the event of an air raid good cover from shrapnel and splinters should be obtained under the concrete stands. Public shelters will be found in St John's Wood Church, Wellington Court, Wellington Road, South Lodge, Circus Road. Spectators are advised not to loiter in the street.

Cometh the Hour . . .

LAURIE MUMFORD

The last ball of the match. England want one run to win.

Medium-pacer Lindsay Tuckett runs up. The ball fizzes down the pitch, swinging in to Cliff Gladwin.

He takes a swing, misses, and the ball bounces off his thigh a few feet in front of the crease.

Alec Bedser charges down the wicket while Gladwin stumbles to the other end. Fielders swoop like sharks . . . but Bedser is home.

So ended the first match of the 1948–49 series between South Africa and England in Durban.

Rarely can the last day of a Test have produced such drama.

The legitimacy of leg-byes has long been a contentious topic in the game, for many feel that they unfairly penalise the fielding side.

Certainly they had a vital bearing on this match. Ten of England's match-winning total of 128 came from them.

This was the first Test between the countries at Durban since the notorious one ten years earlier – which failed to produce a result in ten days.

In contrast, the match, as were all the others in the series, was limited to four days.

England introduced three newcomers to Test cricket – captain George Mann, Reg Simpson and Roley Jenkins.

South Africa won the toss – but it helped little in a heavy atmosphere in which Bedser swung the ball appreciably.

He and Gladwin shared seven wickets as South Africa were put out for 161.

Rain delayed England's reply and the innings was still in its first over when bad light ended play with the score on one.

On the second day Len Hutton and Cyril Washbrook set off with a stand of 84 and, though Simpson fell cheaply, the total reached 144–2 before a thunderstorm ended proceedings.

Two days had gone and considerable leeway had to be made up to achieve a result.

On the Saturday the pitch was all in favour of the spin of Norman

(Tufty) Mann and Athol Rowan who took all ten wickets between them.

Denis Compton, in superb form on this tour, battled away more than three hours for his 72 and it was mainly through him that the good start was consolidated enough to give England a lead of 98.

The pitch proved equally responsive to Jenkins and Doug Wright so that by the end of the day South Africa were 90 for four.

At this point Denis Begbie and Billy Wade became associated on the last morning in a stand of 85, Wade being the only Springbok to exceed 50 in either innings.

Then the spinners stepped in again so that when South Africa were out for 219, England were left 135 minutes to make 128 on a difficult pitch.

Rain washed 12 minutes from their time and a further five were lost while Dudley Nourse, the South African captain, received treatment on the field for a knee injury.

The light was dismal, the ball like soap. Yet both teams pressed on for a result.

Washbrook was dropped, as was Mann. England had reached 49–2 when Nourse called up Cuan McCarthy, a 19-year-old pace bowler playing his first Test.

McCarthy responded by taking the remaining six wickets to fall.

He swept aside the first four so quickly that England staggered at 70–6 with an hour left.

Compton and Jenkins then added 45 before a McCarthy express shot through Compton's guard.

With five minutes left, Jenkins was leg before. Twelve runs were needed and it was raining again. But no one was bothered about the weather now.

Gladwin scooped his first ball to Tuckett at mid-on, but the catch went down and two runs went up on the board instead.

So came the last over with eight wanted from as many balls.

A leg-bye was scampered off the first. The second, hit by Gladwin for four, was almost a catch to Athol Rowan.

Off the third ball another leg-bye but Bedser could not score off the fourth or fifth.

By snatching a single off the sixth ball, Bedser put England level.

A bad return by a jittery fielder made that run possible but when Gladwin failed to score off the seventh ball the batsmen held a mid-wicket conference and decided on a helterskelter whatever the consequences.

Then there was that last supreme moment. Gladwin nurturing the bruise on his thigh as long as he could and proudly exhibiting the spot off which the decisive run was filched.

Tailpiece: Long afterwards, Cliff Gladwin, when asked for his thoughts at that hectic moment, replied gravely, 'I thought – cometh the hour, cometh the man!'

South Africa

FIRST INNINGS			SECOND INNINGS		
E. Rowan	*c* Evans *b* Jenkins	7	E. Rowan	*c* Compton *b* Jenkins	16
O. Wynne	*c* Compton *b* Bedser	5	O. Wynne	*c* Watkins *b* Wright	4
B. Mitchell	*c* Evans *b* Bedser	27	B. Mitchell	*b* Wright	19
D. Nourse	*c* Watkins *b* Wright	37	D. Nourse	*c* and *b* Bedser	32
W. Wade	*run out*	8	W. Wade	*b* Jenkins	63
D. Begbie	*c* Compton *b* Bedser	37	D. Begbie	*c* Mann *b* Bedser	48
O. Dawson	*b* Gladwin	24	O. Dawson	*c* Compton *b* Wright	3
A. Rowan	*not out*	5	A. Rowan	*b* Wright	15
L. Tuckett	*lbw* *b* Gladwin	1	L. Tuckett	*not out*	3
N. Mann	*c* Evans *b* Gladwin	4	N. Mann	*c* Mann *b* Compton	10
C. McCarthy	*b* Bedser	0	C. McCarthy	*b* Jenkins	0
Extras (b 3, lb 2, nb 1)		6	Extras (b 1, lb 5)		6
	Total	161		Total	219

England

FIRST INNINGS			SECOND INNINGS		
L. Hutton	*c* McCarthy *b* A. Rowan	83	L. Hutton	*c* Dawson *b* Tuckett	5
C. Washbrook	*c* Wade *b* Mann	35	C. Washbrook	*lbw* *b* Mann	25
R. Simpson	*c* Begbie *b* Mann	5	R. Simpson	*c* E. Rowan *b* McCarthy	0
D. Compton	*c* Wade *b* Mann	72	D. Compton	*b* McCarthy	28
A. Watkins	*c* Nourse *b* A. Rowan	9	A. Watkins	*b* McCarthy	4
G. Mann	*c* E. Rowan *b* A. Rowan	19	G. Mann	*c* Mitchell *b* McCarthy	13
G. Evans	*c* Wynne *b* A. Rowan	0	G. Evans	*b* McCarthy	4
R. Jenkins	*c* Mitchell *b* Mann	5	R. Jenkins	*c* Wade *b* McCarthy	22
A. Bedser	*c* Tuckett *b* Mann	11	A. Bedser	*not out*	1
C. Gladwin	*not out*	0	C. Gladwin	*not out*	7
D. Wright	*c* Tuckett *b* Mann	0	Extras (b 9, lb 10)		19
Extras (b 2, lb 12)		14		Total (8 wkts)	128
	Total	253			

Bowling Analyses

SOUTH AFRICA – FIRST INNINGS

	O	*M*	*R*	*W*
Bedser	13·5	2	39	4
Gladwin	12	3	21	3
Jenkins	14	3	50	1
Wright	9	3	29	1
Compton	2	0	5	0
Watkins	3	0	11	0

SECOND INNINGS

	O	*M*	*R*	*W*
Bedser	18	5	51	2
Gladwin	7	2	15	0
Jenkins	22·3	6	64	3
Wright	26	3	72	4
Compton	16	11	11	1

ENGLAND – FIRST INNINGS

	O	*M*	*R*	*W*
McCarthy	9	2	20	0
Dawson	3	0	16	0
Tuckett	6	0	36	0
A. Rowan	44	8	108	4
Mann	37·4	14	59	6

SECOND INNINGS

	O	*M*	*R*	*W*
McCarthy	12	2	43	6
Tuckett	10	0	38	1
A. Rowan	4	0	15	0
Mann	2	0	13	1

Fall of the Wickets

South Africa – First Innings

1/9 2/18 3/69 4/80 5/99 6/148 7/150 8/152 9/160

Second Innings 1/22 2/22 3/67 4/89 5/174 6/179 7/208 8/208 9/219

England – First Innings

1/84 2/104 3/146 4/172 5/212 6/212 7/221 8/249 9/253

Second Innings 1/25 2/49 3/52 4/64 5/64 6/70 7/115 8/117

LONDON EVENING NEWS, MARCH 1974

Test Century

GEOFFREY MOORHOUSE

The Centenary Test which starts at Lord's next Thursday will, it is safe to say, be an occasion that every cricket watcher in the country would like to attend. A seat by a television set will be small compensation for anybody who will be unable to tell their grandchildren that they were actually present when England played Australia in the great anniversary match at the headquarters of the game. Cricket has cherished its traditions more than most sports, and nothing in the long history of the game has ever roused as much feeling as Test matches between Englishmen and Australians. This is the strongest as well as the oldest major international rivalry, its origins lying in historical events that have nothing to do with cricket, but which the game has perpetuated: this is where the love–hate relationship between the old colonials and the old imperials has been maintained most steadily, fiercely, warmly and dramatically. Neither the Poms nor the Aussies take kindly to being beaten at cricket by any team, but when one defeats the other the sense of triumph and dismay can assume the proportions of an independence celebration or a national calamity.

It is, in fact, something over a hundred years since the two sides first met. Combat began in Melbourne in 1877, a game that was celebrated three years ago by another centenary match on the same ground, memorably and brilliantly fought to precisely the same result as in that very first Test which the Australians won by 45 runs. They led by two matches to one when their cricketers came here in 1880 and played the first Test on English soil. This was hastily arranged at the Oval on 6, 7 and 8 September at the end of a tour that had been improvised from start to finish, with the Australians at one stage advertising for fixtures because the English counties already had their summer programmes booked up. England, led by Lord Harris, had the three Grace brothers in the side and W.G. hit 152 in the first innings. That was topped by the Australian captain W. L. Murdoch with 153 not out, but in the absence of their great fast bowler, Fred Spofforth (hurt in a game at Scarborough) the tourists were beaten by five wickets before crowds which, according to Wisden, were the largest ever seen at a cricket match – close on 45,000 over the three days.

When the Australians next came to England in 1882 to play a single Test, again at the Oval, 'The Demon' Spofforth was in full working order and finished the game with figures of 14 wickets for 90 runs, bowling with such ferocity that every English batsman might have echoed what The Hon Edward Lyttelton once said after facing him: 'I give you my word that for several overs I stood on the brink of the tomb'. One of the most famous cricket matches ever played, its fortunes fluctuated tightly (Australia 63 and 122, England 101 and 77), and its climax was so nerve-racking that one spectator died of heart failure and another chewed right through his umbrella handle. Spofforth was carried from the field shoulder high when the last Englishman was bowled eight runs short of victory. Within a week the *Sporting Times* had published its famous mock obituary of English cricket: 'Deeply lamented by a large circle of sorrowing friends and acquaintances. RIP. NB – The body will be cremated and the ashes taken to Australia.' Thus a great myth was begun, to be given reality after the third Test at Sydney in 1883, when England took a 2–1 lead in the series. A bail from the match wickets was burnt and its ashes were sealed in a tiny urn which was presented to England's captain, The Hon Ivo Bligh, who later became Lord Darnley. This is the mystical trophy for which English and Australian cricketers have played ever since, though the urn never changes hands whoever wins a Test series; having been left to MCC in Darnley's will, the Ashes have been on display in the cricket museum at Lord's for many years, and there they are likely to stay.

The two countries have now fought 239 Tests, the Australians winning 92 to England's 79, with 68 games drawn, and some finishes as desperately close as that at the Oval in 1882. In the Fourth Test at Old Trafford in 1902, Australia won by just three runs, after Victor Trumper had scored a brilliant century before lunch on the first day at almost a run a minute, and after poor Fred Tate of Sussex had not only dropped a vital catch on the boundary but, last man in for England, had got himself bowled out as well.

Particular players on both sides will be forever associated with certain matches, for great feats or significant failures, or simply for displays of enormous character. Warwick Armstrong, a huge man from Victoria, is remembered not only for leading Australia to the only clean sweep of a full series that has ever occurred (5–0 Down Under in 1920–21) but for his protest at the Oval a few months later against the English authorities' decision to limit the 1921 matches to only three days each, instead of playing to a finish, however long that took, which was the habit in Australia. When the fifth Test was heading for an inevitable draw, Armstrong left his fielding position close to the wicket, strolled over to the boundary and began to read a newspaper. Eddie Paynter, of Lancashire, will never be forgotten for his performance at Brisbane in 1933, when he got out of a hospital bed with England up against it, and began an innings of 83, with the aid of egg and brandy taken between overs at the crease, that laid the foundations of victory. Sydney in 1946 was where Godfrey Evans, keeping wicket for England for the first time, didn't let a single bye get past him in Australia's match-winning score of 659 for eight declared. Brisbane in 1958 was where Trevor Bailey batted remorselessly for seven-and-a-half hours to make only 68.

Those names, and the events attached to them, are among the regular currency of Anglo–Australian Tests; there are many others, and volumes have been written to do them all justice. But in a game which thrives on statistics (down to the calculation someone has made that after the fourth Test at Sydney in 1975, no fewer than 864,000 empty beer cans had to be cleared from the ground), the absolute dominance of some players is reflected in the record books.

The most lustrous name of all remains – possibly for ever – that of Don Bradman, whose batting genius originated in childhood when he would spend hours at his home in New South Wales hitting a golf ball against a wall with a cricket stump. Throughout his first-class career he was to average a century every third innings he played and, although he made only 19 runs in his first Test match against England at Brisbane in 1928, he rarely failed to produce big scores after that. By the time he retired 20 years later – bowled by Hollies, second ball, in his last English Test – his overall Test average stood at 99·94, and against England alone it was 89·78.

It was to counter Bradman's devastating efficiency with the bat that the Englishmen resorted to the strategy of bowling dangerously short and fast down the leg side in the notorious 'bodyline' series in Australia in 1932–33, which all but ruptured diplomatic relations between the two countries. The chief instrument of 'leg theory' was the Nottinghamshire bowler Harold Larwood, but the strategy was wholly that of his captain, the austere Surrey Scotsman, Douglas Jardine, who became the most detested man in the southern hemisphere as a result. Fielding on the boundary at Sydney one day (an act of moral courage in the circumstances), he brushed away an insect which flew round his face, when a voice from the crowd yelled: 'Leave our bloody flies alone, Jardine. They're the only friends you've got round here.' Humour, one of cricket's great graces, has generally broken in even at the most belligerent moments.

Bradman had hit the world's record Test score of 334 just before his 22nd birthday at Leeds in 1930. Len Hutton, curiously, was almost the same age when he made 364 at the Oval in 1938 – still the highest individual score between the two sides – and England crushed Australia by an innings and 579 runs. This is one of two matches that Englishmen prefer to dwell on most, the other being the setting for the most astonishing piece of bowling in the history of cricket.

It was Jim Laker of Surrey who turned the fourth Test of 1956 at Old Trafford into a legend that almost certainly will never be surpassed. England had the very best of a wearing pitch to score 459, and in the event they could have won the match by an innings with little more than half those runs. Laker was virtually unplayable from start to finish of Australia's batting, as wind and sun aided his baffling flight and finger spin. His Surrey colleague Tony Lock took one wicket in the first innings, but Laker collected every other Australian scalp in the match – 19 wickets out of 20 for only 90 runs.

Three great moments stand out in the Test matches played at Lord's. In 1934, Hedley Verity, with left-arm spin, took 14 Australian wickets – including Bradman's – between noon and late afternoon on the same day. In 1953, the obdurate Bailey and Willie Watson came together on the last day when England were 73 for four and heading for defeat. For over four hours they hung on against an attack which included Lindwall, Miller, Davidson and Benaud, and saved the match. In 1972 it was a novice's name that rang out from this ground – the 25-year-old Bob Massie, playing in his first Test for Australia, swinging the ball in extraordinary fashion to dismiss 16 Englishmen for 137 and take his side to an eight wickets win. Lord's, indeed, has usually been a good place for the Australians, who have lost only one Test there (Verity's match) since 1896.

They will therefore go into the Centenary Test this week with a distinct psychological advantage. England might well wish to be playing at the Oval, which has been kinder to them and which historically would be a more justifiable venue; but Lord's can accommodate several thousand more spectators and that, more than anything, has given it what promises to be a splendid occasion. A number of cricketers will be playing who deserve to be listed with the all-time greats of Anglo–Australian Tests. The Australian captain, Greg Chappell is one, and so is their fast bowler Dennis Lillee, who may well be making his last appearance in harness with Jeff Thomson to form one of the most effective of all speed combinations. ('Ashes to ashes, dust to dust,' wrote a Sydney cartoonist after the pair had wrecked England during the 1974–75 series. 'If Thomson don't get ya, Lillee must . . .'). Of England's likely players, Boycott, Underwood and (already) Ian Botham belong with the legendary cricketers. Many more of those will be watching with the rest of us, including old-timers like Bill Ponsford, who will be in a party of nearly 100 ex-players and officials flying across the world for this match. Another legend will, sadly, be performing in his last Test – John

Arlott in the commentary box, who retires after 34 years of illuminating and embellishing the game. What everybody will hope for above all is that this occasion comes as near to perfection as the Centenary Test at Melbourne did three years ago. And all Englishmen should pray that the result, like the one at Melbourne, is the same as in that Test a hundred years ago. RADIO TIMES, 23–29 AUGUST 1980

Hobbs – Master of All Eras

CHRISTOPHER HILTON

He was called simply The Master. You could stretch the English language to describe John Berry Hobbs, but in the end you would come back to those two words.

He played cricket for 30 years, and across that awesome span he mastered generations of bowlers. He played against Fred Tate of Sussex before the First World War and his son Maurice after it.

Some of the bowlers have retreated into the mists of the game. Others – Hirst and Rhodes, Larwood, Gregory and McDonald – are legends still.

It didn't matter what they bowled at the neat, quiet man in the chocolate cap of Surrey and the blue cap of England; or where.

They were his prey at Sydney and Melbourne as well as his beloved Oval; up at Manchester, down at Taunton – where in 1925 he overtook W. G. Grace's record number of centuries.

The figures are staggering and they do not diminish. He scored 61,237 runs and 197 hundreds, and he found three perfect opening partners: Tom Hayward, Andrew Sandham and Herbert Sutcliffe.

With Sutcliffe, he didn't call short singles. The pair ran between the wickets by instinct, swift and sure: a kind of silent, enchanting dance.

But runs – the short singles or the 61,237 mountain – are no measure of Hobbs at all. All avenues lead back to mastery.

On bad wickets, even sticky ones, when the ball snarled and spat and shot, he made hundreds while others (Sutcliffe apart) floundered.

And the most famous of all was at The Oval in 1926, the deciding Test for the Ashes. England, 22 behind on first innings, were trapped on a wet wicket.

A picture of that day returns: the encircling leg-trap, predators with hands outstretched: Arthur Richardson bowling his spin for ten overs which yielded but one run: and Hobbs still there, Sutcliffe still there.

The scorecard proclaims the achievement: Hobbs 100, Sutcliffe 161. The next best . . . 27.

He took it all, as I have said, with a quiet modesty which is dimensions away from sport today. The man who was born in humble circumstances in Cambridge in 1882 made 15 Test centuries, 12 against Australia. He was knighted in 1953.

The Master: each – or any – of his strokes could have been used in coaching manuals. There was a perfection about each movement and mechanism of the man which, in all conditions and against all comers, made him the most complete batsman who ever lived.

How many others, in golf or tennis or soccer or what you will, have achieved that?

Arthur Mailey, the Australian leg-break bowler who savoured his meetings with Hobbs as (almost) pure intellectual combat, actually managed to baffle him a time or two with the googly.

But Mailey understood the immense talent of Hobbs. As he said, by the end of that series: 'My only chance of confusing him in the slightest was by flight variation.'

Most had no chance at all.

He died in 1963, leaving not an enemy in the world. It's a funny thing that those bowlers didn't resent the runs he harvested from them in such abundance.

If you ask, they say, simply, that it was an honour to bowl at The Master. DAILY EXPRESS

Running Scared

PAUL WEAVER

Charlie Griffith watched the third Test between the irresistible force of the West Indies and England's all-too-moveable objects at Bridgetown and the muscles stood out from his bull-like neck as he shook his head in disgust.

'Those England batsmen are bloody scared,' snorted the West Indian giant, and as one of the most feared fast bowlers of all time he can recognise a drop of adrenalin when he sees it. 'All you have to do is ping one delivery past their noses and the next ball they're there for the taking.

'I took a few wickets in my time but I wish I was bowling against this team because I'd get a lot more.

'When I think of the men I had to bowl against in England in 1963 and 1966 there is no comparison. You couldn't frighten Brian Close or Kenny Barrington.

'I remember knocking Kenny down a few times and I don't think he liked facing me, but he never gave up. People don't realise how many runs he scored.

'On my first tour to England, Wes Hall and I hit Close so many times his whole body was black and blue, but he never flinched.

'That's what I call real character and guts – and I reckon Wes was a shade faster than the four quicks we have now, Michael Holding included.'

Griffith, who with an apparent addiction to the sound of collapsing timber now works as sales manager for the Barbados Lumber Company, added: 'You had to work to get those batsmen out. The same applied to Peter May, Ted Dexter, Tom Graveney, Colin Cowdrey and Colin Milburn.

'When I got one of those wickets, I knew I'd bowled well and deserved it.

'But this England team is the weakest I've seen. Judging by the way some of their batsmen back off to square leg instead of getting back and across to get behind the ball suggests to me they're frightened.

'Even Geoff Boycott doesn't get behind the ball like he used to, but he does try. It's just that he's 40 now and he's not quite the player he was.

'Geoff probably thinks he can bat as well as he used to just as I feel I can bowl as fast as before. But it's impossible, and Geoff's reflexes have slowed up just as my legs have.'

Griffith, an extremely fit looking 42, still plays occasionally for his Barbados club, Empire. He played his first cricket for the club as a gentle spinner in the 1950s before he collected seven wickets for one run in a fast bowling experiment.

He was almost unplayable in England in 1963 when he took 119 wickets at an average of 12·83 – including 32 in the Tests at 16·21.

With the majestic Hall, Griffith formed one of the fastest and most fearsome of opening attacks.

He was not so effective on the tour three years later when many experts, including my colleague Richie Benaud, judged that he threw his faster bouncer.

David Gower, at least, has impressed Griffith. 'He has the edge on all the other England batsmen when it comes to ability,' says Charlie. 'I'm delighted to see that he's applied himself more, but he's still too casual.

'He should be ashamed of the shot he played in the second innings when Viv Richards bowled him. He seemed so relieved the quick man had gone that he relaxed his concentration.

'But if he continues to work hard I think he could score Test hundreds almost at will.

'The rest of the batsmen seem demoralised and defeated before they go to the wicket. They've no chance that way.

'I'm also surprised and disappointed by the bad technique of your batsmen. In England, where the ball moves around so much, you need to be tight, but these players seem very loose.'

The West Indian is no less scathing about England's solitary fast bowler, Graham Dilley. 'He's got a lot to learn,' said Charlie, 'and should start by doing something about his action.

'A fast bowler should be exploding in his delivery stride, but Graham seems to slow down as he approaches the wicket.'

Griffith rates Hall ahead of Holding, Andy Roberts, Colin Croft and Joel Garner. He says: 'Wes carried a far heavier workload than any of them, but he accepted it and fulfilled it.

'But Roy Gilchrist was the fastest bowler I've seen. He was only a short man, but his arms were long and his hands used to hang below his knees.'

Griffith is still upset by the uproar his suspect action created in England. 'I was never given a fair break in your country,' he said. 'I was kicked around like a football and it demoralised me. I just wanted to crawl into my shell.'

Many England players must have felt the same way at the end of the third Test on Wednesday. A large English contingent watched the match and the 298-run defeat was one which really sorted out the manic depressives from the boys. NEWS OF THE WORLD, 22 MARCH 1981

An Over to Forget

STEVE WHITING

Ian Botham talked yesterday about: 'The over I want to forget.'

It was the one in the third Test at Bridgetown on Saturday when West Indies' Michael Holding had him dropped, then nearly killed him and then had him caught behind.

Botham said 'I want to forget it. It was one of the best overs I have faced in Test cricket.

'What happened to the ball that got me I just don't know. I don't even know where it came from.' THE SUN, 17 MARCH 1981

LITERARY STYLIST

John Clarke (then *Evening Standard*) on Tony Smith, batting for MCC *v* Victoria, Melbourne, February 1963: Smith is no great stylist. He uses his bat, now like a fireman at work with a hose, now like a frenzied signalman trying to flag a runaway train to a halt.

But, from time to time Smith found shots, as when he drove Kirby, the leg spinner, through the covers, and twice in an over on-drove the medium-paced West for four.

But his great virtue was that he stayed while Graveney composed chapter two of his wonderful essay on the art of batting!

Eric Hollies – a Man for All Cricket Occasions

LESLIE DEAKINS

Famous names from the annals of Warwickshire cricket assembled at Rowley Regis yesterday for the cremation of Eric Hollies, who died last week aged 68.

They paid their last respects to the county's greatest bowler, who captured 2,323 wickets between 1932 and 1957 with his brand of leg-spin wizardry.

Leslie Deakins, who was assistant secretary and secretary during Hollies' years at Edgbaston, offers his special tribute.

I first met Eric Hollies just over 50 years ago when he was attending the old Indoor Cricket School at Edgbaston, which was subsequently destroyed by a German bomb in the Second World War.

I well recall Norman Kilner who was running the school at the time, in conjunction with his County colleague, Len Bates, being tremendously impressed by the bowling ability of the young Hollies, and as a result he made arrangements for the youngster to have a net trial out of doors towards the end of the 1930 season.

This trial was conducted in the presence of several members of the County Club Committee, together with Sydney Santall, the club's senior coach. The young bowler gave an immediate impression of slight nervousness, but I recall this evaporating the moment he had a cricket ball in his hand. He quickly made it apparent to those looking on that he was a bowler not to be missed.

He was, of course, at that time, despite his youth, playing in good class cricket in the Birmingham and District League.

So anxious was his father, 'Billy' Hollies, a lob bowler of considerable skill himself, to give his son every chance to play that when school tended to conflict with cricket he decided it was time for Eric to give up ... school.

Eric was born in Staffordshire on 5 June 1912, and this meant that when Warwickshire offered him an engagement on their playing staff as they did following the trial, he had to qualify by taking up residence in the County.

Owing to this quite extraordinary anomaly in the Rules of the County game which seemed designed to prevent, rather than to encourage, cricketers, it was not until well into the 1932 season that he could appear in the Warwickshire XI. In his very limited appearances at the end of that season he took his first four wickets in the first-class game – a modest preliminary to the great achievements that were to follow.

With more opportunity in the following two seasons his returns were 79 and 87 wickets, before in 1937 taking 127 wickets (the first of fourteen seasons in which he claimed more than one hundred victims).

His ability and form, however, had already aroused the interest of cricket's top authorities and at the end of the 1934 season he was invited to tour the West Indies with a party under the captaincy of his own County captain, R. E. S. Wyatt, and his cricket colleague and fellow spin-bowler, George Paine, was also selected.

Bearing in mind his youth and very limited experience of the first-class game he had quite a successful tour, and in the third Test at Georgetown he returned figures of 7 for 50 in the West Indies first innings.

This performance alone put him in line for further opportunities, but unfortunately injury prevented him accepting selection in the following home series and thereafter his claims seem to have been overlooked and it was 1947 before he was on the Test match scene again when appearing in three matches against the South African touring team.

In the years that followed he eventually brought his tally of Test match appearances up to 13 which the cricket world at large regarded as modest indeed, bearing in mind his very considerable ability in a department of the game in which few succeeded at top-class level.

It was well known that he was never happier than when among his 'ain folk', but when chosen to represent his country at home or on tour, there always followed reports of splendid loyalty, all-out effort, ready and characteristic humour, and tributes to a grand companion on and off the field.

He had a delightful gift of repartee, and using the Black Country idiom which came easily at will, he enlightened many dull moments, made many friends and helped to carry his team mates through a long day in the field.

Perhaps his character and humour were even more developed when we think of him as a batsman. Colleagues in the team were frequently reminded by Eric personally, when anywhere near Stratford-upon-Avon, that it was on that ground he opened an innings for the 2nd XI and made over 20 runs, but in County and Test cricket he continually claimed the right to precede the roller.

In the County game he was a very dominant force throughout his long career and for Warwickshire he took 2,201 wickets which is greatly in excess of the figures of any other bowler for the County throughout its history.

He also holds the seasonal record with 180 wickets in 1946, when he literally carried the County attack on his shoulders owing to the absence, consequent on the War, of other bowlers of genuine ability, and it was frequently felt by those visiting the ground that not only was he bowling continually but also from both ends.

This is to a degree exemplified throughout his career for in eleven seasons he bowled well over 1,000 overs a season, and that includes his final season in 1957 when he also captained the team to bridge the gap between the retirement of Tom Dollery and the arrival of Mike Smith.

His greatest single performance was undoubtedly his 10 wickets for 49 runs against Nottinghamshire, at Edgbaston in 1946, taken without fielding aid: i.e. 7 bowled and 3 lbw.

He will also be remembered always for bowling Bradman second ball in the Oval Test match of 1948 and also in the same season for taking eight Australian wickets for 107 runs in the County game with the tourists.

History and statistics, impressive though they may be, are only a part of the story of Eric Hollies, who developed into one of the game's great characters. Fair-haired, and blessed as a result of long years of early practice with an easy and graceful action, he brought the ball right over the top and possessed much the best bowling action of the right arm leg spinners of his day.

At all times completely loyal to his club and to his colleagues, he was a model cricketer of the very best type, completely unassuming and yet positive when the need arose. No cricketer had a greater love for the game, nor a greater willingness 'to put something back' for the pleasure he had personally derived from playing.

Anecdotes concerning him will pass into cricket legend to give warmth and a touch of the summer to the bare figures which will be posterity's yardstick for measuring his great contribution to the game. We at Edgbaston, however, will always remember him in the mind's eye as we saw him in his great days when the ritual never varied – the removal of the cap, the sweater, the marking of the run, the reflected pleasure in the feel of the ball, the easy run, the smooth action and that unexpectedly vicious follow through.

Eric Hollies, master spinner, will always bowl at Edgbaston for the initiated, and our summers will be made the brighter by his eternal presence, for he is of the very spirit of the game.

SPORTS ARGUS, 25 APRIL 1981

Commentators Bowl Me Over

COLIN WELLAND

Queueing at the gates of Old Trafford in the early summer mornings of '48, loaded up with Tizer and tomato sandwiches, I had two ambitions. One was to open the batting for England, the other – to be a commentator.

I've managed neither, but having spent a day with those who have done both, I'm utterly convinced it's a life to be envied.

Anybody who loves cricket would swap places with them. Anybody.

Today millions of armchair sports fans will settle down in front of their television sets to watch the India versus England Test match from Edgbaston, and Messrs Dexter, West, Laker and Benaud will once again be analysing and commentating on the match for us.

You think you know them, don't you? You've seen them often enough chatting in the front room all day – but you don't, you know.

For a start I now realise how Jim Laker took all those wickets. He chuckled them out. He hunches over the microphone in his shirt-sleeves with that confidential air of someone who has got a new one to tell you.

But he's watching, is Jim, analysing, assessing, and, have you noticed, he's completely cliché free. Because to him each ball is a new experience – and he finds the words to fit.

Ted Dexter, on the box, is staff college material. I drink my beer to attention when he appears. In real life he's younger, more vulnerable, a pip or two down market, but nicer for it.

Richie Benaud strides through the comfortable cluster of BBC cardigans. On screen he's the sort of fellow you'd find yourself trying to please. In reality he has a generous smile and a warm humour, but he's always ready to crack the whip.

Peter West I've known for years. Much less straight down the middle off than on. There's a self-depreciating devil in him but he never allows it air time. Which is a pity.

The 'hellos' over, their attention turns to the task in hand. However they've no more idea of spotting Indian cricketers than we have. They have an expert, Irving Rosenwater, to prompt them, though he himself has no idea what they look like.

Godfrey Evans comes in with the day's odds. A bookie's runner par excellence! Our men like a flutter – especially on Ted's dogs.

The game starts, and, to everyone's disappointment, England are batting. Richie lists the Indian team. It still reads like a menu.

Play commences and the mood immediately changes. The knowledgeable grunts and chuckles tell me there's a lot to learn from the opening deliveries. I watch with ignorance. Thank God for Ted at the end of the over.

I'm now in my element for Boycott's settling in, a homesteader ploughing a furrow for centuries to come. Meanwhile, iced rosé is provided with Westy doing the honours on behalf of Cornhill. It is their party, after all.

I'm feeling a bit of an interloper now that we're into the meat of the afternoon.

Their concentration is complete. They talk, both on and off the mike, of cricket and nought else. For you they pick their words precisely, enhancing the pictures flickering before them. You are well served.

The cricket's as boring as hell at the moment. Brearley's batting like a school kid playing against the teachers.

The day drifts on – old but timeless stories are chewed over lunch. The cricket shimmers and fades in the Edgbaston heat. Six hours talking about this stuff has to be a labour of love.

And it is. These fellows are experts. It's an honour to sit with them – to eavesdrop on their asides – those emotional indulgences the BBC charter just cannot allow.

Like us, they think Brearley's out of his class. That Boycott wants a rocket up his back stroke. That Ghavri might chuck. But no – to you they remain fair, painfully neutral, and save all the juice for the newspapers.

Still, here's power to their eloquence.

DAILY MAIL, 14 JULY 1979

Chris Old: Century in 37 Minutes

Yorkshire's Chris Old yesterday went within two minutes of clocking the fastest-ever century as cricket went crazy at Edgbaston with Geoff Boycott eventually asking Warwickshire to score a mere 338 in 25 minutes and 20 overs and then opening the bowling himself.

But Old could not be blamed for the farcical circumstances in which he all but wrote himself into immortality with a 37-minute century.

As he said after going so close to Percy Fender's 57-year-old world record of 35 minutes for Surrey against Northants: 'It was not my fault how they bowled – when it was there to be hit, I hit it.'

Old blazed six sixes and 12 fours and sprinted through his last 50 runs in just nine minutes. In all, he faced 72 deliveries for his century and, incredibly, took only 21 deliveries over his second half-century which contained four fours and five sixes.

Old was eventually out for 107, caught at long-off when going for another six off John Whitehouse.

Warwickshire, who had declared 149 behind, tried to contrive a positive finish. But Boycott would have none of it and Old was left to gorge himself on the donkey-drops of Rohan Kanhai and Whitehouse, and the unimpressive off-spin of Eddie Hemmings.

Old, who told the Test selectors that he did not think he was fit enough to last out a five-day match, took three sixes off Hemmings – one of which soared over the pavilion – two off Kanhai and one off Whitehouse.

When Warwickshire came out to bat they faced an opening attack of Boycott and Old with their number six and seven batsmen.

Then Bairstow, who had not kept wicket yesterday because of an eye injury, became the first change bowler, and Boycott took the wicket of No 11 batsman Richard Savage, who had come in first wicket down.

Old is now certain to pocket the £250 prize for the fastest 100 of the season – and that may not be too well received by the other two batsmen who had also recorded the fastest centuries of the season off Warwickshire.

On June 26 at Edgbaston, Essex's Ken McEwan scored a century in 94 minutes. On July 9, Somerset's Viv Richards reached 100 in 85 minutes. Both scores occurred in the first innings of the match against serious bowling.

The Six Fastest Centuries:

35 minutes:	P. Fender	Surrey *v* Northants, 1920
37 ,,	C. Old	Yorkshire *v* Warwicks, 1977
40 ,,	G. Jessop	Gloucester *v* Yorkshire, 1897
42 ,,	G. Jessop	Gentlemen of South *v* Players of South, 1907
43 ,,	A. Hornby	Lancashire *v* Somerset, 1905
44 ,,	R. Hobbs	Essex *v* Australians, 1975

How He Did It:

00000100400000010040000004000001020104401601
0421004401 = 50 off 51 balls
00010046160446064160 1 = 50 off 21 balls

DAILY EXPRESS, 6 AUGUST 1977

One Tavern After Another

JOHN ARLOTT

The new 'public bar and concourse', MCC officially assured us in their plan of development, 'will retain the traditional atmosphere of the present Tavern Bar'. More, if semi-authoritative stories are to be believed, the new concourse will be sloped or stepped so that Taverners will not, as hitherto, have to be graded – 'shortest to the front, tallest to the rear' – in order to watch the play over the rims of their tankards.

The positive and practical advantage, however, may not allay alcoholically nostalgic regrets for the Tavern which is gone. These are sentiments which should not be discouraged; certainly not ignored, for they spring from the tenderest of emotions.

Fortunately, however, history may allay these feelings. It would be a short-sighted Lord's Taverner, devoid of feeling for tradition, who was not prepared to consider the feelings of his spiritual predecessors when, exactly one hundred years ago, the original Tavern – for ours was the second – was demolished to make way for the place where he has so often satisfied simultaneously his appetites for beer and batting, tipple and Titmus, or crisps and Compton.

Thomas Lord started to build the first Tavern in what was then open country in 1813, but St John's Wood Church and several houses were going up by the time it was ready for the opening of the present ground – Lord's third – on 9 May 1914. During the week before the opening, according to the *St James' Chronicle:*

'A shocking accident occurred at the New Lord's Cricket-ground public-house, Marylebone Fields. The landlady of the house had occasion to use a small amount of gunpowder, and whilst in the act of taking same from a paper containing a pound weight, a spark from the fire caught it, and it went off with a great explosion. The landlady, her sister, and two little girls who were in the room were seriously burnt. The two former are in a dangerous way. The explosion broke every pane of glass in the room and set it on fire.'

Did no one think it odd that the landlady 'had occasion to use a small amount of gunpowder' sufficient to cause a great explosion? Or take it from a paper containing a pound weight?

The original Tavern was 'a low rustic building' with bow windows, fronted by a row of leafy trees, and the green at the front had tables and chairs for the patrons. By 1838 an assembly room had been built over the parlour, the long room at the end had been turned into a billiard room, and a railed-in bowling green was laid at its western end.

Owen Swift was a boxer, a large, heavy and lazy man who, in his brief career as a cricketer, was extremely reluctant to field. So he used to arrange for an easy chair to be placed outside the Tavern for him and while his side was in the field he would sit back in it, smoking a churchwarden pipe and with a quart pot of porter at his side – a good Taverner. His rest was disturbed on one occasion, if not for good, when one of his opponents lofted a big hit straight into his stomach.

To Swift, and many another, it must have seemed something near desecration when, in 1867, their familiar Tavern was demolished and what was to them the new, and to us the old, Tavern was built on the site.

Taverns – or rather The Tavern – may change: but I doubt there is much change in the character, the pleasure or the habits of those who frequent it: only Swift had a *quart* pot!

LORD'S TAVERNERS BALL, PROGRAMME, 4 NOVEMBER 1968

COME OFF IT

Over the years in Ceylon I have seen bamboo stands fired and burn to the ground within minutes; a woman groundsman prepare a pitch twenty-three yards long, and a near-riot caused by 'spectators' who, charged one rupee for the use of the tree overlooking the ground, found they were expected to fork out another rupee to be allowed to land.

ALEX BANNISTER, DAILY MAIL, 1 JANUARY 1969

Quickies

The Cricket Memorial Gallery at Lord's holds consolation and frustration for hard-pressed England supporters. The Ashes are there, come what may, but the men who won matches are there only in effigy.

There is much W. G. Graceiana – two portraits, one severe, one rather bucolic, and the gold plate which celebrates his hundredth hundred in 1895. The coffin-shaped snuffbox of his brother, the coroner-cricketer, is the most charming of many cricket trinkets. Old bats bear traces of strokes well struck and there's a right-handed smiting stick used by Rick-a-Dick, a star of the Aborigine tourists of 1868.

The old photographs of teams of moustachioed and bearded Victorians may suggest placidity, non-commercialism and good sportsmanship. If so, they mislead. The first England team to tour America in 1859 survived hitting an iceberg en route ... 'All the sea needed was ten minutes of the heavy roller,' says Wisden.

The first England tour of Australia (1861) was sponsored by a commercial firm who sent them when Charles Dickens refused to tour. The Government wanted to stop the 1872 tour of America for political reasons, and the first Australian team to play a Test here (1880) came in a maelstrom of hostility generated by the unruly behaviour of Australian tours the winter before.

DAVID ROBSON, SUNDAY TIMES MAGAZINE

The last time I saw dapper, immaculately dressed Huntley Wright at Lord's was a few days before war was declared (28 August). He probably saw some of the war-time cricket, but I never ran into him again after that Monday morning when the balloon in the Nursery was throwing its shadow of things to come over the Mound Stand.

We watched from the Long Room the gallant Edrich innings, and equally gallant resistance from the tail-enders which helped to foil Surrey. Edrich went from 28 to his century while Gover and Co were capturing the remaining three Middlesex wickets. As the last Middlesex wicket fell, that of Laurie Gray, Huntley Wright turned to me, and with his face expressing tragedy that gained nothing from his seventy years of service on the stage, said, 'When, Oh when, shall we see the like again.' ROY PESKETT, DAILY SKETCH, JULY 1941

Brian Johnston, at Lord's ... 'Lindsay Hassett has not changed his field, except to hurry along two fellows crossing the sightscreen while carrying trays of beer.'

Lincoln City manager, Bill Anderson, takes a cricket team on tour in the West Country, to play Torquay.

Stan Montgomery, Cardiff centre half and cricket pro to Torquay, is desperately batting out time. Anderson calls up Jack Rowley and the field is set.

Journalist John Camkin, keeping wicket, leans over the stumps and says, 'Stan, something's happening here which can't have happened many times before.'

'What's that?'

Indicating Jack Chisholm (Tottenham and Plymouth) and Pat Glover (Grimsby), Camkin says: 'The slips haven't a cartilage between them.'

Montgomery laughed so much he was bowled next ball.

Misprint from a report in *The Daily Telegraph:* The Selectors will be together for the fourth successive year, which constitutes a record. Insole is on the Committee for the 100th successive year, his fourth as Chairman.

Thanks to *The Cricketer* for reminding us that 25 years ago last Tuesday, and on that one day alone, Jack Robertson scored 331 not out for Middlesex at Worcester, and the county made 623 for five wickets. The corresponding fixture this year, a few days' earlier, also produced, by far, the highest-scoring match of the week; but in that and in none of the other concurrent county matches this year did the aggregate for all three days exceed that Middlesex total by more than fifty runs.

While on the subject of high scoring, remember the story of Bobby Abel's historic innings against Somerset at the Oval, just fifty years before Robertson's? He hit 357 not out when Surrey were paying their pros a £1 bonus for every fifty.

Such potential extravagance called for a committee meeting on the spot, at which it was decided that £5 was top whack, come what may.

'Sod em,' said Abel, or some such Victorian equivalent. 'If that's the way they feel, I'll get myself out at 250 in the future!'

THE OBSERVER, 28 JULY 1974

Apropos the recent records of our Test players, it may be of interest that my son, aged 15, now in his school eleven, scored 391 runs in the morning, and 190 in the afternoon.

Unfortunately, his little sister, who did all the bowling, is now in bed, prostrate with fatigue.

LOUIS REID, BRIGHTON ... LETTER TO NATIONAL NEWSPAPER

Godfrey Evans Misses a Chance

JAMES MOSSOP

The first draught ale of another blistering summer's day was being drawn down at the Jolly Drover, a quaint old inn set in a leafy corner of Hampshire.

The talk was of cricket. A conversation prompted by the photographs and cartoons decorating the walls of the 17th century pub where the sheep and cattle drovers used to call on their way to market.

There is Godfrey Evans meeting the Queen. Godfrey Evans smiting sixes. Godfrey Evans diving, falling, running, laughing in the company of such fellow legends as Compton, Edrich, Trueman, Miller, Lindwall and so on.

From the back room the caricature emerges in real life. Godfrey Evans, now 57 but as chirpy as in those days when he was the world's greatest wicket-keeper, is carrying a large and colourful box.

He plonks it on the bar, opens it up to reveal a replica of the Lord's cricket ground, flips a coin and says: 'You bat.'

Within minutes I had scored 50 and he, of all people, had missed a stumping chance. Suddenly I was on the way to victory over a man whose talents alone used to draw me to the Scarborough Cricket Festival for schoolboy holidays.

Godfrey Evans has turned inventor. An ingenious game he calls 'International Cricket' brought enough excitement in half an hour to make the Jolly Drover seem like the Lord's Tavern.

The game is played with dice launched from a small, stationary catapult into the playing area. Already one London store has placed a £1,000 order.

'I first had the idea 20 years ago,' he said. 'On those cricketing days when it rained and we just sat about in the pavilion I used to think that there must be some way this great sport could be transported to the fireside in game form for rainy days and long winter nights.'

Long winter nights. I remember a frosty February in 1947. We set the alarm to rise long before dawn, brewed mugs of tea and glued our ears to the radio. From Adelaide, through the atmospherics, we followed every ball as Evans stonewalled for 95 minutes without scoring while Denis Compton punched out his second 100 of the match and the fourth Test was saved.

This dramatic dawn vigil was brought to mind last Sunday afternoon. On a village ground at Charlwood in Surrey I came across a match of infinite charm.

Beech and chestnut trees ringed the field . . . and my eye caught this Pickwickian character with his eccentric silver, mutton-chop whiskers crouching behind the stumps.

Every ball that flew his way, leg-side, off-side or over the top, nestled safely in his gloves. He seemed neither to move nor sway. The timing was perfect. Fathers were telling their kids that an old master was young again.

It was T. G. Evans. After an hour he took off his pads and bowled a slow mixture, taking four wickets. Then he gambolled at extra cover. 'The eyes have gone. Can't see a damn thing these days,' he kept apologising over his shoulder to no one in particular.

Soon he was strutting out to bat. (He always strutted, still does). By this time I had been recruited as umpire. He scored 12, went for a sweep and was caught off a skier. It was so clean nobody bothered to appeal. Too late to shout 'no ball'.

The old boy was gone. 'I'm as stiff as a wicket,' he said back at the Jolly Drover as he catapulted three fruitless appeals in one over in the International Cricket series. SUNDAY EXPRESS, 11 JULY 1976

Those Damn Yankees Hit Us for Six

LAURIE PIGNON

Now I know that the sun has finally set on the British Empire. The Yanks have licked us at cricket.

We have long learned to live with American supremacy on the tennis court, in the boxing ring, on the golf course and running track.

But 28 years after the US knocked the full England soccer side out of the World Cup we consoled ourselves that there was always cricket. They couldn't beat us at that, we said.

Having watched our three best tennis players, Buster Mottram, John Lloyd and Mark Cox, fail to survive the first week of the US Open, I took a short walk across the railway tracks from Flushing Meadow to the towering Shea Stadium sure in the knowledge that the Yanks would be shown a thing or two when it came to a real game.

But it didn't work out that way. The American All-Stars beat an international side of former Test cricketers by seven wickets.

The world All-Stars were all out for 124 in 33 overs. The legendary Sir Gary Sobers made just three. And when he bowled he was hooked and driven to the boundary.

Former Australian skipper Greg Chappell scored a single and Tony Greig was top scorer with 18.

Yet Sobers and Co had the help of erstwhile England wicket-keeper Alan Knott and fast bowlers John Snow and Andy Roberts.

Not to mention South African opener Barry Richards and such masters as West Indian Roy Fredericks, Australian David Hookes and India's Sunil Gavaskar.

To be fair, the conditions were slightly different from those at Lord's. The pitch was a matting strip laid across a baseball diamond used by the New York Mets.

And every ball was accompanied by a commentary in language which would hardly be understood in the Long Room at Lord's.

The American team were drawn from the New York area which has 70 clubs whose players are, in the main, of Caribbean descent. But their hero was a New Zealander, Dr John Millener, who took four wickets for 13 runs in seven overs.

Greig, who is accustomed to putting a brave face on disaster, told me afterwards: 'I am disappointed at our performance – and surprised at theirs. We made the mistake of not coming here earlier. It is out of season for most of our team and we were not prepared. And most of us haven't played on a matting wicket since we were ten.'

Burt Smith, the president of Cricket Classics Inc., who put on the match kept telling everyone: 'This is my great American dream.'

But for 11 cricketers and a handful of Brits it was a daylight nightmare.

The only mercy is there's a newspaper strike in town. With luck, not too many people will get to hear about it.

DAILY MAIL, 4 SEPTEMBER 1978

I Know What It Is Like To Be Hit by a Bouncer

DENIS COMPTON

Is there a more glorious sight for spectators than a world-class batsman hooking a fearsome bouncer to the square-leg boundary in a Test match?

Pulses race, even if batsmen are forced to take evasive action to prevent the ball from rearing at their skulls. For the bouncer is an important part of cricket.

Take it from the game and fast bowlers lose a legitimate weapon crucial to their armoury. Yet, paradoxically, the ball that sets the nerve-ends tingling is threatening to become a menace.

The treatment meted out by England fast bowler Bob Willis to Pakistan's night-watchman Iqbal Qasim at Edgbaston gave nothing more than a cheap thrill to those baying for blood at the expense of sportsmanship.

First, Willis dug in a bouncer that soared over Qasim's head. Then he went round the wicket to deliver another that struck him full in the face.

Even more disgraceful was that, having felled a 'batsman' who had a tour record of 11 runs in five innings, including three noughts, Willis stood in mid-pitch apparently unperturbed by the sight of his victim writhing in the crease.

It was later revealed that Willis was just as anxious as the rest of us but, while Mike Brearley and England's close fielders rushed to Qasim's side, the Warwickshire pace-man appeared to survey the scene as nonchalantly as a day-tripper watching the pigeons in Trafalgar Square.

It saddens me that many of today's fast bowlers flout the time-honoured code that decrees bouncers should not be fired at nine, ten, 'Jack'.

I know Qasim was showing a pretty straight bat, but Willis, no doubt becoming frustrated, should just have bowled even faster and straighter. But no genuine bouncers.

I would never advocate the use of Grand Prix-style helmets for established batsmen – technique should nullify the risk of injury – but if fast bowlers persist in bumping tail-enders, I would recommend them to wear one of those caged helmets worn by goal-minders in ice hockey.

More important, umpires the world over *must* take a grip on the situation. The Test and County Cricket Board recommended last year that bowlers should be allowed no more than two bouncers in any over in Tests, or no more than three in any two consecutive overs.

Countries were asked to introduce the experiment by mutual agreement. Well, when are they going to start?

The lead should come from the captains. Brearley, perhaps understandably, refused to condemn Willis, saying: 'This was one ball in a Test match and if it hadn't hit him there would not have been all this fuss.'

He went on: 'It is very hard to draw the line between who is a recognised batsman and who is a non-recognised batsman.'

I am surprised that cricketers find it difficult to tell the difference.

Of the England side who played in the first Test, Willis was the only non-recognised batsman. Yet when England played against Australia at Lord's a year ago they had three non-bats – John Lever, Derek Underwood and Willis.

That is not to say that that trio are incapable of scoring runs. Underwood and Lever, in particular, have played some staunch rearguard innings in Tests without assuming the mantle of acceptability as recognised batsmen.

They and their like should be protected by umpires and captains if fast bowlers need to resort to the short-pitched stuff to claim their wickets.

To be fair, dubious tactics are not a new phenomenon. The 'bodyline' series cast a dark shadow across cricket before the war and I can recall Ray Lindwall, perhaps the most sporting fast bowler of all time, felling England's tail-ender Frank Tyson with a bouncer in Sydney in 1954–55.

'Why did you do that, Ray?' I asked at the end of play. 'I wanted to show him how fast I was', was the answer.

It was a rare blemish on an otherwise spotless character.

Lindwall's bouncer was particularly dangerous. It skimmed off the pitch at your throat. I was on the receiving end of plenty in that series in Australia.

In an earlier Test at Old Trafford he sent me packing to the dressing-room with a split forehead after unleashing a series of bouncers. I hooked at a 'no-ball' bouncer and the ball flew into my head off the edge of the bat.

When I returned later with a stitched skull, Lindwall bowled faster at me for a few overs than I had ever seen him before. I finished up with an undefeated 145. You see, I rather expected these tactics from Ray because, after all, I was a recognised batsman.

We have had many great batsmen who were glorious hookers of the short-pitched ball. They relished the challenge and the opportunity to demonstrate their technique. It was a fair contest.

But I know of no tail-ender in Test history who has excelled with the hook or who relished facing balls fired at their heads.

I thought the 'Fast Bowlers' Union' had learned their lesson when Ewan Chatfield, the New Zealand No 11, was injured, almost mortally, by a short-pitched delivery from England's Peter Lever in the first Test at Auckland in February 1975.

Chatfield deflected a bouncer into his face. Bernard Thomas, the MCC physiotherapist, had to administer the kiss of life. It was revealed later that Chatfield's heart had stopped for several seconds.

Fast bowlers would be wise to heed Thomas's words after the incident: 'It was the worst case I have seen and I never want to see another.'

Let us call a cease-fire against late-order batsmen before someone gets killed. This heavy responsibility lies with the captains and the umpires. SUNDAY EXPRESS, 11 JUNE 1978

1911 Hard Hitter

BENNY GREEN

On the morning of 20 May 1911 a young man hobbled over the shingle on Hove beach and strode into the surf. The front was almost deserted. It was the start of a summer whose heat was to become sub-tropical, but that morning the weather gave no indication of the climax to come. Low clouds scudded across the sea's face, and a brisk breeze whipped the breakers into milky confusion. The young man was a perfect physical specimen, just over six feet tall, broad-shouldered and deep-chested, and although in the peak of condition, weighed over fifteen stone. As he cut a furrow through the green water, he seemed preoccupied with the muscles of his right hand which he kept flexing in mid-stroke. After a few minutes he strode back up the beach, threw on his clothes and disappeared into the town.

The name of the lone swimmer was Edwin Boaler Alletson, and although he could not possibly have known it, that swim was the prelude to the one sensational moment in his long life. He survived into his eighties, but only on the day of his swim off Brighton beach was he ever fated to accomplish anything unique. Tomorrow his train would be racketing back to his native Nottinghamshire, his day of fame over.

Alletson was a professional cricketer, a nonentity in a sport then enjoying its Golden Age. The game was crammed with *virtuosi* who could hardly have spared Alletson a glance. English batting was dominated by the Aristotelean logic of C. B. Fry and the budding classicism of the young Jack Hobbs. Sidney Barnes still looked like the greatest bowler of all time, and connoisseurs of spin bowling, perhaps dismayed by the mysterious evolution of Wilfred Rhodes from a great left-arm spinner into a workmanlike batsman, consoled themselves with the delicate art of Colin Blythe. Compared to these men, Alletson was a nobody, a tail-end batsman who drifted in and out of the Notts county side in the years between his debut in 1906 and his retirement in 1914. There were countless professionals like him, honest artisans who appeared on the county grounds of England for a few seasons, gradually faded away and were never heard of again until the death notices, which often ended with a phrase something like 'In his last years he unfortunately fell into poor circumstances.' Nothing seemed more certain that Alletson would be numbered among this anonymous army, for at 27 he was already past the age when any dramatic improvement in his technique might be hoped for. Indeed, it was already five years since Alletson had made one last attempt to turn himself into a cricketer of real distinction. The attempt failed.

Alletson had always dreamed of that succulent slice of cricketing pie in the sky, the fast leg-break, a ball which would turn from leg with the venom of wrist-spin, and yet at a fast-medium pace. But because the leg-break has to be delivered out of the back of the hand, real pace is almost impossible to achieve. In 1906, well aware of this, Alletson began his pursuit of the unattainable. Alletson's father worked on the Duke of Portland's estates up in Welbeck, and now, using his father as wicket-keeper, Alletson spent a winter in 1906 practising his new ball in the orchards at Welbeck.

Progress was slow, but Alletson found that by turning his body at the moment of delivery and swinging his powerful shoulders through a wide arc, he was occasionally able to produce a fast-medium ball which turned from leg. But five years later, in 1911, he had still not acquired the consistency demanded in a match of any consequence.

Notice it was as a bowler that Alletson aspired to power, not as a batsman, which makes his fame doubly remarkable. Reports of the period described his batting as 'orthodox', in the sense that he could play a straight bat in defence. But although his immense shoulders and a freakish armspan of 78 inches made him a powerful hitter when he happened to connect, his batting could never be effective against bowling of any quality because of his inability to use his feet. He never moved to the pitch of the ball, but simply stayed rooted to the crease, driving from there when the chance came. Most bowlers could therefore subdue him quite easily by pitching the ball a shade short or a shade wide.

Alletson was also a good deep field with a safe pair of hands and a strong accurate throw. And that was all. It was not much on which to base a professional career. A summary of his ability would see him as a tail-end batsman who occasionally hit a spectacular drive, a mediocre bowler in a side already packed with good bowling, and a reliable deep fielder. It is no surprise that in his nine seasons with the county he never established a regular place in the side.

Three days before his dip in the sea, the Notts side had arrived at Hove for the annual championship match with Sussex. Doubts about fitness had complicated the processes of team selection, so that not eleven but twelve men had travelled down, two of them nursing minor injuries. One of these was a bowler called Wass, the other Alletson himself, suffering from a sprained wrist. At the last moment Wass was declared unfit to play and Alletson found himself drafted into a side that had been alternately picking and dropping him for the past six seasons.

Notts, a powerful side, champions in 1907 and boasting at least four England batsmen, won the toss on a genial wicket and started well. Then the Sussex bowler Killick enjoyed a purple patch of five wickets for only 14 runs and Notts were all out for 238. Alletson, batting at number nine, was caught off Killick for only seven runs. Sussex now piled up 414 runs in their first innings and took control of the game. By the end of the second day Notts were drifting to certain defeat, and it was clear that the issue would be decided long before the end of the allotted three days. One local newspaper, which had been reporting the match in close detail, ended its comments on the eve of the last day with the words, 'Tomorrow's play promises to be most interesting,' evidently without believing anything of the kind. It sent no observer to the Hove ground on May 20, and no further mention of the match appeared in its columns. The only Press representatives to witness the closing formalities were from the *Sussex Daily News*, *The Nottinghamshire Guardian*, the magazine *Cricket*, and of course the inevitable man from Wisden's Cricketers' Almanac.

On that last morning Alletson was still troubled by his injured wrist, and thought that perhaps contact with sea water might ease the muscles. But he was careful not to prolong his swim. Half the Notts side was already out in its second innings, and he might be required to go in and bat at any moment. When play recommenced on the last morning all went as the experts predicted. More Notts wickets fell, and when the seventh man was out with 50 minutes still to go to lunch and Notts only seven runs ahead, it looked very much as though the players would have the afternoon to themselves.

In the Notts dressing-room the mood was one of cheerful acceptance of defeat. Nothing short of a thunderstorm could save them now, and already the sun was out and the weather steadily improving. A. O. Jones, the Notts captain, having realised the game was lost, no longer bothered to brief his batsmen. Before he went out to bat Alletson asked him, 'Mr Jones, does it matter what I do?' to which Jones replied: 'No, Alletson, I don't think it matters what you do.' Alletson's reply to this innocent remark was the first hint that a thunderstorm was actually coming, although not quite the conventional kind. 'Oh,' said Alletson, 'then I'm not half going to give "Tom" Killick some stick,' with which he emerged from the Hove pavilion and marched towards the wickets carrying a cricket bat weighing only two pounds three ounces, an absurdly flimsy weapon for so huge a bulk of a man.

Alletson started to bat in a manner which he later described as 'normal', scoring 47 runs in the 50 minutes before lunch, including two sixes. During this session, however, two more Notts wickets fell and Alletson was himself dropped twice. When the two teams went in for lunch, Notts had only one wicket left standing and had built up a slender lead of 84. The game was still lost, however, and very few spectators bothered to wait for the afternoon's play. What is more surprising is that three of the four Press reporters followed suit, leaving only one official observer to witness the most extraordinary batting episode in the history of cricket.

At this point an exasperating veil falls over events on the Hove ground. The actual details of play have since been documented and examined, discussed and discussed again with relentless attention to every incident, but as to what, if anything, went on in the pavilion during the lunch interval nobody could be found who remembered. This fact is fundamental to the story of Alletson's great day, because he re-emerged from the pavilion after lunch almost like a man with an extra dimension up his sleeve. No record exists as to what the players were given for lunch, but in view of what was about to happen, nectar and ambrosia seems as good a guess as any.

Three minutes after the resumption he drove the four which gave him his half-century, and from this point on he did not so much assault the Sussex bowling as strew it in gobbets about the field. In no time the game drifted out of reality into the realm of pure fantasy. Five times Alletson drove Killick's bowling into the middle distance. One of his hammer-blows flew right out of the arena, hurtling into the pavilion bar like a shell from a cannon, sending broken glass and cascading whisky all over the premises. Another straight drive went out of the ground completely, soaring over the entrance gates into the street, where it was picked up by a small boy who was later found playing with it down on the beach. A third shot disappeared from view over the south stand, coming to rest on the roof of a nearby skating rink, a carry of at least 160 yards.

Only 13 minutes after reaching his 50, Alletson had completed the first century of his career, by which time the proceedings on the field no longer resembled a cricket match at all.

For one thing, play was repeatedly being stopped because there was no ball for the players to play with, Alletson having despatched five of them out of the ground. Bemused officials wandered about the precincts of the pavilion searching for one or another of these lost balls. In the meantime a subtle change had also came over the fielding side. By now Sussex had forgotten all about winning the match, or even losing it, and could only stand by and watch something they could not believe.

Poor Killick, the conqueror of the first innings, now had only one aim in life, not to get Alletson out, or even to stop him scoring at so hysterical a rate. All Killick asked was to be allowed to get out of the ground alive. John Gunn, one of the Notts batsmen watching this crazy display, said: 'Killick was almost frightened to bowl. I don't think he minded his bowling being hit so much as he was worried Ted might hit one back at him.'

Neither were the fielders much inclined to lend a hand. John Gunn's brother, George, himself a batsman of genius, remembered calling out to Vine, the Sussex deep fielder, 'Look out, he'll hit you any minute now,' to which Vine replied, 'Bugger him. I don't want it.' Gunn goes on, 'The ball fizzed through the fielders as if they had been ghosts. I have never seen another innings like it. One of those drives would have smashed a man's hand if he had tried to stop it.'

Having arrived at his hundred, Alletson now got down to business in earnest. It was now just half-past two, and as he thrashed the bowling the ball could literally be heard humming past the Sussex outfielders. No person or place on the Hove ground was safe. H. P. Chaplin, the Sussex captain, but a spectator that day, described it as 'the most amazing innings ever. Once he just lay back on his heels and pushed and the ball went through the pavilion clockface.' Relph, another of the Sussex fieldsmen, observed, 'He stood up and hit like a giant. I don't think any man could have played two innings like that and lived.'

Years later Relph was asked to recall his impressions of Alletson's exhibition. He said, 'My chief memory is that shower of cricket balls going over the boundary and the crowd mad with delight. It cost us a match we were winning, but I don't think anyone minded about that. It was such an experience to watch it.'

It is perhaps understandable that the more impressionable members of the audience went slightly hysterical, and could no longer make sense of what their eyes showed them. A gentleman called C. P. Foley later dedicated part of his autobiography to a lurid description of the innings, and as he strove to give a true impression drifted from factual reportage into the higher planes of literary invention. 'Time was wasted in trying to prise the ball out of the new stand into whose soft wood Alletson had driven it, no chisel being available.' Perhaps closer to the truth is Foley's observation, 'The fieldsmen and umpires had a very anxious half hour, but by skilful agility managed to avoid contact with the ball, and nobody was killed, or indeed seriously injured.'

By 2.55 Alletson had amassed 189 runs and there seemed to be no known way of getting him out. A Notts rout had been transformed into a Sussex massacre. But then Alletson connected with yet another prodigious drive which the fielder C. Smith caught with one foot over the boundary line and his head resting against the grandstand. The rules of cricket define this as an illegal catch, and Alletson knew this well. But he also knew that time was running short and that Notts still had an outside chance of winning the game, so he acknowledged the catch and ran back to the pavilion. When George Gunn ran after him to tell him he was legally not out, he is said to have replied, 'It's all reet.' Gunn later remarked, 'He had had enough.'

In 90 minutes Alletson had scored 189, the last 142 of them in only 40 minutes. Nothing like it had ever been seen or would be again. Alletson became the most notorious athlete in England. For a brief spell he was what he had always wanted to be, a great cricketer.

And yet, if the hysterical Mr Foley is to be believed, what followed was even more outlandish. According to Foley, who saw the whole business as an epic of Attic proportions, Jones, the Notts captain, told Alletson that from now on his place in the side was assured indefinitely on condition that he went out to hit in every match.

'But,' said Foley, 'after hitting a ball over the clock at Lord's later in the season, he retired into his shell and absolutely refused to hit.'

The facts are rather less dramatic. In his very next innings Alletson once again smashed the ball all over the place, scoring 60 in half an hour against Gloucestershire. But then a certain change of attitude did seem to set in, and gradually his approach to cricket subsided back to the norm. But for the moment the entire cricketing world was in ferment. A fortnight after the record-breaking innings, Alletson, this obscure bottom-of-the-order batsman unable to command a place in the county side, was invited to play in the official Test Trial at Sheffield. He failed, scoring 15 in the first innings and only eight in the second. It was the only occasion in his entire career when he appeared in a first-class match for any other side than Notts.

There are many possible explanations for his return to mediocrity, and the most attractive one of all is that he was still preoccupied with his potential as the bowler of that infallible fast leg-break. Two years later, in

1913, he was finally ready to try his new delivery in a county game, at which fate, which had been so lavish on that day at Hove, finally turned sour on him. At first everything went splendidly. Against Kent he won the match with six wickets for 43 runs, and followed up with four for 17 against Derbyshire. The long hours in the orchard at Welbeck were paying dividends at last.

And then, in the next match against Gloucestershire, he bowled only two overs before the umpire, in Alletson's own words, 'Told me to stop bowling.' Rumours began to circulate that his bowling action was not within the letter of the law. He bowled no more that season. In 1914, against Derbyshire, his captain asked him to bowl again, and once more he was taken off because of the alleged illegality of his action. He never appeared in a first-class match again. At the time of the Derbyshire match he was just 30 years old.

In the Great War he served in the Royal Garrison Artillery, and later went to live at Worksop and work at the Manton Colliery. In 1950, crippled by arthritis, he retired reluctantly to a wheelchair. A visitor described him at this time as 'still tall, dark and huge, his voice deep, his relish for cricket immense, and his humour good'.

As to his one day of glory, it was never quite forgotten, and remains in the record books to this day as the fastest big innings ever played. The only point left unanswered, the one point Alletson was too inarticulate to explain, is the most vital of all. What got into him that afternoon? All he himself ever offered on the subject was that 'after lunch A. O. Jones told me to have a go, and I did. Runs kept coming and I cast care aside and hit harder.'

There is a nice poetic flourish to that last phrase, but it still seems possible that something is missing from the equation. What happened to Edwin Boaler Alletson from 1.30 to 2.15 in the Hove Pavilion on 20 May 1911?

Probably nothing at all, but it is tempting to speculate whether a double brandy slipped into his beer, or a wink from the groundsman's daughter might have had something to do with it. Perhaps some actual metabolic change in his body lasting only a few hours? A metamorphosis caused by something he ate or drank or saw or heard or thought? Absurd to entertain such romantic ideas, and yet why not? When a man suddenly turns into a giant, there is certainly no rational explanation for it. EVERYBODY'S WEEKLY

VIEW FROM THE DEEP

R. C. Robertson-Glasgow on John Hayward, after his retirement: But he was best of all as a spectator with his face balanced like a luminous walrus over the wall by the dressing-room steps.

One Man's Week

The amazing Mike Procter struck Somerset spinner Dennis Breakwell for six successive sixes yesterday during the most outrageous innings of the season.

In what probably qualified for the most sensational piece of big hitting since Gary Sobers took 36 off one over from Glamorgan's Malcolm Nash 11 years ago, Procter went to within seven runs of completing one of the fastest centuries in the history of cricket.

His six sixes in a row came from the last two balls of Breakwell's second over at Taunton and the first four of the next. The buccaneering South African all-rounder deposited his sixes to the distant corners of the ground – towards St James's Churchyard, into the car park, on top of the toilets and one through the open windows of the visitors dressing-room high up in the stands.

Procter tore past his half century within 25 minutes and had advanced to 93 in 46 minutes when he dragged a ball from England's Ian Botham on to his stumps going for another colossal hit.

He made his runs from only 23 scoring shots – eight sixes, nine fours, three twos and three singles. In his 46 marvellous minutes Procter scored all but 14 of a 107-run third wicket partnership with opener Andy Stovold. DAILY MAIL, 29 SEPTEMBER 1979

Tailpiece: A week later, against Warwickshire at Bristol, Procter was at it again. He scored 92 off 45 deliveries in 35 minutes.

Most of his three sixes and ten fours were at the expense of Clifford's off-spin, and poor Clifford ended with 2 for 185. His only consolation was to catch Procter one-handed at mid-wicket off another lusty blow.

Ball by Ball: How Sobers Hit Me for 36

MALCOLM NASH 'EXPLAINS' TO JIM HILL

The over in which Alletson hit E. H. Killick for 34 (including two no-balls) at Hove in 1911 remained a record in world cricket until 30 August 1968 when Gary Sobers hit Malcolm Nash, 28-year-old Glamorgan bowler, for six successive sixes at Swansea. (This record can be equalled, but never beaten, while the scoring and length of over remains unaltered.)

I suppose being hit for 36 runs in one over, as I was by Gary Sobers on Saturday, is getting into the record books the hard way.

But I won't let it worry me. The way Gary was going it could have happened to anyone.

I'd already bowled three overs at Gary and it was pretty obvious that he was looking for quick runs. So I wasn't all that surprised to see the first ball go for 6.

It was a half-volley, anyway, and if you bowl those to a man like Sobers you expect to get hit – though maybe not out of the ground.

I thought about it a bit while I went back to bowl the second ball and decided not to worry but just to keep the ball up to him. This time I flighted it up on a good length and that one went into the crowd over long-on.

As I walked back again I was beginning to wonder where I ought to bowl next. I thought about pitching wide but decided it was my job to get him out and the best way to do that was to keep bowling straight.

So I tossed that one up, too, and watched it sail into the crowd over long-off.

After that, I didn't quite know what to do. I looked hopefully at skipper Tony Lewis, but he just smiled and told me to keep bowling.

I looked down the wicket at Gary and told him: 'I'll bet you can't hit the flood-lights with the next one.'

He just smiled back and said 'That's too high for me.'

So he hit it out of the ground instead. It was a terrific shot. I had decided to bowl this one a bit faster and flatter but I dropped it shorter than I intended. Gary hooked it like a bullet and I swear he had both feet off the ground when he hit it.

By now the crowd were going mad but I was still only thinking about getting him out rather than avoiding more punishment. I kept telling myself how wonderful it would be to get the world's greatest batsman.

I nearly did it with the fifth ball. I pitched it on a good length just outside the off-stump. Gary made his only mistake. He mistimed it slightly and it dropped straight towards Roger Davis who was standing on the long-off boundary.

Roger caught it low down and I thought: 'I've got him!' Then Roger over-balanced and part of his body went over the boundary line, so the umpires decided it had to be another six.

It wasn't until then that I began thinking about a world record. Even then, my only thought was to stop Gary getting it. I still wanted to get him out, so I thought I'd try him with a yorker.

It was a miserable failure. When it got there it was more of a long hop and when Gary swung at it I didn't have to follow the ball to know that that one was out of the ground too.

DAILY EXPRESS, 31 AUGUST 1968

Editor's note: Eight years later, on the same ground, Frank Hayes of Lancashire hit on Malcolm Nash again. He took 34 in one over off Nash, 6, 4, 6, 6, 6, 6.

Both six sixes and 36 runs in an over are world records for a six-ball over. Five sixes in an over were the previous best, by Arthur Wellard (Somerset *v* Kent) off Frank Woolley, at Wells, in 1938; Wellard also hit five sixes (against Derbyshire) off T. R. Armstrong, again at Wells, in 1938. J. D. Lindsay, the South African, did the same (touring Fezela XI *v* Essex) at Chelmsford in 1961.

And the story went round the world after H. B. Cameron, the South African, hit Hedley Verity for 30 in one over in the match against Yorkshire at Sheffield in 1935.

At the end of the over, which had consisted of three sixes and three fours, Maurice Leyland said to Verity, 'Keep going Hedley, you've got him in two minds'.

'What do you mean?'

'He doesn't know whether to hit you for four or for six!'

The Private Test Match

BARRY WILSON

Lionel Robinson was an Australian who tried hard to establish himself as a landed English gentleman. He never quite made it – he had the money but not quite the style. But he did carve a tiny niche in history for himself: he had a passion for cricket and he built an Australian cricket pitch on his isolated Norfolk estate; and in 1921 he staged what amounted to his own private Test match in his own backyard, during the course of which England's greatest batsman played one of the best innings of his career.

Lionel Robinson was born in Ceylon in 1866 but his parents returned to Melbourne when he was a few weeks old. His father became city editor of the *Melbourne Age*; Lionel himself dabbled in financial journalism before moving into stock-broking where he prospered mightily. Before he was 35 burgeoning financial interests brought him to London and he became a powerful figure in the City.

To give substance to his new station in life he sought a suitable country seat. He found what he wanted in Norfolk, in the village of Old Buckenham, near Attleborough, 15 miles south of Norwich. The previous owner of the 2,000-acre estate was the singular Indian antiquarian Freddy Duleep Singh (son of a deposed Sikh maharajah) who, like Robinson, also had problems in gaining full aristocratic acceptance in England (but for duskier colonial reasons; Duleep's more famous son gained another sort of acceptance when selected to play cricket for England in 1929–30).

Without delay the tough, swashbuckling Australian financier tore down the comfortable, elegant Duleep residence, and, in 1906, set about erecting an appropriate home for himself. It is reputed that, in all, he spent close on £1 million. Twice the building was pulled down and started again. At last he was happy with specially imported Dutch bricks and a style which could perhaps now be described as '1930s baroque'. The house had 14 bathrooms – a wondrous Australian novelty at that time.

He had Billy Smith, the local barber from Attleborough, cycle out to the hall every morning to shave him. He employed a superior butler, Royce, who ran the household.

But as a country gentleman, he was neither genial, effortless nor stylish. He was obstinate and aggressive, and known for his abusive slanging matches with staff.

Increasingly, he turned his attention to his sporting interests. He built splendid stables and accumulated a fine and typically successful racing stud. The shooting was extensive. And at enormous expense he built the Old Buckenham Hall cricket ground in a clearing in the wood that surrounded the hall.

Robinson had been a regular spectator at the Melbourne Cricket Ground, and he had watched a lot of cricket in England. He was sick of the slow English pitches. He wanted to build a hard, fast Australian type of wicket, and he reckoned that in dry Norfolk (with rainfall half that in Melbourne) he at least had the right geography. He dredged a lagoon near the house for fine clay as foundation for the wicket area (and the soil mixture was reinforced with chicken netting). After the First World War, to further improve the pitch, he actually imported special turf from Australia.

The pitch proved as fast as Robinson hoped. Part of the original wicket area is still in use, known as the 'Australian end'. Present groundsman Billy Lancaster, who scored a century at Old Buckenham in 75 minutes in 1951, says: 'It's when we use the Australian end that the runs really come.'

Robinson soon made the cricket ground a focus for the sporting fraternity. In the early days the village team (which is now the only one using the Old Buckenham cricket ground) had to play on the village green: the ground at the hall was reserved for the visiting toffs.

Robinson appointed as his personal cricket manager the somewhat boozy but still very shrewd Archie MacLaren, who had been an outstanding bat for England. MacLaren lived in a cottage on the Old Buckenham estate for many years.

It was in the first week of May 1921 that Robinson and MacLaren pulled off their small country coup. They persuaded the touring Australian Test team – the first in England since the war – to play the second match of their tour at Old Buckenham.

The teams for Robinson's Old Buckenham match were formidable: nearly Test match strength. For Australia: W. Bardsley, H. L. Collins, C. G. Macartney, J. M. Taylor, W. W. Armstrong (captain), J. M.

Gregory, J. Ryder, H. L. Hendry, H. Carter (wicket-keeper), E. A. McDonald, A. A. Mailey.

For Mr Robinson's XI: J. B. Hobbs, D. J. Knight, V. W. C. Jupp, E. Hendren, A. P. F. Chapman, J. W. H. T. Douglas, P. G. H. Fender, A. C. MacLaren (captain), G. E. C. Wood (wicket-keeper), C. H. Gibson, J. C. White.

The Old Buckenham match, seen as a full dress-rehearsal for the 1921 Tests, got unusually extensive publicity. Just a few months earlier the Australians had drubbed England in Australia by five to nothing, which is a Test record still not equalled. Could Jack Hobbs, only just past the peak of his powers, cope with the new Australian fast bowlers Jack Gregory and Ted McDonald?

The Old Buckenham cricket ground was nearly four miles from Attleborough railway station. All hireable ponies and traps worked to and fro for the duration of the three-day match. Bicycles, pedestrians, horse-carts and motor-cars crammed the village roads. The Norwich *Eastern Daily Press* recorded: 'There was a great pilgrimage from all parts of Norfolk and the adjoining counties to Old Buckenham yesterday, and as the road traffic drew nearer the magnetic centre the country folk, all wide-eyed, no doubt wondered that a mere cricket match could cause so much commotion and stir ... Never before had so many enthusiasts come from far and near.'

Even for this great occasion Mr Robinson did not depart from his practice of never charging entrance fees (although £163 was collected for the Norwich hospital). About 2,000 people crowded the tiny ground on Wednesday, the first day, but it rained almost continuously. Only 15 minutes play was possible, during which the Australians amassed 18 for no wicket.

The second day, by contrast, was bright, sunny and warm, and from the early morning all roads in the vicinity were thronged. Estimates of the crowd that day varied between 7,000 and 10,000 – undoubtedly still the biggest crowd ever to watch a cricket match in East Anglia.

The *Eastern Daily Press* reported 'This was one of the most wonderful days in the history of Norfolk cricket ... Ranged behind the deep human wall were hundred upon hundreds of motor-cars the roofs of which were converted into stands, and from these lofty perches distant views were obtained of the play. The park trees, now in their May glory of leaf, alone were sacred ...'

For the English partisans the day was glorious in almost every respect; it was to be one of few such days that summer.

Astonishingly, the star-studded Australians were bowled out an hour after lunch for a feeble 136 (Douglas 6–64). This was the team's lowest score of the tour.

When the English team batted Knight was out in the second over. But then Hobbs and Jupp attacked the Australian bowling with a gusto unequalled since before the war. It was this onslaught that provoked Gregory and McDonald to resort to tactics that were to demoralise the Englishmen for the rest of the tour.

At the end of the tour, in which the Australians won the Tests three-nothing, and lost only two of their 38 games, Wisden selected both McDonald and Gregory among their Five Cricketers of the Year, and commented: 'This was maybe the finest Australian team we have ever seen, and it was the fast bowling that made the side so good. Never before have English batsmen been so demoralised by pace ... Never were batsmen so obviously intimidated ... McDonald was probably the finer bowler, but Gregory was far more alarming.'

At Old Buckenham Gregory and McDonald attacked Hobbs and Jupp with quite unprecedented ferocity, on a pitch that was remarkably fast. Both batsmen were hit several times. Both were eventually forced to retire hurt, Jupp with a broken thumb, Hobbs with a recurrence of a thigh strain that put him out of action for two months.

But before he was injured Hobbs showed what a difference he could have made. Several times he hoisted short pitched balls over the beech trees, at least 130 yards from the wicket. He scored 85 in just over 90 minutes. Years later, when asked on television which was the finest innings of his career, Sir Jack said: 'It was in a minor match in Norfolk against the Australians in 1921. Always when I look back I think that was one of my best innings – if not the best. Everything went right that day; all my strokes came easily.'

All was anti-climax when Hobbs left the crease with the score at 125–1. J. W. H. T. ('Johnny Won't Hit Today') Douglas stonewalled characteristically, and old Archie MacLaren, going in last, reminded the crowd of his legendary hitting power before he closed the innings at 256–9. The match petered out in a draw when the rain returned.

Ill-luck now dogged Old Buckenham Hall. The next owner, Ernest Gates, a successful north country businessman, died two years after taking up residence, and his son Everard is remembered in the village for his wild parties, complete with what are still remembered darkly as 'chorus girls'. He sold up in 1937 and Old Buckenham boys' school was started. The Hall was gutted by fire in 1952, after which the school and the thatched cricket pavilion were moved to Brettenham in Suffolk. They're still there.

Today the isolated cricket ground, little more than a fenced off clearing with narrowing boundaries, is struggling to survive even as a village cricket ground. SUNDAY TIMES MAGAZINE, 29 MAY 1977

ADVERT FROM WORLD SPORT

Refined gentleman wishes to meet widow with two tickets for third Test, view to matrimony. Kindly send photo of tickets.

It's Somerset on a Tie-Break

PETER JACKSON

Somerset squeezed into their second Gillete Cup Final amid unbearable tension at Taunton last night, off the last ball of a momentous match.

A marvellous semi-final ended with Essex beaten by inches as their last wicket pair made a despairing dash for the run which would have left them one match from winning their first prize in more than a century of endeavour. With the scores tied at 287, Somerset advanced to the final because they had lost fewer wickets.

Yet Essex had moved within sight of an astonishing victory when pace bowler Colin Dredge began their final over. They needed twelve runs with two wickets in hand as the 10,000 crowd were hushed to silence.

Neil Smith took a single from Dredge's first ball. Ray East edged the second through the vacant slip area for four – seven to win, four balls left. With his next delivery Dredge knocked back East's middle stump.

The crowd shrieked their delight, but there was more drama to come. Umpire David Evans no-balled Dredge's fourth delivery, and Lever, the Essex No 11, lofted it towards the mid-wicket boundary, ran two, and pinched a third by courtesy of Philip Slocombe's overthrow.

The match was now Essex's for the taking, with four required and three balls in which to get them. Smith failed to make contact with the following delivery and scrambled a single off the next which left Lever to score three off the last ball.

Somerset's harassed captain, Brian Rose, stopped to reorganise his field, dispatching his players to all parts of the boundary.

Lever struck his final shot into the mid-wicket area. He and Smith crossed for two and set off in frantic pursuit of the match-winning run when Rose, haring in from the ropes, picked up and hurled his throw towards wicket-keeper Derek Taylor. Taylor gathered cleanly, launched himself headlong at the wicket and broke it a split second before the diving Smith could reach the crease. The crowd greeted their team's passage to their first final since 1967 with a boisterous rendering of their battle hymn, *Drink Up Thee Cider*, pausing only to hear Jim Laker, presenting the Man of the Match Award to Viv Richards, say: 'I have never seen a better, a more thrilling cricket match.'

But despite the hammering administered by the West Indian's 116, and Peter Roebuck's 57, Essex recovered magnificently.

England opener Graham Gooch (61) supervised the recovery after the second-over dismissal of Mike Denness, and he and Ken McEwan drove Essex ahead of schedule with a stand of 61 in 14 overs. McEwan, who had dropped Richards when he had made 22, was dismissed by Graham Burgess when promising spectacular atonement, but skipper Keith Fletcher kept Essex on course.

In 13 overs he and Keith Pont put on 80, until Ian Botham stepped in to run out Pont and take a caught and bowled from Fletcher. His next ball resulted in the run out of Norbert Phillip. Scores:

Somerset v *Essex*
TAUNTON – Somerset won by losing fewer wickets.

SOMERSET	
B. Rose *c* East *b* Pont	24
P. Slocombe *lbw* *b* Phillip	0
V. Richards *c* Denness *b* Gooch	116
P. Roebuck *c* Lever *b* Phillip	57
I. Botham *b* East	7
V. Marks *not out*	33
G. Burgess *b* Lever	5
D. Breakwell *not out*	17
Extras (b10, lb14, w1, nb3)	28
Total (6 wkts, 60 overs)	287

ESSEX	
M. Denness *c* Marks *b* Dredge	3
G. Gooch *c* Taylor *b* Garner	61
K. McEwan *b* Burgess	37
K. Fletcher *c* and *b* Botham	67
B. Hardie *run out*	21
K. Pont *run out*	39
N. Phillip *run out*	1
S. Turner *b* Botham	12
R. East *b* Dredge	10
N. Smith *run out*	6
J. Lever *not out*	5
Extras (b14, lb9, nb2)	25
Total (60 overs)	287

Bowling Analyses

SOMERSET	*O*	*M*	*R*	*W*
Lever	12	0	61	1
Phillip	11	1	56	2
Turner	8	6	22	0
Pont	6	1	35	1
Gooch	12	0	42	1
East	11	1	43	1

ESSEX	*O*	*M*	*R*	*W*
Garner	12	1	46	1
Dredge	12	0	60	2
Botham	12	1	48	2
Burgess	12	1	43	1
Breakwell	2	0	11	0
Marks	1	0	13	0
Richards	9	1	41	0

Fall of the Wickets

Somerset

1/2 2/86 3/189 4/208 5/247 6/255

Essex

1/9 2/70 3/127 4/166 5/246 6/248 7/248 8/266 9/281

Man of the Match: Viv Richards

DAILY MAIL, 17 AUGUST 1978

DESPERATE MEASURES

Surgeon Arthur Dickson Wright, in a speech at a cricket club dinner: 'I was fielding in the slips, listening to a lark. The ball came too fast, and I lost two teeth. If I had had my mouth open another half-inch I would have been in Wisdens for ever!'

Nobby's Greatest Deal – £10 and a Box of Chocolates

IAN WOOLDRIDGE

'HE'S TWICE THE MAN ON A WORTHINGTON'

Advertisement on bill posting featuring E. W. 'Nobby' Clark, the Northamptonshire fast bowler, 1933

While it is only through gritted teeth that I can bring myself to mention this Connors fellow who appears to have inflicted himself on Wimbledon again, one fact of these strange economic times makes it unavoidable.

If Connors were suddenly to declare a passion for *Gutglo* – the new proved, patented and about-to-be-marketed stomach powder for men on the move – it would be worth about £100,000 to him in the current fiscal year.

All he would have to do would be to go on court wearing *Gutglo* insignia neatly embroidered just above his tennis elbow and they'd send him the money. Such is the power of pirate advertising which has been having a field day during the television transmission from Lord's and Wimbledon this week.

Well, maybe he'd be required to spread a little charm at a couple of *Gutglo* Press receptions and get his personal manager to send a goodwill telegram to the annual *Gutglo* shareholders meeting. But that would be the extent of it. *Gutglo* would immediately be demanded by an entire generation of schoolboys, none of whom had stomach ache, and some of whom, so help us, would actually like to grow up like Connors.

There are certain cynics, of course, who see nothing strange about Connors receiving five times as much for these services as the British Prime Minister receives for doing whatever British Prime Ministers do these days. I am not one of them.

I am particularly not one of them after talking yesterday to Mr E. W. Clark, who, at 74, is currently enjoying the second-best years of his life sea-angling daily off the Dorset coast near Swanage.

The first best years of his life were circa 1928–35 when, as contemporary photographs will confirm, he was certainly the most handsome if not the fastest of the great bowlers then available for England.

Indeed, Adonis may not have been too strong a word for him, for he was tall, blond, supremely athletic and strikingly strong, as he needed to be in an era when his immediate competitors numbered men like Larwood, Voce, Bowes, Allen and Farnes.

It was during this period of which we write that Messrs Worthington, makers then, as now, of a most reputable beer, were looking for a tall, blond, supremely athletic and strikingly strong man to assist them in an advertising campaign.

They considered Harold Larwood, they considered Bill Voce. They considered Bill Bowes, Gubby Allen and Ken Farnes. Eventually they approached E. W. 'Nobby' Clark, of Northamptonshire, and announced: 'We have chosen you from all the others to receive the honour of representing the manly qualities of our product.'

Thus it came to pass that between 1931 and 1933 Mr Clark, photographed in the act of delivering another express delivery, became one of the best known figures in the country.

Above the caption 'He's Twice the Man on a Worthington', he appeared on posters in Carlisle and Torquay, on hoardings in Margate and Birmingham, on motor buses plying from the Elephant and Castle to Kilburn. He decorated bleak walls in Swansea and drew jealous glances from lady typists on their way to work in Nottingham. Naturally he was much displayed in his home town of Northampton, as he was on almost every station on London's already extensive Underground.

On the way to the pub, prison, the dole queue, Charlie Chaplin's latest or Buckingham Palace it was almost impossible not to break stride for a second glance at Nobby Clark bowling better than ever on beer.

So it seemed only right, in these mad days of sporting advertising, to honour the precursor and the father of it all.

Mr Clark was in fact a little sad yesterday because his dog had just died, but we talked of cricket in the old days for a while and he cheered up with the memories.

Eventually we got around to discussing money and I asked him what he was paid for an advertising campaign that lasted for three summers and embraced the whole of Britain.

'Well,' said Mr Clark, 'I don't suppose the lads would do it for what I got. One Christmas they sent £10 for me, and a box of chocolates for the wife.'

Upon which remark we return you to Wimbledon where, from time to time, Mr Clark's successors actually play a little tennis.

DAILY MAIL, 24 JUNE 1977

ALL PLAYERS NOW

The first-class amateur cricketer 'condemned' to lose his status by the counties last November, awaits the final sentence by the MCC Committee today.

They must ratify the decision.

Members of the MCC Committee hold different views on the proposed class-less cricket society, but they will be guided by the fact that the Advisory County Cricket Committee are clearly in favour of removing the last remaining distinctions between amateurs and professionals.

DAILY MAIL, 31 JANUARY 1963

Cricket, Lovely Cricket

JOHN THICKNESSE

For the thousands of West Indians who have made their home in London, there is just one place to be on this mid-summer Friday – Lord's cricket ground in the Borough of St Marylebone, where the Second Test between England and the West Indies is in its second day.

Only a fraction will be there in the flesh, but in spirit *all* will be. Because to the West Indian, cricket is nearer a religion – and more of a way of life than either.

He is taught to play as soon as he can run, and play he does, in the streets and on the beaches, in tiny hidden clearings amid the waving sugar cane, anywhere in short where there is room to swing a bat.

Under Clive Lloyd's captaincy, West Indies are a powerful combination in the match at Lord's today, with many a household name among them. And their brightly clad supporters, drawn from the lovely archipelago that forms a daisy-chain across 1,500 miles of Caribbean, are rightly proud of them.

Yet some, the older ones, will look with wistful eyes on the huge fast bowlers, Andy Roberts and his cortege, and sigh for the days when cricket was a game of sublety and greater charm, the days of the three W's and Ramadhin and Valentine – the days of West Indies' first victory over England in this country, at Lord's in 1950.

What a victory it was. West Indies won by 326 and their 20-year-old pair of spinners – those 'two little pals of mine' immortalised in calypso – delivered between them more overs than all the West Indian bowlers put together in the First Test of the present series, at Trent Bridge!

Sonny Ramadhin's was an amazing story. A shrimp of five feet four inches, he was discovered in minor cricket in Southern Trinidad, removed to Port of Spain for two trial games – and picked for England on the strength of five dozen overs of assorted right-hand spinners.

The Lord's Test was the eleventh first-class game of his career and it enriched him by a wicket for each game against batsmen who for the most part had only a vague idea which way the ball was spinning. By the end of the series he had 26 wickets in four matches and became, unchallengeably, the greatest coup by a panel of selectors in the history of the game.

Alf Valentine was a loose-limbed six-footer from Jamaica, who by a twist of fate had been born just three days earlier than Ramadhin at the far end of the Caribbean, who bowled slow left-hand and could spin the ball on a looking glass.

He had seven wickets at Lord's and in the series 33, still a West Indian record against England.

For England the match was a calamity. But more than that, it was a shock, because a fortnight earlier they had won the first Test at Old Trafford by 202, and clearly hadn't an inkling what a bundle of trouble they were up against in little 'Ram.'

The Lord's Test turned the series. West Indies, served by the late Sir Frank Worrell's beautiful 261 at Trent Bridge, won the third Test by ten wickets, and the fourth at the Oval by an innings and 56, where England followed on despite Sir Leonard Hutton's 202 not out.

In four matches West Indies used 12 players, England 25. And not one of them played in all the matches.

Of the England team defeated at Lord's, four are familiar figures on the Test and County circuit, Alec Bedser and Sir Leonard as selectors, Godfrey Evans as the source of all wisdom on behalf of Ladbrokes, and Bill Edrich as a man-of-the-match adjudicator in the one-day competitions.

And in spite of the fact that sportsmen, more than most, tend to cultivate collective amnesia where their (infrequent) failures are concerned, they, and many of their team-mates, retain clear memories of the match – in the cases of Hutton and Evans, unique ones.

'In the second innings I was bowled by one of the few balls I ever lost in flight in all my career – by Valentine bowling from the nursery end,' said Hutton. 'There had been complaints about the height of the sightscreen and the ball must have come out of the crowd behind it.

'The wicket was a good one and the outfield fast as well. I felt I could have played Val and Ram until the cows came home!'

Evans, who was 29, and at the top of his wonderful form as England's wicket-keeper-batsman, has even better reason for remembering the match. 'It was the very last game in which I ever wore a flannel cricket shirt,' he laughed.

And all because he missed stumping Clyde Walcott, manager of the present West Indian team, on his way to 168 not out.

'It was a quarter of a century ago, but it's so clear in my memory it might have been last week,' Evans reminisced. 'Roly Jenkins beat Clyde with a googly when he was 57. I took it cleanly over the leg stump – but when I tried to stump him my gloves got caught up with my shirt. From then on I always wore a cotton shirt that hugged the figure. It wasn't the last stumping I missed, but it was the last for that reason!'

Cyril Washbrook, who made 114 in England's second innings, and was one of the few to emerge with credit, recalls the shrewdness of John Goddard, captain of West Indies, in bowling Ramadhin from the pavilion end, where in those days there was no sightscreen.

'It was very difficult to spot the legbreak from the offbreak because Ram had a quick little action and it was hard to see his hand against the dark pavilion. I learned to judge him by his trajectory, his stock ball, the offbreak, was the lower one, the legbreak more tossed.

'Both he and Val were remarkably accurate and seemed to keep going for ever. At Trent Bridge in the next match they bowled unchanged from 11.30 to quarter to four! I never experienced anything to equal them in all my years of cricket.'

MCC's President in 1950 was Sir Pelham Warner, who was born in Trinidad in 1873, and learned his cricket there. Norman Yardley, England's captain, remembers 'Plum' making an impassioned speech in the West Indies dressing-room afterwards, saying how thrilled he was that they should break their duck at Lord's.

'It was very friendly in those days; none of the aggro you are inclined to get now. John Goddard was a good friend of mine. They all seemed to be good blokes.'

Roly Jenkins remembers hundreds of jubilant West Indians running across the centre of the ground to dance in front of the pavilion – and the police vainly trying to stop them. And Hubert Doggart, just down from Cambridge, recalls Everton Weekes 'grinning at me from silly mid-off – most friendly – just before Ram got me out for nought!'

These days, sadly, it's not so friendly: spare a drop of sympathy for England's batsmen as they try to dodge the 90 mph bouncers of the West Indian fast bowlers.

They will do their best not to look scared. But they would so much rather face Ramadhin and Valentine 'killing them *softly* with their spin'.

The astonishing West Indies bowling figures:

	First Innings				*Second Innings*			
	O	M	R	W	O	M	R	W
Jones	8·4	2	13	1	7	1	22	0
Worrell	10	4	20	0	22·3	9	39	1
Valentine	45	28	48	4	71	47	79	3
Ramadhin	43	27	66	5	72	43	86	6

EVENING STANDARD, 18 JUNE 1976

Val without Sonny

BRIAN GLANVILLE

Alf Valentine has a clerkly look about him. With his spectacles, his slenderness, his largely receded hair, you would expect to find him working in – say – the Town Hall in Palermo, rather than tormenting batsmen with his slow left handers.

At 33, he's making his first tour without his 'twin' spinner, Sonny Ramadhin, who stands by, up in the North, and he confesses, in his slow, shy way, he will miss him.

'Oh yes, we were always room-mates, and we got on well. Yes, well, you know. I've been playing with him all the time. I'd think, if this chap bowls a maiden, or takes a wicket, I want to do a bit more. When a chap's bowling ragged, your competition's really not there, and you've no standard to set yourself.'

'And yet,' said his captain, Frank Worrell, 'in this sort of contest there's no rivalry.'

'No rivalry,' said Valentine.

'I've never heard either chap begrudge the other's performance,' Worrell said. His view is that, on the ecstatic 1950 tour, and for years after that, 'these chaps did not know how good they were'. Valentine confirms it. 'Even now I can only vaguely remember the 1950 tour. I just bowled.'

The 1957 tour wasn't as happy; Valentine's admirers believe he was badly under-bowled. 'I played two Test matches and 12 games in all. The first was against Essex – Ilford – and it was raining.

'Ball wet, cold fingers,' said Worrell. 'Val started off and bowled two full tosses.'

He was quickly and traumatically taken off. I asked if the experience of that tour undermined him.

'I thought so,' he said, 'because I probably believe I lost my confidence, really, in what I could do as a bowler.' But he found it again in the Lancashire League, and has regained his old pleasure in cricket, even if he finds celebrity a trial. 'If you let yourself go, you're a nut: if you're reserved, you're still a nut.' SUNDAY TIMES, 26 MAY 1963

INSULT TO INJURY

During a break through rain at a charity cricket match at Coventry in 1942, that indefatigable cricket story-teller, Frank Chester, one of the greatest-ever umpires, who had only one arm to signal with, a relic from the First War, told this epic:

Pre-War County match at Headingley, and Lol Larwood was getting a bit of a tonking from Yorkshire. Out comes Wilfred Rhodes, and his mannerism of pointing his left toe in the air annoyed the usually mild-mannered Larwood.

Walking back, Larwood said to me, 'I'll soon knock that bloody toe down.' Which he did, next ball.

Rhodes hopped about, in agony, then finally makes signs of resuming his innings. I looked down the pitch and asked, 'Are't all right, Wilfred?' 'Aye'.

'Can you walk, Wilfred?' 'Aye'.

'Well, walk Wilfred, you're out lbw'.

Tribute to Harold Gimblett

ALAN GIBSON

Harold Gimblett, who was remembered yesterday in a memorial service at Taunton, was a little like Hamlet playing – no, not the clown, but possibly Laertes. He batted most of the time like some lusty country lad, without a care in the world, though I am not suggesting his style was bucolic. Most of those who watched him, and even met him, at least casually, took him for a cheerful extrovert. But he was a man who thought a lot, who fretted a lot, all the more because he struggled to present a calm, bold front to the outer world.

I do not claim to have known him specially well, but once, when I was in a mental hospital, and feeling very sorry for myself, he wrote me a letter full of understanding and wise advice, and thereafter we sometimes talked of mental problems. It did not come as a total surprise that he died after taking an overdose. He had been suffering acutely from arthritis, which provided Giant Despair with a spur.

Harold was born in 1914, in Bicknoller, a Quantock village. The story of his entry to first-class cricket has often been told, but is always worth re-telling.

He was a promising player from an early age and made a reputation in Somerset village and club cricket. The standard of such cricket in the West has long been high.

At the beginning of the 1935 season, he was offered a month's trial with Somerset. A fortnight passed, he had not been chosen for the county side and had been warned that his contract was unlikely to be renewed.

Then Somerset found themselves a man short, not an improbable situation in those days, for the match against Essex at Frome. Gimblett was summoned from the family farm near Watchet.

He went in at No 8 when the score was 107 for 6, and made a century in 63 minutes which, as it proved, was the fastest of the season.

For this he won the Lawrence Trophy. E. H. D. Sewell, in one of his books, mentions how fortunate it was that journalists whose task it was to log every innings, remembered to jot down Gimblett's entry. He made 123, with three sixes and seventeen fours. Gimblett then went to Lord's and scored 50 against Middlesex.

By that time he had become a wonder boy. A chartered aeroplane flew to Somerset, so that he could be photographed on the family farm. The Press rang with his praise. I do not think that this treatment did him or his cricket much harm, but equally it did no good, and it left him vulnerable when, inevitably, he could not live up to that remarkable start. His average at the end of the season was under 20; a useful beginning, really, but so much had been unwisely expected.

In 1936, I went to Taunton School, making my first proper acquaintance with Somerset. The Day Boys, were, of course, full of Gimblett, though it was sometimes said he was conceited (I don't think we knew the word 'big-headed' then). This was an unjustified view, but it was held, if only because small boys, being what they are, they were disappointed he did not get a hundred in every innings, and again, it did nothing to help Gimblett.

Nevertheless he had a good season in 1936, and played the first two of his three Test matches, against India. If he had been playing in August as he had done in May, he must have had a very good chance of going with G. O. Allen's side to Australia. He played for England once against the West Indies in 1939. He had not been unsuccessful (192 runs, average 32·00) but did not play for England again. He was chosen as late as 1950 against the West Indies, but withdrew through illness the day before the match. It was difficult in those immediate post-war years, with Hutton and Washbrook present, for other English opening batsmen to get a look in.

But if his Test career was a disappointment, he holds three Somerset records, the most runs (23,007), the most centuries (50), and the highest score (310 not out). A useful life's work there.

As he became older, he became less of a dasher, unless the mood took him. It was not often we saw him use the hook, which had been one of his favourite strokes. He reduced its use, I believe, on the advice of Walter Hammond who had taken the same advice himself half a generation earlier. It was possibly a wiser decision for Hammond than Gimblett, not because Hammond was so good at all the other strokes, but because Gimblett, even more than most batsmen, liked to be in command, liked to be seen in command, and never played better than when he felt he was in command; and the hook is a commanding stroke.

He died loved by some, liked by many, admired by countless. I should be surprised if he had an enemy. SUNDAY TIMES, 28 MAY 1978

NEGATIVE RESPONSE

Everyone, including the Australians, likes to see our oldest umpire, Alex Skelding, of the grey hair, white boots and many jokes, who keeps things lively during dull periods. He broke a leg during the close season, but now, at 68, is dodging about as sprightly as ever.

We at the ringside know Skelding chiefly for his downright megaphonic harangues directed at the high and lowly – it matters not which – who move behind the bowler's arm. In the middle they hear more.

Neil Harvey, who at Leicester, broke the wicket with a long throw-in, was told: 'Not out. It's a photo finish, young man, but we can't wait for the camera, so it's still not out.' DAILY EXPRESS

Like a Bag Bursting

R. C. ROBERTSON-GLASGOW

We lost to Leicestershire in the first match of the Weston-super-Mare Festival. It was a bad batting match, especially for the older gentlemen, our Ernest Robson and their J. H. King, ninety-five years between them, making only one run in their four innings. King made up for it by doing the hat-trick in our second innings, the third wicket of the feat being also his hundredth of the season.

He was surrounded by congratulations and his face was illuminated by triumph as I walked to the crease, a possible fourth in hand. But I corrected his exuberance by hitting my first ball out of the ground and over the pavilion at mid-wicket. I added one more, then was feebly caught and bowled by Ewart Astill.

In the Leicestershire second innings I took 5 for 33, and caught G. B. F. Rudd, 71, in the deep field with a sound like a bag bursting.

FROM '46 NOT OUT' (HOLKS AND CARTER), 1948

Editor's note: It was my sheer joy as a young writer to sit next to 'Crusoe', as he was affectionately known, in the Press Box and to listen to the wit and laughter that followed, in which he always joined with a happy guffaw.

During a wartime match he said to me, quite seriously, as a young ex-Etonian batsman walked to the wicket at Lord's: 'He was sent down for seeing his girl friend off in broad daylight on Windsor Station.'

Says I, 'That was a bit fierce?'

'Not when you remember he was in his pyjamas at the time!'

You Aint See'd Rockhampton

ALEX BANNISTER

Listen, pardners, you ain't see'd nuthing of this little ol' game of cricket unless you bin and see'd it played in a mighty cattle town like Rockhampton, where all the saloons have half-size swing doors and the Northern Express whistles down the main street once a day.

Dear friends and neighbours have bin so mighty kind taking the international visitors round the gold mines (no free samples by request) and pineapple plantations and such, and affordin' them enough time to squeeze in a couple of days ball play.

The Mayor has said not once but several times that it's a mighty international contest, and a mighty international contest it is.

The Old Show Ground, where the rodeos are held and prize bulls shown off, looks a mighty fine picture with the hills in the background, and a strange strip of green straight from the botanical gardens with stumps at each end filling the middle.

Maybe it doesn't remind the Englishmen of Lord's or Sydney Stadium, and maybe the outfield where the grass has been beaten to death by a thousand hooves, is a bit rough. But Rockhampton has really got one up on Lord's, Sydney and other famous grounds, for where else is staged rodeo and cricket?

Maybe, too, the folks here are more sympathetic to the ball players than the city slickers, and it was a change for them not to be told to hit every ball outa the ground – jist every other one.

There were some jokers sittin' on top of the pens used to prison the bucking broncos who started ahowlin' and ahollerin', but when Peter Loader offered them the use of his bat they sorta laughed and quietened down mighty fast.

The crowd saw some fine catching by the Country Boys, and I guess if the Englishmen had done as well back in the city last week they might not have lost that Test match.

Mighty innings too, came from Edrich, Hutton, May, and Wilson, but Graveney (stumped 29) missed a fine opportunity of match practice when he went acharging down the pitch like a mad bull. Maybe he was mad about sump'n, and that sump'n could have been the non-stop and loud background of radio commentary which accompanied the play.

Now and agin they broke in with race results and fishing prospects, and I guess the Englishmen now know what makes the broncos buck.

Then, I suppose, apart from radio they don't go in for new fangled notions here, for this contest is being fought with old fashioned wickets which are eight inches wide instead of nine, and an inch shorter. The rest of the world changed in 1931.

But what does a little ol' inch matter in a Mighty International Contest like this? DAILY MAIL, 6 DECEMBER 1954

Editor's afterthought: Rockhampton also produced Rod Laver, and called him the Rockhampton Rocket!

WELL-PLACED SHOT

Robin Jackman, Surrey all-rounder, hit an all run six, without overthrows, in yesterday's John Player League match against Yorkshire. The runs came from a square cut at the Oval, where the wicket was pitched on the edge of the square. 10 JUNE 1974

Two Bats in the Boot

A car belonging to Denis Compton, Middlesex and England cricketer, was stolen from Park Road, near Lord's yesterday. He had driven to London to go to Lord's, and to attend the Lord's Taverners Ball at Grosvenor House.

Last night he said, 'I stopped for a quarter of an hour on my way to Lord's. When I came back the car was gone.' The loss of the car, a Hillman convertible, was reported to the Marylebone Lane Police Station.

In the boot was a cricket bag, which he planned to use on the Australian cricket tour, but apart from a new pair of batting gloves he had been breaking in, it contained only practice gear – boots, a sweater and two bats. His main equipment was at Grosvenor House, where he was staying last night. Compton is due to leave tomorrow to join the MCC team in Australia. When the team sailed he remained behind for treatment to his knee. DAILY TELEGRAPH, 19 OCTOBER 1954

Editor's note: This cutting arrived with a letter to me from retired *Daily Express* Sports Editor, W. R. Simmonds:

'To call your attention to heading in today's *Daily Telegraph*. It does not mention how many in the belfry!'

Dolly's Revenge

IAN WOOLDRIDGE

County cricket is not always the languid exercise in impeccable behaviour that its loyal chroniclers would have you believe. It may now be revealed, for example, that the match between Yorkshire and Worcestershire at Hull (6–9 July 1974) had some of the undertones of Mafia gangwar.

The records show that Yorkshire, batting first, were all out 101. At one stage in their reply Worcester were 57 for 5. Then came the most significant innings of the summer.

Basil D'Oliveira strolled to the wicket, amiably warned his opponents of his intentions, and proceeded to smash their bowling all over Yorkshire. He kept on doing this for well over six hours, by which time he had made 227, the highest score of even his remarkable career.

Worcester won the match by a long street and went on to become champions.

What inspired this spectacular retribution by a man whose sportsmanship is so legendary that he has been known to hit a breezy 100, and then laughingly throw his wicket away?

It would appear that in the general atmosphere of carping which prevailed on the field, one Yorkshire player's standards of etiquette lapsed so badly that he actually suggested D'Oliveira was out when he wasn't. D'Oliveira decided to administer some summary justice.

At his age, which I suspect is nearer 50 than 40, it was a stunning performance and one which caused vast amusement throughout all the cricketing counties except Hampshire.

Dolly's revenge of course cost them the championship.

DAILY MAIL, 4 OCTOBER 1974

Jack Hobbs' Last Match

IAN PEEBLES

'At the start of our second innings the Australians gathered round Jack Hobbs and gave him three very warm cheers. I think he was also greatly affected by his reception, for, having made nine, he played on to Alan Fairfax.

'It was a charming gesture to a great player and our side did the same to Don Bradman in 1948, but I feel it might be as well to leave the salute until the player concerned is out, and actually retiring from the scene. It must be rather trying to address oneself to the serious business of batting while under the resulting nervous tension.

'We lost the next whole day through rain. Then, after the rain we were caught on a real sticky wicket and beaten by an innings. I did not receive a ball second time, but did manage to grab one of the stumps as a souvenir. It had one shortcoming in my eye ... it was one of the old fashioned small size!' PICTURE POST, 1953

O-O-O-O-Oh Dear, Sussex!

JAMES CONNOR

Sussex lost their first four wickets for no runs in an amazing start to their John Player League match against Surrey at the Oval yesterday. Arnold Long, former Surrey keeper, and successor as Sussex skipper to Tony Greig, won the toss – and wished he hadn't.

Four Sussex men were out with just thirteen balls of the game gone.

Their first run just had to be . . . a wide! But the recovery lasted for only another three runs. The fifth and sixth wickets tumbled with the score at four.

Left arm seamer David Thomas started the ducking and weaving with a spell of 4–1 in three overs. The eighteen-year-old finished with 8–4–13–4.

Shell-shocked Long, who stopped the rot with 33 to carry the Sussex score to 99–9, said: 'The ball was moving a bit, but there was nothing in the wicket really. There was a silly run out, two good balls, and two bad shots. The Surrey chaps were a bit surprised too.'

Sussex's timetable of woe, which ended in a seven-wicket defeat, went like this:

0 for 1: John Barclay was caught second ball of the match, by David Smith off Thomas;

0 for 2; Imran was taken behind the wicket by Jack Richards next ball;

0 for 3; Mendis was run out off the last ball of the second over;

0 for 4; Jerry Groome was caught by Geoff Howarth off Thomas from the first ball of the third over;

4 for 5; Paul Parker was caught behind by Richards off Thomas;

4 for 6; Mike Buss was bowled by Robin Jackman.

THE SUN, 29 MAY 1978

Frogs Stopped Play

Andy Sandham, the Surrey batsman, was in the England team playing in South Africa during the 1922–23 tour. He had been having quite a successful time, and when the last Test at Durban came along, many thought that England would win fairly easily.

In South Africa then they had the habit of completely covering the wicket some days before a match, so when England won the toss and decided to bat first, a large army of coloured lads set to work to take up the large sheet which covered the wicket and ground surrounding it.

At last Andy Sandham, partnered by A. C. 'Jack' Russell, of Essex, took his place at the wicket ready to face S. J. Snooke, the South African fast bowler.

Snooke took his usual pacey run up to the crease and hurled the ball down with plenty of force behind it. You can imagine Sandham's surprise when the ball, after pitching, slowed down almost to a crawl.

He said nothing, just played the ball back to the bowler. The same thing happened next ball, so the English batsman walked down the pitch to investigate.

Imagine how he felt when he saw a moving patch in the middle of the pitch. Closer investigation showed it was a hill of little green frogs!

The match was held up while the groundsman called upon his small army of assistants who gathered two pails full of those little creatures. Yes, frogs did actually hold up a Test match!

EVERYBODY'S WEEKLY

Loive Air Bluddy Flies Alone

Approached by reporters to comment on the near-death of an Australian batsman at the hands of an English bowler, England captain Douglas Jardine, who led the 1932 'Bodyline' team, replied:

'I never speak to reporters.'

'Ah yes,' replied the reporters, 'but you ought to know that we are Australians.'

'In that case,' said Jardine, 'I never speak to Australian reporters either.'

In Sydney, in that same series, Jardine, as usual, walked out to bat wearing a silk scarf, a gaudy Harlequins cap symbolising ultimate privilege and the kind of haughty expression affected by English butlers opening front doors to Americans.

He was welcomed by the absolute silence of uncompromising hatred.

Half-way to the wicket an Australian insect had the temerity to buzz round Jardine's face. Jardine made his only mistake of a long and arduous tour. He raised a languid hand and dismissed it from his presence.

'Hey, Jardine,' blistered a voice from the infamous Sydney Hill, 'loive air bluddy flies alone.'

I Bowl to Hit Them

STEVE WHITING

Dennis Lillee may not be playing against England any more. But the great Australian fast bowler is still letting slip a few bouncers at us Poms, even if they are mainly verbal.

In his new book, 'The Art of Fast Bowling,' Lillee recalls the time he sent the British Press scurrying for their typewriters with the comment that he bowled bouncers to hit the batsmen.

He says: 'I make little of the criticism that flowed from many English writers who had earlier said nothing of the intimidating bowling of John Snow.

'Nor do I make anything of those who say that fast bowlers do not set out to hit a batsman when they send the ball whizzing round his ears at 80 mph.

'As far as I'm concerned, if you are a very fast bowler and you send the ball down short of a length you are trying to hit the batsman. It is just a matter of whether you are prepared to be honest about it.'

That, strangely, is the only controversial remark in an uncontroversial book, which is a revealing insight into everything concerning fast bowling – and a few of the things concerning Lillee himself.

THE SUN, 27 APRIL 1978

Editor's note: Lillee did say, however:

'Find me the man who can embody all these attributes and I will show you the acme of perfection in fast bowling:

The breath-taking run-up of Wes Hall;
The silk-smooth delivery of Ray Lindwall;
The blistering pace of Jeff Thomson;
The firebrand aggression of Freddie Trueman;
The scintillating swing of Alan Davidson;
The devastating cut of John Snow;
The nagging accuracy of Brian Statham;
The lethal bouncer of Charlie Griffith;
The demoralising yorker of Andy Roberts;
The unstinting stamina of Mike Procter;
The sheer brilliance of Keith Miller.'

FROM 'THE ART OF FAST BOWLING', BY DENNIS LILLEE WITH IAN BRAYSHAW, LUTTERWORTH, 1978

Sans Mouvement Mecanique

My recent story about the difficulty the French Customs experienced in categorising a hovercraft reminded a reader of the problems he had in 1925 when trying to take a cricket bat through Customs at Calais.

Was it for hockey, they wondered, or tennis? Baseball, perhaps? No, it was for cricket. Impasse. Finally my reader was given a list of customs duties, thousands of pages long, and told to find a category.

After a long period of deliberation he came up with a suggestion. He had to pay 1·25 francs, but was allowed through with his 'engin sportif sans mouvement mecanique.'

PETERBOROUGH, DAILY TELEGRAPH, 11 AUGUST 1979

Champshire

The ghosts of the Hambledon Men must surely have staged an Old Boys reunion as the moon rose last night over Broadhalfpenny Down.

It was in Hampshire that they cradled the game that was to encircle the globe, outlive dictators, and stir passions in the most puritanical soul.

They were craftsmen, carpenters and gardeners, who, in their parochial pride, forged a team that could vanquish all England.

Yesterday another such team, after 66 years of toiling and spinning, regained the old glories for Hampshire.

They are among the least fashionable of cricketing counties. They are a team without a contemporary Test star. They have been led by daredevil dash. They have snatched victories with declarations that solemn men deemed suicidal.

We should raise our tankards today to the players of Hampshire. The toast should be 'The *teamsmanship* that led to a triumph in the finest traditions of cricket.'

DAILY MAIL LEADERETTE, 2 SEPTEMBER 1961

And Colin Went to Church

FRANK ROSTRON

On this New Year's Day, Colin Cowdrey, just 22, awoke to find himself the cricketing hero of 1955.

The Australian newspapers this morning re-echo the tremendous ovation yesterday that greeted his superb Test century, made in adversity. It was one of the most stirringly emotional scenes I have ever seen on a sports ground.

In the baking sunshine of an Australian summer afternoon 63,814 people stood bareheaded, as though welcoming new royalty to the preserves of cricket immortals. For minutes, they stood in summer dresses and shirtsleeves, their sun-reddened faces alight with enthusiasm as they cheered the Test colt who must be destined to become a Test giant.

This was the sort of adulation they reserved for Bradman in his heyday.

The surprising inside story is that Cowdrey, like Hutton, was suffering from a touch of influenza. After his innings, Cowdrey admitted, 'Yes, I felt pretty awful really. My head was heavy, but it got steadily better until I forgot about it.'

Last night, when most of the Test players had gone to bed early, and the rest of Melbourne was waiting to see the New Year in, Cowdrey went off on his own – to a church service.
DAILY EXPRESS, 1 JANUARY 1955

Mike Brearley, Cricketer

DAVID BENEDICTUS

And it's not for the sake of a ribboned coat,
Or the selfish hope of a seasons fame,
But his Captain's hand on his shoulder smote,
Play up! Play up! and play the game.

The Captain of England? Why, he should be blond and swashbuckling and arrogant, but he's greying and looks a bit lugubrious. As for arrogance, he's having to learn it the hard way.

He tells how, in Greig's reign – 'the Prince Charming, the Golden Giant who comes from afar to set to rights our tottering state' – the English players got green cars, but when Brearley took over the captaincy a lady in Preston sent them all hand-knitted socks. It seems that self-effacement comes naturally. Tom Brown, not Flashman. Ridiculous, really, when you consider.

After four years as a classics scholar at Cambridge, during which time he amasssed more runs than any student before or since, Brearley earned a first in classics and a two-one in moral science. Shortly afterwards he came joint top in the Civil Service examination.

As Captain of Middlesex he took the county from 16th place to the Championship in 1974, to 6th in 1975, to win it in 1976, and to share it with Kent in 1977. As Captain of England he won back the Ashes and he has yet to lose a Test. Knitted socks indeed!

He says he's 'learning to accept success. When people clap you, you have to learn to bask in it. I wasn't able to at first – I hadn't had much practice'.

But surely when Middlesex ... 'Oh yes, they clapped then. But what was nice about it was that it stopped people talking so much about the great days of Compton and Edrich.'

I had just been talking about the great days of Compton and Edrich. I stopped.

Brearley's father and paternal grandfather were fine cricketers. His mother was a netballer. Both parents are mathematicians. They come to see him often at Lord's, bringing his two younger sisters. On a few occasions Brearley *père* and Brearley *fils* shared stands when they both played club cricket at Brentham; nice that, if your family are proud of you, maybe you can afford to deprecate your own achievements just a bit.

And then there's the tiresome business of Brearley being a philosopher. He taught the subject for three years at Newcastle University. It makes it difficult to make snap judgements about things. Did I play well? That rather depends on what you mean by *play* and it rather depends on what you mean by *well*. And when you get right down to it, who am I?

Brearley might still be struggling with such conundrums had not Middlesex offered him the captaincy. Philosophy or cricket?

'I used to be high-minded about it. I had this silly idea that sport was slightly second rate'. But cricket gives a lot of people a lot of pleasure, while philosophy ... the captaincy settled it.

I had driven him to London's Camden Town. He had worn his seat belt. He had just learned that the bruise on his finger where he had been struck by a ball from Alan Ward was worse than a bruise; the bone was chipped and he would miss the two one-day Tests against Pakistan, maybe more. Not easy to be philosophical about when you have just recovered from a broken arm. (But Brearley is not injury prone. His record over 17 years has usually been good.)

When we reached his unarrogant flat, where he lives alone – rumpled bedclothes in mid-afternoon, unwashed plates on the kitchen table – I made a beeline for the bookshelves. Books tell you a bit about what a man is, a great deal about what he wants to be.

I spotted Games People Play; the Divided Self; Human Aggression; the Art of Loving; Perspective in Group Therapy – we'll come to that – The Miracle Worker; The Poems of W.H. Auden. I wondered what books Greig and Boycott have on their shelves. One of the advantages of cricket in England is that you get plenty of opportunities to read.

Over a lemon squash we talked about cricketers. Greig he admires for his strength. So strong as a captain that he was able to defend the weaker and less popular members of the side. Loyal. Strong socially too. Loves parties and is very good at them. Has done the things you are not supposed to do, and so can understand the temptations that beset those who haven't. Was not a democratic captain.

Brearley believes in involving his team in both strategy and tactics, although he has become less democratic on the field. He likes to consult Clive Radley, who fields near him in the slips. Does he consult Boycott? 'That's not so easy. He doesn't field so close to the bat.' (The contrast between Boycott and Brearley is the epic one of North *v* South, Player *v* Gentleman, yet both are perfectionists, both have an intelligent approach to the game.)

'Success and failure in cricket are related to the success and failure of personality, and the most serious shortcoming in a cricketer is *selfishness*.

It's a team game, but the major confrontations are between individuals.' A captain requires a tough hide. Brearley ruefully admits that the constant battling does take its toll. Fast bowling, bad pitches, newspaper journalists, commentators all beat you down. When Brearley took over at Middlesex Mike Smith remarked: 'That's not a crown on your head, it's a coconut.'

Brearley: 'I have to try to take criticism as less hostile than it sounds – a lesson I learned from my philosophy tutor before I gave my first paper at the University of Oregon. It's all too easy to become paranoid.' I wondered if that helped with fast bowling – no use being paranoid there.

Brearley, as you must have noticed, wears protective headgear against fast bowling. The polythene shell was designed by Bill Swanwick, the man who makes protective headgear for epileptic children. As the bowler starts his run up, Brearley hums the cello passage from a Rasumovsky Quartet, and feels a little safer.

'I'm not scared of fast bowling – I'm apprehensive. You have to cut out the areas of risk. Prepare to go back – you can always come forward at the last moment. Make them bowl *at* you. The books tell you to get behind the ball, but if you do, you get hit on the chest; much better give yourself room to cut or get inside the ball to hook – I worked that out against Lillee at Perth. But there's nothing much you can do about bad pitches.'

It seems that there is a sort of pleasure to be got out of fast bowling, seeing them off is one of the nicer moments! But there's a subtler pleasure, an intellectual, even an aesthetic pleasure to be got from slow bowling. Once in Poona, Brearley made 200, playing as well as he ever has, after a shaky start.

'Prasanna was bowling his off spin, and after he'd bowled a good one, and I'd played it well, there'd be a little nod of his head and a look of mutual recognition would pass between us. It's like when Rava Shakar is playing on his mat (his pitch!) surrounded by his acolytes, there's a slight smile on his face and a wagging of his head. It's as if he is saying I'm a beautiful player and *you're a beautiful listener*.'

I was enjoying this exposition; in my miserable exploits on the cricket field I had experienced something similar, but now we were interrupted by a man calling about a bed.

'I'm having it made specially for me,' said Brearley with pride. 'The space underneath is to be used. I don't like wasting space.'

'What are you using the space for?'

'Drawers.'

We talked about money. Brearley wants money. One of the reasons he didn't join Packer is that 1978 is his benefit year and he didn't want to forfeit what could be as much as £30,000.

He wants the money for when he leaves cricket, for his work with disturbed adolescents, the psychotherapy which is his great love. For a year he was a nursing assistant ('that's the lowest of the low') at Hendon, and it's not put him off. But that wasn't the only reason why he didn't join.

He admires Packer for a number of things, not least for making the world realise that cricket was being undersold and cricketers underpaid. It's not generally known how underpaid they have been. Few county cricketers receive more than £60 a week, and even top players do well to exceed the national average wage. They are also away from home too much for comfort.

Two years ago, Knott and Underwood, the best in the world, played eleven Tests and received £7,600 each for the year. But since Packer, the sponsors have moved into cricket and the rewards are becoming more realistic.

A Test player now receives £1,000 per Test. But the price for being properly appreciated seems to Brearley unacceptably high. For if television is permitted to dictate how cricket will be played the whole rhythm of the game will alter. Short run-ups, mikes round cricketers' necks, cameras in the dressing room, an artificial encouragement of the aggressive instincts in players – these and other more radical changes will have to be faced.

What Brearley loves about English cricket is 'the real, rooted, regional traditional thing'. He means unpredictable pitches, unpredictable weather, wistaria, bird song, and inevitably a certain measure of incompetence and monotony. but in the modern world it is necessary to be tough and arrogant in defence of the *status quo*. Indeed, the pressures for change are so great that it's often easier to become radical. Brearley does not entirely support the cricketing establishment either. He is 'not wildly attracted to either the dark suit and striped tie ... or the snappy cerise and crocodile skin shoes.'

He is learning the necessary toughness and arrogance, although as yet it doesn't show. But he wins Tests and Championships and Ashes and his batting average continues to improve (although a Test century would be nice). Under that diffident exterior there is a resolute spirit. Philosophy is a tough training. And if you are used to handling disturbed adolescents, Packer may not seem so very formidable after all. (Review of 'The Return of the Ashes', by Mike Brearley and Dudley Doust, published by Pelham Books, 1978) RADIO TIMES, 8–15 JULY 1978

PROTECTIVE HELMETS WANTED

India, 66–2, are crawling towards a draw with England. A fight breaks out in the crowd. Police charge. Says Graham Dilley, helping Don Mosey describe the scene: 'At least they're stepping up the baton rate.' BBC COMMENTARY, 26 DECEMBER 1981

My Heroes Made Life Hell

BRIAN CLOSE

I was a very young 19 when I sailed for Australia in October 1950. True, I had played for England. I had achieved the first-class double.

I had my Yorkshire cap, and I had played representative football in Holland and Scotland.

And I had had a decent education which had equipped me for an academic or professional career had I not opted for full-time sport.

But I was an inexperienced youth, who had had very little opportunity to develop any sort of worldliness.

The MCC party included giants who were more or less names on cigarette cards to me ... Denis Compton, Cyril Washbrook, Douglas Wright, Freddie Brown and of course Len Hutton.

I badly needed advice. I was desperately anxious for one of those great players to take me under his wing. But none of the senior players offered me a word of advice about anything.

I was lacking in discipline in that I didn't know how to conform on that voyage to Australia. No one told me what was expected of me, so I just did my own thing as they say.

I played in six of the first eight matches. I was not in the first Test team, nor had I expected to be. My form was inconsistent.

Against New South Wales Country Districts I made 105 not out, but during the innings I strained a tendon in my groin. Before the second Test I went through a series of movements to test my fitness. I thought that I was fit but as I dashed back, twisting to take a catch during fielding practice, I felt my groin go again.

Freddie Brown called me over, 'How bad is it?'

'It's still there, but I think it's only slight.'

'That's a pity – as an all rounder you could be invaluable in balancing the whole side up, if you were fit.'

Not wishing to let the side down, I answered, 'It should be all right if I have it strapped.'

It was one of the great mistakes of my life.

I was out for a duck. In retrospect, I think that, as a captain, I would have killed anybody who told me he was fit enough to play when he wasn't. But I was 19. I badly wanted to play in a Test match against Australia.

If I was ever big-headed in my life it was at that moment when I thought my enthusiasm and natural ability, in which I had boundless confidence, could take me through a Test in Australia with a groin injury, however slight.

I went in with four balls to go before lunch, when we were 54 for 4. I was strung up.

I was out to a loose one, and England were 54 for 5. When I got back to the dressing room, there was a deathly silence. I sat in the dressing room through lunch almost in tears.

I missed the fourth Test, then went to Melbourne where I bowled 33 overs against Victoria. By now my leg was dragging as I ran.

Finally at Geelong, I felt something completely snap. I collapsed, couldn't get up and had to be carried off the field. I lay on the table for the rest of the day, sick and feverish with ice-packs being applied to my head. And at the end of it the senior players gave me a solid cursing.

There were one or two occasions on that tour when I felt so completely out of my depth that I even contemplated killing myself.

Freddie Brown, Len Hutton, Cyril Washbrook, Reg Simpson, Denis Compton – you made my life hell. DAILY EXPRESS, 19 APRIL 1978

Eddie Paynter's Epic

Eddie Paynter was in hospital suffering from tonsilitis during the fourth Test at Brisbane on England's 1932–33 'Bodyline' tour.

Bill Voce came to the hospital to tell him that England were in trouble, so little Eddie asked for his clothes.

The ward sister, knowing that Eddie had a high temperature, refused, so he went off in his pyjamas and dressing-gown. He and Bill Voce took a taxi to the ground to find that England had slumped to 198 for 5.

Paynter went straight in to bat, saw out the day's play, and the following day helped Hedley Verity put on 92, in what proved to be an Ashes-winning tail-end partnership. Eddie scored 83. And he used every drinks break to gargle and take aspirin; 'It sweated all the fever out.'

This story was retold in the Sun *when Eddie Paynter died, at Keighley, Yorkshire, in June 1979.*

PAGING NUMBER NINE

Bat and Breakfast: Despite morning rain, Surrey resumed their first innings promptly against Oxford University at Guildford, where their total stood at 368 for five wickets.

For the first time in the match, Mallett and Travers, the Oxford fast medium bowlers, were able to extract some life from the pitch. A fine ball from Travers which lifted quickly soon beat Barton, and a catch at the wicket disposed of Bernard Constable at the same hotel.

PRESS ASSOCIATION REPORT MISPRINT

Cricket's Funniest Innings

ROY PESKETT

'I'm going to watch the Australians at Leyton.'

That remark, to his parents, by a young Gidea Park, Essex, bank clerk of 19, settled his destiny.

He did go to watch the Australians. He left the bank. Within two months he was playing county cricket, and in five years he was in the England team holding a regular place until Hitler's scheming ambitions forced England's sportsmen to play another, and greater, game.

Ken Farnes was the name of this young bank clerk who became England's fast bowler. Who bowled for England, flew for England. And died for England.

The cricket career of young Farnes was all too short, as was his flying career, for he was killed in a flying accident only a month after winning his wings. That was on 20 October 1941, when he was just three months over thirty.

The story of his cricket life started on the village green at Gidea Park, with its high grass and snug thicket, its hollow walnut tree and huge spreading elm, so vividly described in his own book, completed and published not long before his death.

Farnes loved the green. In fact, he loved cricket altogether, whether it be school, village green, country house, county, or Test. He was a happy cricketer, happy even in failure.

Who could fail to be thrilled by this tall, lithe youngster moving up to the wicket with his easy and economical run up, his beautifully controlled delivery, hair waving, his faultless follow through . . . his joy at the conquest of a batsman, his singular lack of despair at the ball which missed the stumps by a coat of varnish, his failure to complain should a chance be lost or a run fumbled.

He was a real son of the Empire. He played for England in Australia, South Africa and the West Indies. He learnt to fly in Canada, and did some of his training in America.

Farnes, born and bred in Essex, spent his schooldays at the Royal Liberty School, Romford, and his spare time in playing cricket. On leaving school he joined an insurance office, then a bank. When the break came he decided to become a schoolteacher, which meant a training period at Cambridge. It was then that he, to his immense delight, got his first chance in the county side.

During the summer of 1930, Farnes was on holiday at Minehead when he received a telegram asking if he could play in the Essex county side against Gloucester at Chelmsford.

So, for the first time, Ken Farnes met the Essex side, the men to whom he was unknown and they but names to him. His start in county cricket was inconspicuous, except that it showed that he would never be played for his batting alone. He claimed that during his career the only man who ever got more ducks than him, was H. D. 'Hopper' Read, also an Essex fast bowler!

That first afternoon, against Gloucester, Farnes was put in at No 7, the highest position he ever occupied for the county. His strokes were weird, but he managed to score eight, which in fact was higher than some of the higher up batsmen!

His bowling start was no picture book story. He was hit all over the field, and finished with no wickets for 60. Altogether a depressing start, yet he was a happy man when he drove back to Gidea Park with his family that evening. He had played for the County!

In his book 'Left Behind in Civvy Street', Ken Farnes described one of his own innings, which convulsed everybody on the ground (except the luckless bowler) and which must have qualified as one of cricket's funniest ever innings.

'I was once the scapegoat in a scene of more sustained mirth than I have ever known at a cricket match, when batting against Derbyshire at Chelmsford.

'I was determined to hit the ball, but every time I did, it went vertically up into the air. My first ball was from Copson. Tommy Mitchell came in so close in the gully that I could have tweaked his nose.

'The ball hit the shoulder of my bat and bounced gently up and over Tommy's head, and landed about a foot behind him. The next over I faced Alf Pope. Each time I struck the ball it was a balloon. Each time a fielder circled underneath it, waiting, and down she went.

'Amid huge gusts of laughter from the holiday crowd I was finally caught at the second attempt, and everybody doubled up, except Tommy, whose face was black after he had dropped me twice!

'We ran two each time the ball was in the air, and so, plus a snick for two also, my total was fourteen!'

DAILY SKETCH, 27 OCTOBER 1941

SEE TOMORROW'S PAPER

The Test at Nottingham takes my mind back to the last Test there against the West Indies seven years ago. Shackleton, Hollies, Jenkins, Yardley and myself tried desperately to dislodge Frankie Worrell and Everton Weekes, who figured in a partnership which no one who saw it will ever forget.

Worrell made one stroke which left all the fielders gasping. It was a six *off the back foot.* Roley Jenkins, the unfortunate bowler, watched the ball disappear into the crowd behind him, and said, 'I just don't believe it.'

Whereupon the late Frank Chester, the umpire, said: 'I'm still going to give six, Roley!' ALEC BEDSER, NEWS OF THE WORLD, 7 JULY 1957

Fifty Years of Hollywood Cricket

DICK ADLER

Los Angeles in 1931 offered just about everything that anyone – even an Englishman – could ask for. There was soft, sweet air and 350 days a year of sunshine. Oranges dropped into your outstretched hand. The movies gave a young man with good features and his own dinner jacket a chance to supplement the remittance from home. The only thing missing, really, was organised cricket.

The game had been played in the Los Angeles area in a sporadic fashion since just before the First World War, but keeping any sort of a league going proved to be more bother than anyone cared to cope with. Then, in 1931, a 68-year-old actor called C. Aubrey Smith was brought to Hollywood by MGM to re-create the role in *Bachelor Father* which he had played on the London and New York stage. Within months, California cricket was a going concern.

Waiting for his family to follow him, Smith settled first into a large and comfortable set of rooms in the St Francis Apartment Hotel on Hollywood Boulevard near Western Avenue, across the street from the famed Central Casting office. It was here, on a soft spring evening in 1932, that 20 assorted Englishmen and one American with a shared passion for the game gathered to form what would soon become the most highly-publicised cricket club in the world.

Most of the avid cricketers were actors: Alan Mowbray, Melville Cooper, H. B. Warner, Pat Somerset, Claude King, Derek Reeves, Douglas Walton, Herbert Mundin and Boris Karloff. Writer P. G. Wodehouse was on hand (a generous cheque of his paid for much of the initial equipment), along with various other Englishmen who worked behind the cameras as assistant directors and grips. The lone American was 19-year-old Bill Feeder, then a budding journalist and now a vice-president of the Rogers and Cowan publicity organisation. Feeder's room-mate, Dickie Carpendale, also 19 and the son of a retired British admiral who was Controller of the BBC, brought him to the meeting as he thought it might make a story.

'Even though he was 68 when I first met him, Smith had the physical stamina of a 35-year-old,' Feeder recalls. 'He had a reputation for being very careful with his money, but he was extremely generous to English actors in need. He would always give them a bed and meals until they got set up. His apartment soon became the unofficial meeting place for people just off the boat.'

Even before the full flush of his Hollywood career – almost a hundred films in the next 18 years; pictures like *Morning Glory*, *Lives of a Bengal Lancer*, *Little Lord Fauntleroy*, *The Prisoner of Zenda*, *Little Women* – Charles Aubrey Smith was a figure of legendary proportions. The tall, lordly actor had conquered the stage and made a sizeable splash on the silent screen. But playing the perfect English squire or general was only a small part of his life. The son of a Brighton doctor, Smith first excelled on the cricket pitch at Charterhouse. He polished his skills at Cambridge, then was captain of the Sussex team and an All-England touring squad to South Africa. The high point of his playing career, he often said, came when he played against Dr W. G. Grace.

Virtually everyone who met Smith was charmed by the combination of gruff, beetle-browed exterior and the expansive warmth and good humour underneath. 'I used to call him "Sir" even before he was knighted; he played my father so many times,' David Niven recalls.

Smith became an ardent admirer of his adopted land. 'I love it for all it contains that *isn't* like England,' he once told a reporter. 'The climate, the sunshine, the beauty of the place. My wife and I have built a house above Beverly Hills, at the head of a canyon overlooking the sea – perfect!'

That house, where Coldwater Canyon joins Mullholland Drive, was called The Round Corner – because Smith was known as 'Round the Corner Smith' in his fast-bowling days – and boasted a weathervane in the shape of a cricket bat. When the Hollywood Cricket Club became part of folklore the house was the social centre of the British Colony. At that first organisational meeting in his St Francis apartment, Smith was primarily a keen cricketer anxious to have a bash at his favourite sport, and even willing, with 'Piggy' Wodehouse, to help defray the expenses.

Bill Feeder recalls that only one small touch of social snobbery surfaced at that first meeting. 'Someone said, "What about this fellow Pratt who calls himself Karloff? Understand he's a keen cricketer. But is he the sort we want? Drives a cement truck, I'm told, and besides, with that face, who knows if he's even British?" Someone else coughed to let the speaker know that Karloff himself was sitting in the corner, and the subject was dropped.'

Boris Karloff had been hanging around Hollywood since 1917 and now his career was just about to take off with a Howard Hawks film called *The Criminal Code*. He became one of the Hollywood Cricket Club's most loyal members and played the game through the Second World War, until at last his legs gave out and he was forced to watch from the side-lines. One of his proudest moments came toward the end of his life, when he was made an honorary umpire at Lord's. Friends said he enjoyed that more than any good review. And the highest praise he could think of after seeing a stage performance by Laurence Olivier was, 'And to think – he wore my boots!' referring to a time when Olivier had played with the Hollywood Cricket Club.

Any remaining traces of snobbery among the Hollywood members soon disappeared when they learned that many of the teams they were to play against were made up of British servants from some of the great homes in Pasadena, Santa Barbara and San Diego. And, at least once, the Club played against Jamaican-born railway porters in San Francisco.

To begin with, the Club's home pitch was several miles from Hollywood – on the grounds of the new UCLA campus in Westwood. A sympathetic college official got them permission to play there and, as David Niven remembers, 'Crashes were frequent on Sunset Boulevard on Sunday afternoons when amazed drivers were distracted by the sight of white flannel trousers and blazers on the football ground of UCLA.'

Then, in 1933, the British consulate in Los Angeles helped the Club to secure a strip of Hollywood's own Griffith Park, much more suited to their rising fame and affluence. They named it the C. Aubrey Smith Field by what is said to have been a unanimous vote, and with matching funds from the park commissioners soon erected a $30,000 clubhouse. Smith wept openly at its dedication.

By that time, the regular playing membership included Smith, Nigel Bruce, the newly-arrived David Niven, Stanley Mann, Basil Rathbone, Melville Cooper, H. B. Warner (who played Christ in De Mille's silent version of 'King of Kings') Boris Karloff, Errol Flynn, Murray Kinnell, Reginald Owen, Pat Somerset, W. J. Cowen, and Halliwell and Peter Hobbes. 'But the real star of the team,' reported the *Los Angeles Times*, 'is a young dentist from South Africa named Gene Walsh.' Walsh's office, at Hollywood Boulevard and Highland, was a gathering place for Club members, who often could be seen practising batting in the corridors.

By then, Bill Feeder had moved on and actor Claude King, known as 'The Old Bensonian' because of his public-school cricket career, had become the team secretary. King arranged matches with teams from British Navy ships which touched at San Pedro and Santa Barbara, and with the crews of British passenger liners. The Hollywood squad seems to have held its own; journals of the period record such triumphs as winning three out of five matches against Victoria and Vancouver in an invasion of Canada in the summer of 1936. Tommy Frebairn-Smith, King's successor as secretary, remembers: 'I think it was on this same tour that Errol Flynn and his great chum, the actor Frank Lawton, had to be disciplined by Aubrey. He was always pretty severe with the team, made them go to bed at nine before a game. Of course, Chaps like Flynn and Lawton didn't like that; they snuck out after lights out.' Smith once sent Flynn home on the train from Santa Barbara because there was a hint of alcohol on his breath, and also he was improperly dressed.

Frebairn-Smith recalls a moment in 1936, during a match in Santa Barbara, when 'a little old gentleman in a Charterhouse tie came up to bat. "Spread the field!" Aubrey ordered, so we did. Well, this fellow couldn't hit a thing. "Spread the field, Aubrey?" I said to him afterwards. "Well, dammit, he was senior to me at Charterhouse, and he used to hit them out of the grounds," said Aubrey, who was 73 at the time.'

As the Hollywood Cricket Club's fame grew, helped by the publicity generated by the studios of its more celebrated members, the social side became as important as the cricket. On any given Sunday in Griffith Park, watchers might include Olivia de Haviland, Greer Garson, Benita Hume, Gladys Cooper, Merle Oberon and Evelyn Laye, along with non-playing but fervent fans like Montagu Love, Herbert Marshall, Henry Stephenson, Walter Pidgeon and P. G. Wodehouse. 'There was a bonhomie, a cameraderie that you just don't see today,' recalled one regular, Doc Severn, just before his recent death at 92. 'True, most of the famous actors weren't great cricketers, but they talked a fine game. Like Boris: he didn't get many runs, but he was very stylish. Once, after finishing a cut, he hit a lady in the crowd. Aubrey rushed out to apologise, but she said, "My dear sir, it is an honour!"'

Canadian actor Ted du Domaine recalls several occasions when some of the Hollywood players would follow a match with a poker game at Boris Karloff's house in Toluca Lake, next door to W. C. Fields. 'At that time, Boris was put on a very strict allowance by his business manager,' says du Domaine. 'All he got was $25 a week for his spending money. So he worked out a scheme where I was to be his secretary, at $50 a week. Then I had to kick back half of that to him.' It was du Domaine who once bowled out a very surprised Don Bradman when the great Australian cricketer came to play at Hollywood in 1932.

When actor Gilchrist Stuart arrived in Hollywood in 1939, the Club was in full flower. Stuart, who died in 1979, remembered the ritual of going up before C. Aubrey Smith for the brusque but good-hearted grilling that preceded membership in the Club and the British Colony. 'All he wanted to know was where you'd gone to school and whether you played cricket. Everything else was irrelevant.'

The Second World War ended the glorious days of the Hollywood Cricket Club. Some of the younger men went off to serve; Aubrey Smith (knighted in 1944), Nigel Bruce and Boris Karloff finally were forced to admit that their playing days were over, although they could be spotted in the stands almost every Sunday. By 1950, a new generation of cricketers had begun to take over, solid, middle-class British and colonial types who recognised some of the famous faces in photographs on the clubhouse wall but couldn't quite put names to them.

Ironically, in this its 50th anniversary year, the Hollywood Cricket Club won't be playing at the C. Aubrey Smith Field in Griffith Park. Late in April, the Los Angeles City Council rescinded the Club's permit and turned the land over to a corporation which plans to build a $3 million equestrian centre. Woodley Park, a large stretch of grass in that part of the San Fernando Valley known as the Sepulveda Basin, will be the setting for this summer's matches – including special anniversary visits by touring teams from Kent, Vancouver and Australia House. They'll be facing a different sort of Hollywood team than in the old days:

the secretary is a CPA, the best fast bowlers are an Indian student and tool grinder from Barbados, and several of the players are British engineers who came to join the California aerospace boom of the 1960s.

So stables will soon stand on the site of the clubhouse whose dedication made Aubrey Smith weep, and horses will trot where Willie Bruce and Boris Karloff once bowled and batted. Still on a recent Sunday, when visiting British actors Anthony Andrews and Ian Bannen stopped by to watch a final practice session, if you listened carefully you might have heard on the wind just the whisper of an old gentleman shouting: 'Spread the field, chaps! Spread the field!'

SUNDAY TIMES MAGAZINE, 31 MAY 1981

Botham's 100th Test Wicket

DUDLEY DOUST

The date: 2 August 1979. India stand at 96 for 9 in their first innings. Botham's figures of 19–9–35–5 mean that he needs only one Test wicket to take 100 in record time.

The spinner Bedi comes in, chin up, patka held high. His swinging swagger belies the fact that he is among the poorest batsmen in Test cricket. His Test average, about 9·5, is inflated beyond his talents, for he goes in last, and sometimes the Indian innings dies at the other end.

To bowlers, Bedi is a sure wicket, a knock-over, Marilyn Monroe drugged! Botham again implores Lever to bowl wide to Bedi. He won't. Bedi lasts two minutes, four balls, before being clean bowled by Lever. India 96, and all out.

Lever makes a poor show of contrition as England come off the field. 'Sorry, Both,' he says. 'You'll have to wait until next digs.'

With only eighty minutes until stumps, Botham is aware that his work is done for the day. But it has been a good day, by any Test standards ... 19–9–35–5.

As he walks through the pavilion his father, come from the Guests Q Stand, walks over to him and says, 'Bad luck,' consolingly, 'but never mind.'

Botham climbs the flight of stairs, and, as England go out and make 53 runs for the loss of a wicket, he sits by himself in the changing room. A feeling of melancholy sweeps over him, followed by a rising sense of anger.

Five wickets. *Five wickets.* He curses. 'I've just got five bloody wickets in a Test innings and people are disappointed,' he says to himself. 'This record thing is getting to everybody. And it's beginning to get to me.'

'IAN BOTHAM, THE GREAT ALL-ROUNDER', CASSELL, LONDON, 1980

The date is 5 August 1979. And this is how Alex Bannister recorded the taking of the record 100th wicket in the next day's DAILY MAIL:

Ian Botham, the 23-year-old Taunton Tiger, bowled his way into the record books with the fastest 100 wickets in Test history. Botham, starting his dazzling Test career on 28 July 1977, has taken only two years and nine days to reach the milestone – 133 days fewer than West Indies' Andy Roberts, who took two years and 142 days to take 100 wickets.

To mark the occasion Botham was presented with a medallion by Selectors' Chairman Alec Bedser after play when India, 323 behind, had reached a commendable 196 for two. Bad light ended play thirteen minutes early.

'The record was on my mind as I went out,' said Botham. 'But I was just happy to bowl and delighted when I finally reached the hundred. I'm not a records man so that I can't tell you who I've beaten.

'All I know is that the important thing is for England to win the match. I would have been quite happy for Mike Hendrick to have gone out and got all ten wickets. It's a team game.'

Both Botham and Roberts were in their 19th Test, but are well above the achievements of George Lohmann, who had his 100th in 16 Tests in the last century. England's Sydney Barnes and the Australian C. T. B. (The Terror) Turner needed 17 matches, and Colin Blythe, the Kent left-arm spinner, also had 100 in 19 Tests.

It was a remarkable over which gave Botham his record – and the added distinction of being the youngest Englishman to take 100 wickets – and cost India the dismissal of their prime batsman, Sunil Gavaskar.

England were anxiously contemplating another mammoth score from Gavaskar when he started swinging his bat as if in a tight last over of a John Player League match.

Astonishingly, he offered three chances in four balls. The first whistled high to Derek Randall at deep point and was too hot to hold. The next ball flew to Mike Brearley at first slip. Again the chance was unacceptable. The third ball lifted and passed Gavaskar chest high, and now thoroughly unsettled, he edged the fourth low to Brearley's left hand – a brilliant catch.

How he reached the 100

1977	Australia (2 Tests)	10 for 202
1977/78	New Zealand (3 Tests)	17 ,, 311
1978	Pakistan (3 Tests)	13 ,, 209
1978	New Zealand (3 Tests)	24 ,, 337
1978/79	Australia (6 Tests)	23 ,, 567
1979	India (2 Tests)	13 ,, 271
		100 (average 18·97)

6 AUGUST 1979

Cricket Report 1896

This is a report of the two days Surrey trial match . . . the First Twelve v *Next Seventeen, from the very first issue of the* Daily Mail, *Monday, 4 May 1896 . . . priced One Halfpenny.*

Bitter, easterly winds are scarcely a pleasant accompaniment to cricket, but they were present in profusion at Kennington Oval. Whether what we may fairly term, in a comparative sense, the inclemency of the weather had a greater effect on the older hands than on the younger it is hard to say; but certain it is that the Surrey 'Next Seventeen' had decidedly the better of the argument in their match with the First Twelve. With another half-hour for play the youngsters would have gained a brilliant victory.

The famous Surrey wicket-keeper, Henry Wood, officiated in the match in the unusual position for him . . . that of umpire. His accustomed place was filled by Keeley, a young player who had never hitherto found himself associated with the First Eleven of Surrey. His selection for this match caused more surprise, and not a little discussion. C. Marshall, Wood's understudy last year, was available, indeed, he figured on the more numerous – and more successful – side, and his display was certainly a better one than that of Keeley.

Another player to assist the First, whose place is by no means assured, was Nice. This young player took part in one match for the county last year, against Hants at the end of the season, when he took three wickets for 63 runs. As he has always done well for the Second Eleven he may have further trials; but his performances last week were not such as to encourage the hope that he will immediately become a regular member of the team.

Remembering that the bowling to which they were opposed was Surrey's best, it must be admitted that the most commendable achievements in the batting were those of W. G. Baker, Thompson and J. S. Lohmann. The first named got his runs in the best style, and, if he were somewhat over careful, the importance of the occasion, to him, should be borne in mind.

During nearly the whole of Saturday the First Twelve were at the wicket, and we had an opportunity, in the first place, of seeing what sort of form the champions were in with the bat and also what the outwork of the youngsters was like. I think the general impression was – it was mine at any rate – that the old and tried players were for the most part the more short of condition and practice, and that on the whole the second team men again made the better show.

Holland and Hayward, whose styles at the wicket are very similar, played excellent cricket, the cutting of both being a delight to the critical eye; but, hampered more than usual by the number of fielders, they found runs very difficult to get. Whilst Braund was bowling, particularly, the score of each rose very, very slowly, Hayward travelling rather the faster.

The popular old stager, Robert Abel, created a favourable impression in his first innings, his timely cutting, occasional hard driving, and generally careful play being pretty much what it has usually been. He, too, found that the bowling was too good to take liberties with – not that Robert would be reckless under any circumstances. In the second innings he was unfortunate enough to get Lees's very best ball right into his wicket before he had had time to settle down, but he had given evidence enough at his first innings that he was fairly fit this early in the season.

Mr W. W. Read probably blames himself more than most men usually do when they are sent back without making runs, for he twice practically threw his wicket away. In the first innings when he had two to his credit Hayes gave him a nice tempting ball which it would have been no surprise if W.W. had sent to the boundary. It was a ball to hit and evidently he wanted to hit it, but possibly the number of men out in the open caused a sudden perturbation in his mind. At any rate he hesitated – and at cricket he who hesitates is lost. A tame pat back into the hands of Hayes was the result here, and Mr Read walked back to the pavilion smiling at his own simplicity.

Street and Smith, who had both been but a few days back from South Africa but had each found time to take unto himself a wife, were perhaps scarcely expected to show his true form so soon. Smith was at the wicket a long time in the first innings, but he never seemed very happy and was a little lucky to get as many as fourteen.

The best display of hitting in the First's initial innings was given by Mr K. J. Key, who hit the ball to all parts of the field while he was in, and eventually fell to a very fine catch by young Lohmann at cover point or extra cover. He was snapped up at the wicket soon after arriving in the second innings.

Turning now to the Second Team's bowlers, there were plenty of them of fair merit but I fancy Braund was the only one of outstanding ability. He has a free style, bowls rather faster than medium, right hand, with an off break. His was the bowling which caused the experienced hands the most trouble, and he got his fair share of wickets. W. G. Baker was probably the next best, though Lees, Higgins and Thompson all showed more than average capacity.

I should have picked out young Plaistow as an exceptionally good bowler but for his frequent habit of pitching the ball very short. His good balls were very good ones. He bowls left hand, with a free swing, medium pace and apparently breaks both ways.

The two days trial at Kennington Oval resulted in a draw, the Next

Seventeen wanting 26 runs to win with fourteen wickets to fall. Overnight the Seventeen had completed an innings for 251 and dismissed two of the Twelve for 33 runs. Abel added sixteen before being caught at point, and subsequently Holland and Mr Key batted well. The innings closed for 138 and the First had to follow on. Abel and Street were soon sent back, but a prolonged stand was made by Hayward and Holland, and, Lockwood hitting well, the total reached 164. The Seventeen were left to get 52 to win and only half an hour to bat, but half the requisite number were scored and the game was left drawn. Scores and bowling:

Next Seventeen

FIRST INNINGS		SECOND INNINGS	
Baldwin *c* Holland *b* Richardson	10		
Braund *b* Nice	12	*b* Lockwood	7
Ayres *b* Smith	14	*not out*	4
Higgins *st* Keeley *b* Abel	15		
Henderson *b* Abel	12		
Hayes *st* Keeley *b* Abel	0		
Mr H. R. Parker *b* Abel	0		
Baker (W. G.) *b* Richardson	38		
Mr W. T. Osborn (capt) *c-b* Lockwood	4		
Lees *c* Street *b* Lockwood	6		
Thompson *c* Hayward *b* Richardson	46	*c* Key *b* Richardson	0
Marshall *c* Hayward *b* Nice	5		
Baker (A.) *c* W. W. Read *b* Lockwood	6		
Lohmann *not out*	38	*not out*	5
Plaistow *c* Holland *b* Abel	1		
Hussey *b* Lockwood	0		
Keene *b* Lockwood	15		
Extras	29		10
TOTAL	251	(for two wickets)	26

The Twelve

Abel *c* Baldwin *b* Plaistow	23	*b* Lees	0
Street *c* Braund *b* Keene	4	*b* Braund	0
Hayward *c* Hussey *b* Thompson	17	*b* Braund	48
Holland *c* Marshall *b* Braund	24	*c* Hayes *b* Lees	63
Brockwell *c* Ayres *b* Plaistow	1	*c* Marshall *b* Braund	0
Lockwood *c* Ayres *b* Plaistow	0	*not out*	30
Mr W. W. Read *c* and *b* Hayes	2	*lbw b* Lees	4
Mr K. J. Key (capt) *c* Lohmann *b* Hayes	27	*c* Marshall *b* Braund	1
Nice *b* Braund	0	*c* A. Baker *b* W. G. Baker	5
Smith *c* Braund *b* Higgins	14	*b* W. G. Baker	2
Richardson *c* Ayres *b* Lees	1	*b* W. G. Baker	0
Keeley *not out*	2	*c* Thompson *b* W. G. Baker	3
Extras	23		8
TOTAL	138		164

Bowling Analyses
Next Seventeen

	O	M	R	W	O	M	R	W
Richardson	22	6	63	3	5	1	7	1
Nice	18	8	37	2				
Smith	16	4	32	1				
Lockwood	19·1	9	35	3	5	9	9	1
Abel	19	5	46	5				
Brockwell	12	7	9	2				

First Twelve

	O	M	R	W	O	M	R	W
Keene	23	16	8	1	16	3	26	0
Lees	22	11	21	2	27	16	22	3
Higgins	9	0	23	0				
Thompson	5	0	11	1	6	0	18	0
Plaistow	15	5	24	3	7	2	24	0
Braund	12	7	11	2	14	1	45	4
Hayes	6	1	11	2				
Baker W. G.					6·3	1	13	4
Hussey					4	1	8	0

Plaistow bowled a no-ball　　Lees bowled a no-ball

The 'Walk-Off' and the Ashes

BRIAN JOHNSTON

Commentating on winning the Ashes at the Oval in 1953 is a moment I shall never forget but one which I was lucky enough to be able to repeat when England regained the Ashes in the Seventh Test at Sydney in February 1971. Once again – this time on radio – I was able to describe the final ball which brought the Ashes back to England. Even without that special quality which the Ashes gives to Test Matches this was one of the most tense and closely fought Tests I have ever seen and like all really great games the fortunes of the two sides changed almost hourly throughout the five days.

To the relief of the England camp, Australia dropped Lawry and failed to select McKenzie. Had they played I feel sure the result would have been different. This is not a criticism of their new captain, Ian Chappell, who did a very good job and, on winning the toss, put England in to bat. England were without Boycott who had broken his arm, and on a lively pitch in a humid atmosphere had only scored 11 for 1 wicket at the end of the first hour. Luckhurst, for once, failed. Had McKenzie been bowling he must have taken some wickets. As it was, the inexperienced opening pair of Lillee and Dell bowled too short and were very wild in their direction.

Even so, England struggled for most of the day. Edrich made 30 and Fletcher 33, but with d'Oliveira out for 1 they were 69 for 4 when Illingworth came to the wicket to play yet another of his rescue-act innings. Hampshire went for 10, but Knott lasted over an hour for a useful 27. By this time the two spinners Jenner and O'Keeffe were bowling really well. The pitch was taking spin and the innings closed for 184 with Illingworth eighth out, bowled by Jenner's googly for the top score of 42. Jenner and O'Keeffe each took 3 wickets, and Chappell's gamble had come off in spite of the poor support from his fast bowlers.

But Illingworth was luckier with his. Both Snow and Lever took a wicket in the half hour left for play, and at the close Australia were 13 for 2 with both Eastwood and Stackpole out.

There was a hard tussle the next morning and in the 2 hours before lunch Australia added 71 and lost the wickets of nightwatchman Marsh and their captain, Ian Chappell. But after lunch Walters and Redpath added 63 in the first hour. Walters led a charmed life, being missed at slip off Underwood and at deep third man by Underwood off Willis. It also looked as if Knott had stumped him when he took a ball in front of the stumps off a mishit from Walters who was out of his crease. But it was great cricket to watch and a fascinating battle between the footwork of Redpath and Walters and the flight and change of pace of Underwood.

He got them both in the end, Walters going yards down the pitch only to be stumped, and Redpath giving a catch to the bowler when he had made 59. At tea the score was 165 for 6 representing a considerable drop in the scoring rate – only 18 runs coming in the second hour. O'Keeffe was soon out after tea, and with Greg Chappell and Jenner together the new ball was taken.

Then followed the famous 'walk-off' incident. I was broadcasting at the time so most of what happened is clear in my mind. For the rest I have checked and double-checked what happened out in the middle. I have set out the facts below so that you can judge for yourself and make up your own mind what you would have done had you been the Captain in Illingworth's place – always remembering that you have a chance to sit back and think whereas he had to act on the spur of the moment.

The first two overs with the new ball were bowled by Snow and Lever with no suspicion of a bouncer. With the seventh ball of the third over, Snow, however, did bowl a bouncer at Jenner who ducked into it, was hit on the back of the head, collapsed and had to be carried off. The crowd naturally enough booed and shouted, roaring their disapproval of Snow.

While the new batsman Lillee was on his way out to the wicket, Lou Rowan, the Umpire at Snow's end, told Snow that he should not have bowled a bouncer at a low-order batsman like Jenner. Snow became incensed at this and asked Rowan in not too polite a way whose side he thought he was on. Umpire Rowan then seemed to lose his temper and in what appeared to be an emotional decision, promptly warned Snow under Law 46 Note 4 (IV) for persistent bowling of short-pitched balls.

Then it was Illingworth's turn to protest at what he considered a wrong interpretation of the Law. How could *one* bouncer come under the heading of persistent? Unfortunately, in the heat of the moment, Illingworth also became annoyed and was seen by thousands on the ground and tens of thousands on television to wag his finger at Lou Rowan. Amid a storm of booing – I've seldom heard such a noise on a cricket ground – Snow completed his over by bowling one ball at Lillee. He then turned to go off to his position at long leg. When he had got half-way there some beer cans were thrown in his direction from the small Paddington Hill to the left of the Noble Stand.

Snow turned back and returned to the square where Illingworth told the Umpires that he would not go on playing until the field was cleared of the cans. The team sat down while this was being done by the ground staff. After a few minutes the ground was clear and Snow set off again for long leg.

I remember saying on the air at the time that I thought the whole incident was going to end happily as members in the Noble Stand and people on the hill started to applaud Snow and a man stretched out over the railings to shake hands with Snow. Snow went up and shook hands but a tough-looking spectator who had obviously 'had a few' then grabbed hold of Snow's shirt and started to shake him.

This was the signal for more cans and bottles to come hurtling on to the field, narrowly missing Snow. Willis ran up and shouted something to the crowd. Then Illingworth came up, saw the bottles flying and promptly signalled to his team to leave the field. The two batsmen and the two umpires stayed on the square. Then the two umpires made their way to the pavilion – the first time they had left the square since the trouble started. Rowan made it plain to Illingworth that if he did not continue he would forfeit the match and an announcement was made that play would be resumed as soon as the ground had been cleared, not only of the cans and bottles but also of a number of spectators who had clambered over the fence.

This, in fact, took only 10 minutes and Illingworth led his men back 13 minutes after leading them off. In the remaining 40 minutes the England side somewhat naturally seemed to have lost their zest, and Chappell and Lillee added 45 runs so that Australia finished the day at 235 for 7 – a lead of 51.

That was the incident as I saw it, though it is true to say that opinions differ about what exactly did happen. I said at the time, and I still believe, that Illingworth was right to lead the side off. Not only was it becoming dangerous with bottles flying around, but this action so stunned the crowd that the throwing stopped immediately and play was very soon restarted. In other similar circumstances in the West Indies, the fielding side had stayed on the field and play was abandoned for the day.

There was, of course, no excuse for Illingworth to argue in such a demonstrative manner with the umpire. He has since publicly said he was sorry he acted as he did and also conceded that he should have gone back to the square and warned the umpires that he was taking his team off. But he had to make a quick decision and it is surprising that neither umpire left the square at any time to go to deal with the incident at the trouble spot. Illingworth and Snow have also been criticised for Snow's return to long leg after the first lot of cans had been thrown at him.

There are two views about this. As captain, you either take the peaceful way out and give way to force and threats, or you stick to your right to place your fieldsmen where you like. And finally, Snow was criticised for going up to the fence and accepting the proffered handshake. Who can say what the reaction would have been if he hadn't? I apologise for dealing at such length with this unhappy incident and now you must judge for yourselves. Meanwhile, let's get back to the cricket which continued on the Sunday morning.

Lillee was out to the first ball of the day, caught by Knott off Willis, who 2 overs later bowled Greg Chappell behind his legs for a fighting 65. Jenner came in at the fall of the first wicket, showing no after effects from his injury and he made a bright 30 before being last man out, bowled by Lever. Australia were all out for 264, giving them a lead of 80 runs, and in the 70 minutes before lunch, Luckhurst and Edrich put on 60 with the former playing some brilliant strokes. He was out soon after lunch for 59, Fletcher made 20 and by tea England had made very slow progress to reach a score of 130 for 2.

Two more wickets – Edrich 57 and Hampshire 24, fell before the close when England were 228 for 4 – leading by 149 runs. They owed a lot to d'Oliveira and Illingworth who stayed together for the last hour and a half and added 64. However, next morning, Illingworth was soon lbw to Lillee for 29 and d'Oliveira caught in the slips off Lillee for 47. Only 34 runs came in the first hour – Knott making 15 of them. England had still not anywhere near enough runs. However, Lever and Snow each hit out scoring 17 and 20 respectively, but when England were all out for 302, they had lost their last 6 wickets for only 73 runs, O'Keeffe with 3 more wickets again looking the most dangerous Australian bowler.

Australia needed 223 runs to win in 15½ hours (a sixth day could be used if necessary) – an easy enough task most people thought, even though Australia had not got the steadying influence of Lawry.

They made a bad start – Snow yorking Eastwood for 0 in the first over. But then came tragedy for England. Stackpole hit a short ball from Lever high in the direction of long leg. Snow ran in to make the catch but came too far. He turned to try to make the catch before the ball went over the boundary but somehow overbalanced and caught the little finger of his bowling hand in the fence and broke it. He went off in great pain with the bone protruding through the skin – a horrid sight.

Umpire Lou Rowan signalled 6 although in fact the ball had hit the fence and had not gone full pitch over it. This was the testing time for England, already without their best batsman and now cruelly robbed of their best bowler.

But Illingworth outwardly remained as calm as usual, though what he was thinking one can well imagine. Were the Ashes going to slip away from him after all? But the team rallied round him magnificently, Lever soon got Ian Chappell for 6, Illingworth himself had Redpath caught for 14 and bowled Stackpole, sweeping, for yet another fine innings of 67. At the close of play, Australia were 123 for 5 with Chappell and Marsh the not-out batsmen. The other wicket to fall had been Walters who again showed his dislike of fast bowling. This time he played an incredible shot – an upper cut – off a short ball from Willis and was caught chest high on the boundary in front of the pavilion at *third man*!

So with two days to go if necessary, Australia needed exactly 100 to win with five wickets left and it was really anybody's match, with Australians tending to think England would win, and vice versa.

Once again the England side backed up Illingworth superbly and he himself, in his longest bowling spell of the series, bowled magnificently. Underwood bowled Marsh, hitting desperately across the line, for 16, and the score was 131 for 6. Knott stumped Chappell off Illingworth – 142 for 7, but O'Keeffe put up a stout defence and had been in for nearly an hour when Illingworth brought on d'Oliveira who virtually finished off the match.

He dismissed O'Keeffe and Lillee in successive balls and though Dell saved the hat-trick and hung on with Jenner for twelve tense minutes, at 12.37 it was all over and the Ashes were ours. Jenner snicked a ball on to his pads and it flew to Fletcher at silly point who made the catch and the England team made straight for their captain, Illingworth, and carried him off the field.

England had won by 62 runs and what a wonderful cricket match it had been. It was of course a personal triumph for Illingworth who led his team magnificently in the field, encouraging and sustaining their morale. In addition he had borne the brunt of the bowling after Snow went off and his second innings figures of 20–7–39–3 did much to win the match.

But it was also essentially a team effort and I shall always be glad that I was there to share their happiness in their hour of triumph on bringing back the Ashes to England after twelve years.

The Seventh Test Match

Played at Sydney, February 12th, 13th, 14th, 16th and 17th. England won by 62 runs.

England

Batsman	First innings		Second innings	
J. H. Edrich	*c* G. Chappell *b* Dell	30	*c* I. Chappell *b* O'Keeffe	57
B. W. Luckhurst	*c* Redpath *b* Walters	0	*c* Lillee *b* O'Keeffe	59
K. W. R. Fletcher	*c* Stackpole *b* O'Keeffe	33	*c* Stackpole *b* Eastwood	20
J. H. Hampshire	*c* Marsh *b* Lillee	10	*c* I. Chappell *b* O'Keeffe	24
B. L. d'Oliveira	*b* Dell	1	*c* I. Chappell *b* Lillee	47
†R. Illingworth	*b* Jenner	42	*lbw b* Lillee	29
‡A. P. E. Knott	*c* Stackpole *b* O'Keeffe	27	*b* Dell	15
J. A. Snow	*b* Jenner	7	*c* Stackpole *b* Dell	20
P. Lever	*c* Jenner *b* O'Keeffe	4	*c* Redpath *b* Jenner	17
D. L. Underwood	*not out*	8	*c* Marsh *b* Dell	0
R. G. D. Willis	*b* Jenner	11	*not out*	2
Extras	(*b* 4, *lb* 4, *w* 1, *nb* 2)	11	(*b* 3, *lb* 3, *nb* 6)	12
	TOTAL	184		302

Australia

Batsman	First innings		Second innings	
K. H. Eastwood	*c* Knott *b* Lever	5	*b* Snow	0
K. R. Stackpole	*b* Snow	6	*b* Illingworth	67
‡R. W. Marsh	*c* Willis *b* Lever	4	*b* Underwood	16
†I. M. Chappell	*b* Willis	25	*c* Knott *b* Lever	6
I. R. Redpath	*c* and *b* Underwood	59	*c* Hampshire *b* Illingworth	14
K. D. Walters	*st* Knott *b* Underwood	42	*c* d'Oliveira *b* Willis	1
G. S. Chappell	*b* Willis	65	*st* Knott *b* Illingworth	30
K. J. O'Keeffe	*c* Knott *b* Illingworth	3	*c* sub *b* d'Oliveira	12
T. J. Jenner	*b* Lever	30	*Fletcher b* Underwood	4
D. K. Lillee	*c* Knott *b* Willis	6	*Hampshire b* d'Oliveira	0
A. R. Dell	*not out*	3	*not out*	3
Extras	(*lb* 5, *w* 1, *nb* 10)	16	(*b* 2, *nb* 5)	7
	TOTAL	264		160

Fall of Wickets

England – First Innings

1/5 2/60 3/68 4/69 5/98 6/145 7/156 8/165 9/165 10/184

Second Innings

1/94 2/130 3/158 4/165 5/234 6/251 7/276 8/298 9/299 10/302

Australia – First Innings

1/11 2/13 3/32 4/66 5/147 6/162 7/178 8/235 9/239 10/264

Second Innings

1/0 2/22 3/71 4/82 5/96 6/131 7/142 8/154 9/154 10/160

Bowling

AUSTRALIA	O	M	R	W	O	M	R	W
Lillee	13	5	32	1	14	0	43	2
Dell	16	8	32	2	26·7	3	65	3
Walters	4	0	10	1	5	0	18	0
G. Chappell	3	0	9	0				
Jenner	16	3	42	3	21	5	39	1
O'Keeffe	24	8	48	3	26	8	96	3
Eastwood					5	0	21	1
Stackpole					3	1	8	0
ENGLAND								
Snow	18	2	68	1	2	1	7	1
Lever	14·6	3	43	3	12	2	23	1
d'Oliveira	12	3	24	0	5	1	15	2
Willis	12	1	58	3	9	1	32	1
Underwood	16	3	39	2	13·6	5	28	2
Illingworth	11	3	16	1	20	7	39	3
Fletcher					1	0	9	0

Umpires: T. F. Brooks and L. P. Rowan

'ALL ABOUT CRICKET' BY BRIAN JOHNSTON, W. H ALLEN AND CO. LTD., 1972

Since those early days Surrey County Cricket Club, which was formed as it is today in 1845, had made wonderful progress. Their headquarters, Kennington Oval, was once a market garden. This magnificent enclosure, if it could speak, would have plenty of stories to tell. Of thrilling matches; of gallant and wonderful cricketers. Few grounds have a greater attraction for the Southerner than the Oval, despite the fact it is surrounded by flats – and the famous gasometers.

It was in 1852 that Surrey shocked the sporting world when they beat the England team by an innings and twenty-eight runs. One of their star players in this victory was Julius Ceasar. No, he was not the famous Roman general, but a cricketer of real ability. Ceasar was one of the hardest batsmen to get out, and for four years he had the distinction of being unbowled. Another Surrey star who deservedly holds a proud place in cricket annals is Charles Lawrence. It was Lawrence who, after winning cricket fame in England with Surrey, went to Australia, where he taught the Aborigines the art of cricket. Lawrence had the honour of being the first captain of Australia – and what a 'Test' team he brought over!

The team was composed, in the majority of cases, of Aborigines. Their cricket ability was far from outstanding, but, before every match the natives used to give boomerang displays for the entertainment of spectators!

Without any doubt, however, the greatest cricketer of all time was Jack Hobbs.

To commemorate the great service Jack Hobbs did to cricket – and sport in general – the Surrey club have honoured Hobbs by dedicating their new entrance gates to the Oval to him. It was P. G. H. Fender, for so long his captain, who said: 'He who has not known Hobbs has not lived.'

Of their present side, Surrey owe much to the great-hearted fast bowling of Alf Gover. Season after season Gover runs up to the wicket – and, except for last season, when an injury laid him low, gets either a hundred or two hundred wickets a season.

EVERYBODY'S WEEKLY, MARCH 1945

AS TOLD TO . . .

Reported by Richie Benaud: Scene in deserted Press Box during an Australian Test, with famous ex-player sitting alone. The covers are on because of driving rain. Enter an attendant: 'What are you waiting for? There is no play today.'

'I'm waiting for my "ghost" to write the message for me!'

Wides

R. C. Robertson-Glasgow, one of the greatest humorists cricket ever knew, told many self-deprecating stories about himself. While up from Cambridge before the War, he played for Somerset against Yorkshire.

With the first two balls of the innings, he got Sutcliffe and Barber, the latter off a catch during which Percy Holmes crossed over.

Before starting his run up, 'Crusoe', as he became immortalised, was approached by the Somerset captain, John Daniell, and told, 'You'll make history if you start a county match with a hat-trick.'

Crusoe used to pause, and then say, 'Next morning Holmes resumed on 300.' I once challenged Crusoe as to facts, saying that I couldn't find the score in Wisden's. His eyes twinkling, Crusoe guffawed, then said, 'My boy, never let the facts spoil a good story!'

Richie Benaud, in a TV eulogy on Ken Barrington, MCC Assistant-Manager, who collapsed and died at Barbados in March 1981:

'Ken Barrington spent a week under my tuition trying out my "flipper" ball. At last he was ready to go into action, at the Oval, for Surrey in a county match.

'When he went on to bowl, he whispered to Tony Lock, "Fifth ball". So as he ran up to dispense the fifth ball, Lockie moved even closer at short-leg.

'It was a full toss past Lockie's nose, with the batsman trying to smash it for six.

'Lockie had recovered by the time the ball was returned from the boundary, and he said to the world, admiringly: 'It took Benaud twelve years to perfect. Ken does it in a week!"'

The *Daily Express* quoted R. W. V. 'Cocky' Robins on a phenomenal innings by Jim Smith, the comfortably built Middlesex fast bowler. It was in a charity match between a Middlesex eleven and a Harrow School XV: We were batting out time, having won the match, and when I went in at 5.50, with forty minutes left (I batted one handed because of a recently broken thumb), Jim Smith was fifteen not out.

At 6.30 when stumps were drawn I had scored 7 and Jim's total was 183. Sixes flowed like singles. One of his straight drives smashed a stump in half, and another split the bowler's hand wide open. I'll never forget the last two overs. I took a single off the first ball of the last-but-one over; Smith hit the next five for six. I missed the first ball of the next over, scored a single; and he hit the next four out of the ground!

Late Night Centenary Chat Show

DENIS COMPTON

Perish the thought but I trust that Buckingham Palace have made arrangements for the Queen to stay anywhere but the Hilton Hotel, Melbourne, during the Centenary Test celebrations next weekend.

For the Hilton will be no place for the faint-hearted or for ladies, and certainly not for monarchs or heads of State at a time when the hotel is playing host to nearly 200 former Test cricketers.

Veterans of epic Tests between England and Australia will be encamped together for the duration of this specially arranged Test Match. And the occasion bears the hallmarks already of becoming the most glorious red-letter chapter in the history of cricket.

We will see five days of champagne cricket, topped-up with a heady draught of instant nostalgia, laced with a generous measure of joyful reunions, and given a final splash of the unexpected.

Tall stories, funny stories, tales of woe and glory, some true, some embellished but all gems that never made Wisden, will go on into the early mornings long after the night chill has settled on the Melbourne ground.

Sir Len Hutton will rub shoulders with his old adversary and friend, Sir Don Bradman. Percy Fender, now 84, will no doubt snatch a quick look on arrival at the Melbourne ground on which he scored a valuable 59 and took five wickets for England in 1921.

And when I board the Qantas Jumbo at Heathrow this afternoon I will be looking for that great little left-hander of the 'thirties – Eddie Paynter.

He's now 75 but he will not have forgotten young Compton's first Test against the Aussies. It was at Trent Bridge in June 1938 and I was lucky enough to score 102, but even more fortunate to have made them in a record fifth-wicket partnership of 206 with the Lancashire midget, Eddie, who ran me off my feet, and went on to score 216 not out.

Bill Edrich, who toured Australia in 1946–7 and 1954–5 has a 'shopping list' of old pals to seek out, including two he spent hours studying from 22 yards, Messrs Lindwall and Miller.

I might even bump into the commissionaire who gave me so much trouble on the 1950–51 tour, led by Freddie Brown.

He was the man who barred my entry to the ground in Melbourne during the third Test after the England players had posed for a team picture outside the ground.

As I had been waylaid by a friend, I did not go back to the dressing-room with the rest. And when I did try to go in this commissionaire demanded to see my pass. I had left it in the dressing-room.

'But I'm Denis Compton,' I said.

He replied: 'I know your bloody name, chum, but if you haven't got a pass you can't come in.'

I argued for 10 minutes before finally requesting him to send a message to Freddie Brown stating that I would be unable to take any further part in the Test.

I added a postscript, suggesting that if Mr Brown wishes to reply I would be in my hotel room writing letters.

The commissionaire looked utterly bewildered, and as he rocked on his heels I took action. I vaulted the turnstile into the ground!

I scored a century on my first appearance in Melbourne, hitting 143 out of 220 in three hours for MCC against Victoria in 1946–47.

Eighty thousand people watched our third Test in Melbourne that year. Australian crowds always quicken my pulse, especially those in Sydney.

Who will forget the famous 'Hill' crowd's amazing performance in the second Test of 1946–47. The game coincided with a celebrated abortion case in Australia.

England were in terrible trouble in the match. Sid Barnes and Don Bradman established a fifth-wicket record Test partnership of 405, each hitting 234. Barnes batted more than 10 hours and Bradman for more than six.

We were on our knees in the field; it was suddenly very quiet, when a wag on the Hill shouted: 'Why don't you Pommies call for Nurse Evans? She'll get the bastards out!'

Freddie Trueman described the Melbourne ground as the finest sports arena in the world on the 1962–63 tour. The tour manager, the late Duke of Norfolk – 'Dukie' to Fred – had reminded the tourists of their responsibilities as ambassadors.

In Perth, Fred assured them that their lager was as fine as any he had drunk; in Adelaide, he admired the local wines, but by the time he got to Sydney diplomacy was wearing thin.

What did Fred think of 'Our bridge?' 'Your bridge?' cursed Fred. 'Our bloody bridge, chum. Bugger it, Dorman and Long, a Yorkshire firm, built it, and you still ain't paid for it!'

David Sheppard, now the Bishop of Liverpool, had interrupted a clerical career to make that tour. He had had a long absence from first-class cricket and, not unexpectedly, dropped a few catches.

After one bad miss, Fred, the unfortunate bowler, said: 'Kid yourself it's Sunday, Rev., and keep your hands together.'

The variation of that anecdote, again attributed to Trueman, is that Sheppard caught Lindsay Hassett at leg slip in England. A brilliant catch and as Lindsay walked back to the pavilion, Fred turned to him and said: 'Bad luck, Lindsay. When the Rev. puts his hands together you have no bloody chance.'

I shall arrive in Melbourne wearing a watch that was 30 years old last month. There is only one other in the world like it – and that is worn by Arthur Morris, the former Australian opener.

We were presented with them after we had each scored two separate hundreds in the fourth Test in Adelaide in 1946–47.

But I must also confess to the nightmare series of 1950–51 when I scored just 53 runs in eight Test innings at an average of seven. My scores were 3, 0, 0, 23, 5, 0, 11 and 11 not out.

Don Bradman was very kind in that personal crisis. He invited me to his hotel room to offer words of encouragement and some sound advice.

'You're playing across the line, Denis,' said the great man. He then produced a bat from under his bed to demonstrate his point.

Yes, the old England cricketers will more than hold their own in the verbal exchanges in the lounges of the Hilton with Hassett, Lindwall, Miller and Co.

And I'm confident that Tony Greig's team, fresh from their 3–1 thumping of India, can upset the form-book in the Test beginning on Saturday.

So, charge your glasses gentlemen and let battle commence in what promises to be the longest late-night chat show in history.

SUNDAY EXPRESS, 6 MARCH 1977

Lord's Crowd Boo Big Brother

ROY PESKETT

Until the West Indians from Brixton and other London surrounds brought their lively calypso music and the insidious rhythm of rattled Coca-Cola tins to Lord's it was almost a sin to make a noise during a game of England's national sport: cricket.

But there was one unforgettable incident at Lord's during a war-time game when the man who was later to become the most popular sportsman at Highbury as well as Lord's was soundly booed.

Yes, Leslie Compton, sunny-tempered elder brother of Golden Boy Denis, was the man who fell foul of the crowd one August afternoon in 1943.

Leslie normally kept wicket in those war-time charity matches, but with Leslie Ames available, the big Middlesex cricketer and Arsenal footballer fielded in the deep.

With the batsmen from all over the world representing the Dominions going pell-mell for runs to reach the 359 England had set them for victory, Learie Constantine, already established as a darling of the crowd through his brilliant all-round cricket, sliced a tremendous hit towards the pavilion.

Learie having already got two huge sixes and obviously prepared to give the Lord's crowd an exciting session, the Tavern fans cheered what they fully expected to be another six.

But Compton, judging the hit to perfection, slowly ambled back until his broad back was resting against the white painted fence which enclosed the members' seats in front of the pavilion.

Then, just as the ball was roaring into the scattering members, Leslie reached his left hand up nonchalantly, and grabbed the ball for a marvellous catch.

Then, instead of the deserved applause, there were shouts of 'not out', which turned to booing as Learie Constantine started to walk to the pavilion. He grinned as he approached the fielder, and patted Compton on the back as he passed on to the dressing-room.

Meanwhile the bowler, Alec Bedser, later Chairman of the England selectors, led the applause for one of the greatest catches ever seen at the headquarters of world cricket, which not even Hitler and his mob could close down.

As the explanation went round in the excited buzz, some of the protesting members looked sheepish. Constantine was out fairly, and it was a good clean catch.

The Law concerning this point is clear . . . if the fielder makes a catch without stepping out of the field of play, even if leaning against the boundary, the batsman is out.

That match, containing some of the world's greatest pre-war and post-war players, was as exciting as any staged in peace-time.

Final Scores:

England 324 for 9 dec (Ames 133, D. Compton 58, Dr C. B. Clarke 4 for 89)
and 150 for 6 dec (R. W. V. Robins 69 not, E. R. T. Holmes 45 not)

The Dominions 115 (D. Compton 6 for 15)
and 351 (C. S. Dempster 113, K. Sismey 70, Dr C. B. Clarke 52)

England beat the Dominions by eight runs.

RECALLED BY ROY PESKETT FROM HIS MATCH REPORT IN THE SUNDAY GRAPHIC, AUGUST 1943

RETURN UNKNOWN

As his South African born successor Tony Greig struggled to extricate England from an innings defeat, Scotsman Mike Denness is telling an amusing story of how he received a letter addressed, simply, to 'M. Denness, Cricketer.'

Inside was a short note: 'If this gets to you, the postman thinks more of you than I do.'

The Don Did Not Think He Was Out

MAURICE TATE AS TOLD TO ROY PESKETT

England 658 for eight wickets, declared – Australia 138 with Brown, Fingleton and, best of all, Bradman back in the pavilion. There you have the first chapter in the Trent Bridge Test story – a story that makes bright week-end reading for those of us who aren't Australians. If there were some of us who thought Wally Hammond, in his first appearance as an England skipper, left the declaration a bit late, there can be no grumbles now. Certainly the Australians are right up against it.

Dismissal of The Don means much. And Bradman must still be wondering how it all happened. Here's how I saw it. Sinfield made the Bowral Boy play forward to an off-spinner, and the stroke was made too soon. The ball flicked the bat and cannoned off Don's pads into Ames's hands. There was a half-hearted appeal, and, glory be, it was answered rightaway with Umpire Chester raising his finger! Bradman didn't see the old, heart-breaking sign (Sinfield was in the way) and a quick glance at the square-leg umpire must have reassured him. Then Sinfield moved, leaving Chester in clear view – and Don had to go.

I don't suppose the 30,000 crowd were grumbling. They've seen a day of records. And England records, at that! First, there's a world's best for any Test with four individual hundreds in an innings. We can thank Barnett, Hutton, Paynter and Compton for that. Next, Eddie Paynter, making his Test come-back hit 216 without defeat to beat the previous England record of 182 not out by fellow left-hander Phil Mead at the Oval in 1921.

That's not all. England beat the previous highest total against Australia by passing the 636 made at Sydney in 1928–29. And, just to make weight, the Paynter–Compton stand of 206 gave us a new one to talk about for the fifth wicket. They shattered the 192 put on by Len Braund and R. E. Foster on the Sydney ground 34 years ago.

Paynter's brush with O'Reilly and Co was the big thing of the day, and I'm not forgetting that Denis Compton got a century in his first England match. Eddie only gave one real chance – then Barnett fumbled the ball when he might have stumped the Lancashire lad. There was a dash of Frank Woolley about his strokes.

It was good to see this batsman whom England has so persistently forgotten, master the attack. Here, for me, at least, is a memory of Paynter to store alongside that fighting knock he put up for Jardine's team 'Down Under'. Paynter was a sick man that time, getting from his bed to show real Lancashire grit. Yesterday, he was fighting fit, and the only sick ones, I reckon, were the Australians. Say what you like, Clarrie Grimmett was missed. Frank Ward isn't a Grimmett by a mile, and I fancy that O'Reilly missed the support of the 'Little Gnome'.

The ground was as full as makes no difference when Bradman led his men out. Fleetwood-Smith bowled an over from the pavilion end to Paynter before handing over to McCabe, who shared the new ball with McCormick. Paynter faced the fast bowler with plenty of confidence, and beautifully cut him to leg for two – a dash by Hassett saving the boundary.

Compton carried on where he left off on Friday night, square-cutting McCabe for six in two balls. The Australians' fielding was not up to standard, and Umpire Chester showed them the way, when stopping a hard return from Hassett! The throwing was loose, especially from close in, when the batsmen were trying short runs.

Compton had the real hall-mark of class in his strokes and sped to his century, while Paynter watched him from the other end, content to crack the loose one.

The little left-hander usually contrived to face McCabe, and a punch through the covers flashed to the boundary like a bullet. Paynter had a lucky escape, though, when his score was 88, being beaten by McCabe's faster ball. And, with the batsman well out of his crease, Barnett fumbled the ball, and finally dropped it!

Apart from this let off, neither man looked uncomfortable, and at the end of 35 minutes 51 had been added. O'Reilly had entered the lists by then, his sleeves rolled up and a broad grin on his face. Compton played the great attacker like a veteran, and Paynter, farming the bowling, took 14 off O'Reilly's third over – three 4s and a 2.

The Lancashire lad reached his hundred in this over. Bradman brought Fleetwood-Smith back at 477, but the flow of runs had in no way decreased, and at ten minutes past twelve the partnership for the fifth wicket had reached 200.

It was a new record for the series, breaking the 35-year-old figures of 192, put up by R. E. Foster and Len Braund at Sydney.

Compton soon followed his partner to the three figures reaching his first Test century with a square-cut for 4 off O'Reilly – 102 out of 205.

A great start to the Middlesex boy's Test career. He shared in a stand of 206 in 2 hours 20 minutes. Hitting fifteen 4s Compton never blinked an eyelid when facing O'Reilly, picking out the wrong 'un brilliantly.

Ames was quiet at the start, but Paynter went merrily along. His hooking was especially pleasing to watch, but he nearly tried it once too often, almost kicking his own wicket down when hooking O'Reilly to the fine leg boundary.

Bradman seemed to be bitten by the bad-fielding bug. He gave Paynter four over-throws with a searing throw-in which nearly knocked O'Reilly's fingers off.

Ames was batting well after a quiet start and showed confidence in jumping out to drive O'Reilly. With both men using the covers as the route to the boundary O'Reilly changed his field in an effort to stop the steady flow of runs. To Ames he had two short-legs, silly mid-on, deep fine mid-on, short-slip, backward point, mid-off, cover and extra cover, doing without one of the short-legs when Paynter was facing him.

Ward was brought on for Fleetwood-Smith at 520 and proved the better bowler in the pre-lunch session. Paynter never looked like getting out, but Ames left shortly before lunch. He was bowled off his pads when trying to hit for his 50. It had been a very useful knock at the right pace. It was made in 55 minutes, this wicket adding 90.

McCormick seemed to be slower than usual, although taking a full 25 paces run. Greatly to the surprise of the crowd and, incidentally, myself, Hammond continued to bat on after lunch, although everything cried out for a declaration. Shortly before three o'clock, after Verity – bowled by Fleetwood-Smith – and Sinfield – lbw to O'Reilly's straight through ball – had gone, Paynter reached his 200 amid tremendous cheering.

When Hammond said 'Enough!' Paynter was still there, unbeaten with 216 against his name. What a grand innings! And to think that Paynter has been passed over repeatedly since his brave showing 'Down Under'.

Wright had helped Paynter add 32 for the ninth wicket. Eddie got 30 of these runs, by the way, but I take off my hat to the Kent man for keeping his end up.

Batting five and a half hours, Paynter scored his runs all round the wicket. Besides a 6 and a 5 (four overthrows) he cracked on 26 fours. However, mere figures cannot really tell you the magnificence of his innings, a best bit of England batsmanship – and Lancashire batsmanship, too!

When Australia began their formidable-looking task, Farnes, from the Trent Bridge end, opened to Fingleton, who took a single off his first ball. The Essex amateur, bowling just outside the off stump, had a bad first over, Fingleton taking 5 (including a hard-run 3) while Brown pushed a single. Hammond took the other end and bowled a maiden to Brown.

Farnes' second over was much better, and Ames made two strong appeals for lbw and a catch at the wicket off Brown. But umpire Emmot Robinson just gazed at the sky. Brown was not comfortable, and when another ball hit him low down on the pad it seemed as if the entire crowd appealed.

So cautious were the Australian openers in the first half-hour that only 24 runs were scored. Then Hammond gave way for Sinfield to send down his first over in Test cricket. Sinfield, who bowls off-spinners to an orthodox field, seemed a trifle faster than usual, but was played quietly and confidently by Brown.

At 27 Hammond replaced Farnes with Wright at the Trent Bridge end. Another debutant Test bowler. His first ball, a foot outside the off stump was pasted to the off boundary for 4 by Brown who then took a single off the third ball. The next beat Fingleton, who, trying to force

Wright's googly through the covers, edged it on to his wicket. One for 34, last man 9!

TEST SCOREBOARD

England

FIRST INNINGS

L. Hutton *lbw b* Fleetwood-Smith	100
C. J. Barnett *b* McCormick	126
W. J. Edrich *b* O'Reilly	5
W. R. Hammond *b* O'Reilly	26
E. Paynter *not out*	216
D. Compton *c* Badcock *b* Fleetwood-Smith	102
L. Ames *b* Fleetwood-Smith	46
H. Verity *b* Fleetwood-Smith	3
R. Sinfield *lbw b* O'Reilly	6
D. Wright *not out*	1
Extras	27
TOTAL (8 wkts dec)	658

Fall of wickets

1/219 2/240 3/244 4/281 5/487 6/577 7/597 8/626

Bowling Analyses

ENGLAND – FIRST INNINGS

	O	M	R	W
McCormick	32	4	108	1
O'Reilly	56	11	164	3
McCabe	21	5	64	0
Fleetwood-Smith	49	9	153	4
Ward	30	2	142	0

Byes, 1. Leg-byes, 22. No balls 4 (McCormick 3, O'Reilly 1)

Australia

FIRST INNINGS

J. H. Fingleton *b* Wright	9
W. A. Brown *c* Ames *b* Farnes	48
D. G. Bradman *c* Ames *b* Sinfield	51
S. J. McCabe *not out*	19
F. Ward *not out*	0
Extras	11
TOTAL (3 wkts)	138

Then came Bradman! And what an entry. Forcing his way through the crowd round the pavilion steps, the Don faced a battery of cameras on his way to the wicket, cheered at every step.

Don didn't seem any too sure of himself. Wright had him in two minds more than once. Without a run to his name he seemed to give a chance to Farnes at short-leg, and at 7 Wright failed to hold a hard return. Right after that Don's defence was beaten, but Ames was unsuccessful in his appeal – both for stumping and catching!

After tea Bradman was still shaky, and it took 110 minutes for the score to reach 50. Wright, turning his leg-break sharply and swiftly, wanted plenty of watching, and Sinfield kept a fine length.

Bradman got 51 out of the first 111, having passed 50 out of 84 in 70 minutes. And then he was out. A ball from Sinfield, a yell from Ames – and up went the umpire's finger. Bradman had been caught in quick-silver style. Just to make sure, Ames also whipped off the bails in a stumping attempt. Bradman had hit five 4s, the score being 111 when he left.

Next in was Stan McCabe, who got off the mark all right. With Brown resolutely going towards his half-hundred, the total stood at 123.

Wally Hammond was using his bowlers well and it was a shrewd bit of captaincy that saw Farnes change to the pavilion end. Instantly the move met with success. Brown glanced the ball and there was Ames to make the catch. 134–3–48. England had their tails up.

Batting 100 minutes, Brown hit a couple of boundaries. His innings was sound enough. And now what? There had been a couple of appeals against the light while Brown and McCabe were together, and I didn't think that Bradman would risk one of his recognised run-getters in the waning minutes. I was right.

Out came Frank Ward as stop gap. Farnes attacked him with three slips and a couple of men in the gully, while two fieldsmen were close in on the bat on the leg side. Ward pegged away to keep his end up, and though he didn't break his duck he certainly stayed there till the close.

Australia thus finished 520 behind with seven wickets standing. Good for England, though we can't start talking about victory yet awhile.

REYNOLDS NEWS, 19 JUNE 1938

Editor's Note: That was my first-ever report of a Test match acting as 'ghost' for Maurice Tate, one of England's greatest ever Test players.

On the Monday, Stan McCabe proceeded majestically to his greatest Test innings scoring 232. At one point Don Bradman ordered the rest of the team out on to the dressing-room balcony, and said: 'Watch this and remember – you will never see a better innings than this.'

Many years later the Don said: 'I see no reason to change my mind!'

Final scores: England 658–8 dec, Australia 411 (McCabe 232) and 427–6 (Brown 133, Bradman 144 not out). Drawn.

Epic at Lord's

E. W. SWANTON

There were so many memorable things about the Lord's Test match of 1930 that the picture of it, in all its splendour and excitement, remains fresh in the mind's eye to this day. It contained some wonderful batsmanship by some of the greatest players in the game's history, and for all four days the sun poured down on what was then the largest crowd (115,000) ever to see a cricket match in England.

There were four hundreds, by K. S. Duleepsinhji, Woodfull, Bradman and Chapman. 'Duleep's' 173 came in his first Test against Australia, and Bradman's 254 was at the moment of its making the highest score ever made by an Australian in a Test. Yet England, whose two innings totalled exactly 800, were brought, on the fourth and last day, from the brink of defeat to a real prospect of a draw, and when finally the ending of their second innings at half past three meant that a definite result was certain it seemed for a palpitating half-hour that they might even defy all possibility and snatch a victory.

That did not happen, but when young McCabe made the winning hit in the evening sunshine to give Australia their first win in England in nine Test matches there was such an aura of content at a battle bravely fought, such a sense of honour being satisfied all round, as characterises only the great sporting occasions.

This, however, was not only in itself a tremendous contest that put the emotions under the severest strain from first to last; it was also one that marked, and was seen to mark by all who were at Lord's on Saturday the 28th and Monday the 30th of June, the arrival of a cricketer of unique gifts whose play would henceforth dominate the game as it had not been dominated since the era of W.G. Don Bradman had come to England two months before, a young man of 21 who, after being dropped for one match during the Australian series of 1928–29, had scored a hundred in the fifth Test. Here he had opened the season in a burst of glory at Worcester, reached a thousand runs by the last day of May, and followed this with a hundred of rare skill and maturity that came near to denying England victory in the first Test at Trent Bridge. 'Plum' Warner was already announcing the arrival of a new star of extraordinary brightness. But it was this Lord's innings that clinched the matter.

When in Australia nearly seventeen years later, with almost every batting record then to his name, and his fame supreme, I asked Don what was the best innings he had ever played. He said at once 'My 254 at Lord's,' going on, characteristically, to give his reasons 'because I never hit the ball anywhere but in the middle of the bat, and I never lifted one off the ground until the stroke from which I was out.' Bradman's innings turned the match and made the foundation from which Australia were to regain the Ashes. But before passing on to the story of the game let us make a brief survey of the company.

The England XI, led by Percy Chapman, contained Jack Hobbs, greatest of all professional batsmen, at the age of 47 playing in his tenth and final series against Australia. It contained in Maurice Tate probably the finest bowler of his type ever seen. It contained two of the greatest all-round cricketers of any country or generation, Frank Woolley and Walter Hammond. It contained 'Duleep', whose illness at the height of his powers was soon to deprive the game of a genius. It contained two of cricket's immortal characters, 'Patsy' Hendren and George Duckworth. Not least it contained as many as five present or future captains of England – Percy Chapman, Jack White, 'Gubby' Allen, Walter Robins and Walter Hammond.

Allow for the enthusiasm of youth, and the enchantment that time lends to the distant view, and it seems an incomparable collection of talent and personality. Note, by the way, that Herbert Sutcliffe and Harold Larwood are missing, both because of injury. The latter, contrary to general belief, was as a rule expensive on the English Test wickets of his day, but Sutcliffe, of course, was and had been since 1924 the inseparable complement to Hobbs. How he might have relished England's long rearguard in the second innings!

If some of the Australian names by comparison suffer a little lustre and tend to be dwarfed by Bradman, they likewise include a rich assortment of the great. When has Australia had a better opening pair than Woodfull and Ponsford, a finer wicket-keeper than Oldfield, a leg-spin bowler superior to Grimmett, batsmen more gracious in style than McCabe and Kippax?

Vic Richardson, Woodfull's successor as captain and for long a commanding figure on the Australian scene, and the bowlers Wall, Fairfax and Hornibrook complete the 'dramatis personae' of the Lord's Test of 1930. It is, by the way, a rather sad coincidence that although the England team was senior in age to the Australian – only two of the latter, Woodfull and Fairfax, have passed on, whereas three only of their opponents, Allen, Robins and Woolley, have survived.

Frank Woolley, whose eightieth birthday will shortly be upon us! He it was who began this game on a note of such transcendent quality that though his innings was inconsiderable in the context of the final score, it remains clear in the minds of anyone with whom one ever discusses the match – and not least the Australians. The circumstances of Woolley's opening the innings with Hobbs – the only time he went in first for England in 64 Test Matches – are worth a short digression. From 1909 to 1926 inclusive Woolley played for England 52 times successively. His omission at the age of forty-one from the MCC side to Australia in 1928–29 led to what in those days of more reticent cricket writing passed for an uproar.

For Woolley was not only an idol in Kent, he was an institution among cricket crowds everywhere, a debonair, exciting punisher of every sort of bowling whose batting flourished in an atmosphere of charm and personality that set it right apart. Denis Compton had his army of devoted 'fans' and so did Walter Hammond, but neither even of these, I think, commanded quite such a following as Woolley. And among their number I was as a young man – and still am, in upper middle age – not the least ardent and faithful.

Woolley had been discarded for Australia, be it added, at the end of his most triumphant season. In 1928 he made 3,352 runs, an aggregate which then had been only once exceeded. The following summer, when the South Africans came, he was omitted from the first two drawn Tests wherein the English batting did not greatly distinguish itself. Recalled at this point he led the way with three characteristically easy, majestic innings of 83, 95 not out, and 154 which paved the way to the two victories that settled the series, and at the same time, as it was felt from Blackheath down to Dover, put the selectors in their places.

But in the first 1930 Test at Trent Bridge the great man had fallen for 0 and 5. Again he had been omitted, in favour this time of 'Duleep', and was only drafted back when Sutcliffe dropped out. This, then, was for Woolley and for all his array of worshippers the crucial appearance. He was forty-three, certainly, but these were not the days when a man was thought to be 'over the hill' in his middle thirties. Why, Hobbs, his only superior in terms of fame and achievement, who was now accompanying him to the wicket, was nearly five years older.

Wall, from the Pavilion end, began the game with a maiden to Hobbs. Fairfax bowled at the other, and Woolley simply leaned on his first ball and sent it flashing up the hill to rattle among the seats under the Grand Stand balcony behind cover point. (I know because I was sitting there in the Press Box annexe.) The next three-quarters of an hour were pure heaven. Even the dismissal of Hobbs, soon caught behind off Wall, seemed a relatively minor incident as one watched the Australian attack plundered with a succession of strokes that held the crowd in wonder and fascination.

Forty minutes after he had received his first ball, his score now 41, Woolley faced Fairfax who had taken over from Wall at the Pavilion end. Fairfax dropped one a little short and Woolley came down on the ball and cut it left-handed just behind square with the speed of light. No gully could conceivably have arrested the stroke, but Wall had retreated until he was almost a pitches length from the bat. Instinctively he grabbed at something red hurtling straight at his boots, and incredibly the catch stuck. So ended one of the little masterpieces of batting, and the hundred before lunch – before one o'clock, I daresay – that never was.

Hammond batted hesitantly. At this stage of his career he was in Tests at home only a shadow of his great self, probably because he was trying to repeat the very cautious methods he had employed to make his huge scores on the flawless Australian wickets of 1928–29 when time was no object. When he was drawn forward by Grimmett and bowled off his pads England were 105 for three. But Woolley had lit the torch, and it was the batting from now on that held the stage throughout the game.

So far as the two England innings went this was despite the excellence of Grimmett. The wicket was particularly comfortable in pace but the little man kept pegging away from the Nursery end, using all his resources of spin and flight, bowling a little 'flatter' and faster to the quicker-footed, tossing the ball a little higher to the rest and giving it an accordingly sharper tweak. He was the foundation of the Australian attack of 1930, and it was the punishment he took after lunch at the hands of Duleep and Hendren that put England, temporarily at least, on top. No one was more nimble at coming to meet slow bowling than little Patsy, while the lithe Duleep, with his oriental speed of eye, though he moved much more deliberately, achieved the same results.

These two made 104 together in an hour and a half. However, the new ball accounted not only for Hendren but also for Chapman and Allen, the latter playing in his first Test match. For a second time the innings was set on its feet, thanks now to Tate. Many a great bowler fancies himself as a batsman but few of his kind have been as effective as Maurice, who in his youth used to open the Sussex innings and over his Test career had the more than useful average for a number eight bat of 25. No stylist, he played straight in defence and gave the half-volley a hearty thump. In a boyish way Maurice had a keen sense of theatre. The scene and the situation were just up his street. The seventh wicket added 98 in seventy minutes, and, when Tate left, Duleep embarked on an all-out assault.

There is some uncertainty over the tactical plan late in the day which at this distance cannot be exactly determined. This was only the second four-day Test to be contested in England, and the critics all had different ideas as to how it should be planned. At six o'clock, so legend has it, Archie Maclaren, the arch-pundit, was brandishing his umbrella in the Long Room and declaiming that 'Percy must be mad'. A declaration was the obvious policy, thought he, with the aim a couple of wickets before close of play.

Did Duleep receive a hurry-up signal from the dressing-room balcony? Evidence is conflicting, but when at quarter past six he was caught at long-off by Bradman off Grimmett, his uncle, 'Ranji', though expressing the greatest pride in his nephew's achievement, is said also to have exclaimed, 'the boy was always careless'. Well, the careless boy had made 173 in five hours, and, far from declaring, Chapman let the innings run its course next morning.

By close of play that hot, eventful Saturday everyone, including presumably Maclaren, was a little wiser about the waging of a four-day match, at any rate when Bradman was around. Who does not remember the Saturday of his first Lord's Test? With me the picture of this one stands clear: the crowd in baking heat, spilling out on to the grass, watching quietly while Woodfull and Ponsford laid their careful foundations, equally at home against all the English bowling except for an occasional tester from Tate; the inspection of troops by the King in mid-afternoon, the small, slight, bearded figure of King George with grey bowler hat, button-hole, and rather high walking-stick, moving up and down the lines of the teams while the crowd stood, thankfully taking the chance to stretch their legs; the fall of Ponsford to the first ball afterwards, caught Hammond, bowled White – the origin, this, of the tradition that the monarch's visit is generally worth a wicket to England; and finally the brilliant, relentless taking to pieces of the England bowling by Bradman.

Over his career Bradman was rarely a spectacular starter. His innings tended to come gradually to full glory from quiet, methodical beginnings. But now he almost leapt down the pitch at White's first ball, reached it on the full-pitch and smacked it crisply to the boundary under the Nursery clock-tower. This was his first sight in England of 'Farmer' White, whose length and wonderful control had pegged down the Australians so completely on their own wickets the previous year. Bradman literally jumped at the chance of showing his mastery, and White was known afterward to say that such was Don's speed of eye and foot he believed he need never have let him bounce unless he had wanted to. But Bradman was equally at home with everyone, and while Woodfull, almost unnoticed, pursued his worthy way the runs accrued at a remarkable rate at the other end.

In the last two hours forty minutes of play Australia went from 162 for one to 404 for two: 242 runs, of which Bradman's share was 155. In fact he caught up Woodfull who, having had three hours start, was stumped off Robins for 155 just before the close. The implications of Bradman's assault were quickly realised. My predecessor, Colonel Philip Trevor, remarked in Monday's *Daily Telegraph* that no one before had seen a side get more than 400 in a Test in England, 'and at the end of the second day's play have to ask themselves if they are going to be beaten'.

M. D. Lyon was contributing a daily piece to the news pages, and alongside a report of how a sun-bathing 'club' was attacked and beaten up by a crowd of outraged citizens at the Welsh Harp at Hendon, he glanced prophetically, and with the most accurate insight, into the immediate future. 'Suppose Australia add a further 330 runs by five o'clock,' he wrote, 'then Woodfull will be able to declare with perfect safety, for they have an innings in hand, and England will be batting under a severe psychological disadvantage, with only a draw or defeat the possible result.'

In fact Australia made 325 more and declared at the tea interval, with all sorts of records lying strewn in their wake; notably, Bradman's 254, the highest Test score in England and the second highest in England–Australia matches, while 729 for six was the largest of all totals by either side in either country. And there was the somewhat grim comedy of the delay in finding the figure seven for the hundreds column on the Tavern score-board. Kippax, batting with the utmost polish, scored almost run for run with Bradman in their long partnership for the third wicket, whereafter all the Australians who got to the crease made runs and made them fast. This was despite a high standard of English fielding, wherein Chapman was the brightest ornament. It was a superb one-handed catch by the captain, wide to his right, at silly-mid-off that at last disposed of Bradman.

The Australian run-rate over their innings was just over 70 an hour, probably the most rapid in the history of Anglo-Australian Tests – and be it noted that England in those less sophisticated days bowled their overs at only a fraction under 23 an hour. Twenty-three! The attack, well-assorted in method if expensive in result, comprised Allen, Tate, White, Robins, Hammond, and Woolley. Your modern cynic may remark that had the captain and his bowlers connived in 'going slow', and delivered, say, at the average rate of the recent series in Australia, the protraction of the Australian innings would have resulted in England easily saving the match. But let me not philosophise painfully about that!

As it was, England's task was in the highest degree formidable, and at nightfall it was still more so with Hobbs bowled round his legs sweeping at a ball that pitched in the follow-through marks and Woolley out hit wicket, having brushed the stumps with his leg as he forced Grimmett to the mid-wicket boundary. Hammond and Duleep lasted out and next morning took the score to 129, but with both of them, and Hendren also, out with 147 on the board England was apparently sliding fast to an innings defeat.

Now came the last of the batting episodes that lifts this game high among the classics. Allen, with a hitherto unsuccessful first Test behind him, joined Chapman around 12 o'clock, their side still 157 runs in arrears. The stand began inauspiciously, for Chapman, misreading Grimmett's googly, so his partner maintains, at once spooned the ball up into the covers where Richardson and Ponsford each left the catch to the other. Thus reprieved, Chapman turned his particular attention to Grimmett while Allen batted in an orthodox and attractive way.

At lunch both had reached 50, and only 42 were needed to make Australia bat again. We had seen some intelligent aggressive cricket, with Allen mostly at the Nursery end taking the faster bowling while Grimmett was attacked by the left-hander. But here is another tactical curiosity. 'Gubby' Allen was under the impression all the morning that so far as possible this was the plan that was being followed, but when on going out again in the afternoon he asked whether they should carry on as before, Percy surprised him by saying, 'Oh, you can't do that in a Test match.' Chapman had great personal qualities as a captain – indeed, in my time I doubt that England has had another as good when all virtues are weighed in the scales – but his make-up was an unusual mixture of the shrewd and the naïve.

As it happened, Allen was soon out, but Chapman went from strength to strength, hitting four sixes and 12 fours in an innings of 121 that lasted just over two hours and a half. There could be no clearer example of the old axiom about attack being so often the best mode of defence.

Chapman's play, sketchy at first and growing in power and certainty the longer he batted, was of course just the medicine the crowd were praying for. In particular they enjoyed his onslaught on Grimmett, who was in almost permanent occupation of the Nursery End, and whose spin down the Lord's 'hill' the right-handers found so difficult to confront. Here Chapman was at an advantage, for to him the ball turned in, towards the bat, not away, threatening its outer edge for a catch at slip or behind the wicket.

Chapman, thrusting out his right leg to cover the stumps – and not incommoded, incidentally, by the present Law which came to pass a few years later – either stunned the ball, or hit it with a full swing into the country down by the Mound Stand and the Tavern.

After lunch he discarded the Cambridge Quidnunc cap of blue with the vertical yellow stripes which was his normal wear, and the change in appearance was symbolic. Bare-headed, literally, he went for the Australian bowling, hitting Grimmett not only into the boundary fence but over it into the crowd. Did not one such blow whistle through the narrow aperture between the score-board and the Tavern and land in St John's Wood Road? Such details are not easy to confirm getting on for forty years later, but I fancy so. At all events the bombardment in that quarter was pretty severe, and it was fine disciplined hitting calling for a nice co-ordination of cool head and eye attuned. This undoubtedly was Chapman's finest hour. When at last Chapman was caught behind the wicket there was now a real chance of saving the game, but Robins, with the impetuosity of youth, called White for a hard hit to Bradman lying deep at mid-off, and 'the Farmer', in his fortieth year, was easily beaten by a fast return. This incident, followed as it was by an ill-judged rebuke in the dressing-room between innings from 'Shrimp' Leveson-Gower, the chairman of selectors, and a characteristically blunt rejoinder by Robins, caused the latter's dropping for the subsequent Tests of the series – but he still had a dramatic part to play in this one.

Australia went in half an hour before tea, needing only 72 to win, but the wicket after all the traffic of the four days and having been baked by unusual heat was now definitely dusty. Robins was brought on for the fifth over and at once should have had Woodfull caught at mid-on. But with the next ball Robins bowled Ponsford, while at the other end

Bradman was marvellously caught in the gully by Chapman off a genuine late cut. Robin's wrist-spin for several overs continued to look infinitely dangerous, and the crowd was on tip-toe of excitement. Duckworth caught Kippax off him (22 for three) and if the 'keeper could have taken a second chance offered by Woodfull, Australia would probably have been struggling for their lives. But the magic moment passed, Robins' length grew uncertain, and the placid Woodfull was sensibly supported by McCabe.

So Australia coasted home, and, though there was some grumbling afterwards about the poor state of English bowling, no one grudged the winners their success: certainly not Chapman, who after winning six successive Tests against Australia now found himself on the losing end for the one and only time. 'It has been a great match,' he said, 'and I think that the people who came each day to see it must have been well rewarded by the fine struggle they saw. Australia fully deserved their victory, for they played splendid cricket at every point.' Woodfull's comment was equally congratulatory and generous. Those were courteous days.

ENGLAND

	FIRST INNINGS		SECOND INNINGS	
1.	Hobbs *c* Oldfield *b* Fairfax	1	*b* Grimmett	19
2.	Woolley (F. E.) *c* Wall *b* Fairfax	41	*hit wkt* *b* Grimmett	28
3.	Hammond *b* Grimmett	38	*c* Fairfax *b* Grimmett	32
4.	K. S. Duleepsingji *c* Bradman *b* Grimmett	173	*c* Oldfield *b* Hornibrook	48
5.	Hendren *c* McCabe *b* Fairfax	48	*c* Richardson *b* Grimmett	9
6.	A. P. F. Chapman *c* Oldfield *b* Wall	11	*c* Oldfield *b* Fairfax	121
7.	G. O. Allen *b* Fairfax	3	*lbw b* Grimmett	57
8.	Tate *c* McCabe *b* Wall	54	*c* Ponsford *b* Grimmett	10
9.	R. W. V. Robins *c* Oldfield *b* Hornibrook	5	*not out*	11
10.	J. C. White *not out*	23	*run out*	10
11.	Duckworth *c* Oldfield *b* Wall	18	*lbw b* Fairfax	0
	Extras (b2, lb7, nb1)	10	Extras (b16, lb13, w1)	30
	TOTAL	425		375

AUSTRALIA

	FIRST INNINGS		SECOND INNINGS	
1.	W. M. Woodfull *st* Duckworth *b* Robins	155	*not out*	26
2.	W. H. Ponsford *c* Hammond *b* White	81	*b* Robins	14
3.	D. G. Bradman *c* Chapman *b* White	254	*c* Chapman *b* Tate	1
4.	A. F. Kippax *b* White	83	*c* Duckworth *b* Robins	3
5.	S. McCabe *c* Woolley *b* Hammond	44	*not out*	25
6.	V. Y. Richardson *c* Hobbs *b* Tate	30		
7.	W. A. Oldfield *not out*	43		
8.	A. Fairfax *not out*	20		
	Extras (b6, lb8, w5)	19	Extras (b1, lb2)	3
	TOTAL (6 wkts, dec)	729	(3 wkts)	72

C. V. Grimmett, P. M. Hornibrook and T. Wall did not bat.

Bowling Analyses

ENGLAND – FIRST INNINGS	O	M	R	W
Wall	29·4	2	118	3
Fairfax	31	6	101	4
Grimmett	33	4	105	2
Hornibrook	26	6	62	1
McCabe	9	1	29	0

Fairfax bowled 1 no-ball

SECOND INNINGS	O	M	R	W
Wall	25	2	80	0
Fairfax	12·4	2	37	2
Grimmett	53	13	167	6
Hornibrook	22	6	49	1
Bradman	1	0	1	0
McCabe	3	1	11	0

Wall bowled 1 wide

AUSTRALIA – FIRST INNINGS	O	M	R	W
Allen	34	7	115	0
Tate	64	16	148	1
White	51	7	158	3
Robins	42	1	172	1
Hammond	35	8	82	1
Woolley	6	0	35	0

Allen bowled 4 wides and Robins 1 wide

SECOND INNINGS	O	M	R	W
Tate	13	6	21	1
Hammond	4·2	1	6	0
Robins	9	1	34	2
White	2	0	8	0

Fall of the Wickets

England – First Innings 1/13 2/52 3/105 4/209 5/236 6/239 7/337 8/363 9/387 10/425

Second Innings 1/45 2/58 3/129 4/141 5/147 6/272 7/329 8/354 9/372 10/375

Australia – First Innings 1/162 2/393 3/585 4/588 5/643 6/672

Second Innings 1/16 2/17 3/22

FROM 'I WAS THERE', BY TELEGRAPH SPORTSWRITERS, FONTANA BOOKS, 1967

PUN TIME

COBBERSWOLLOP! For Australia it was the sackcloth – and for England the Ashes. In Jubilee Year England is no longer down under. We've beaten the old enemy at cricket – and things are starting to look up on all fronts.

Better trade figures. Better pound. Better economic outlook. ALL THIS AND BETTER CRICKET TOO.

A winning soccer team is good for any town. And a winning cricket team is great for Britain. Mike Brearley's magnificent eleven regained the Ashes at Headingley yesterday with their third Test victory in a row. Some hat-trick!

As the new captain Brearley has done wonders in moulding an England side we can all be proud of. After all that Pommy-bashing from an Australian Cabinet Minister last week the patriotic boot is now on the other foot.

The wizards of Aussie have been sent Packering.

DAILY MIRROR LEADER, 16 AUGUST 1977

Vintage West Indies Batsman

LETTER TO THE EDITOR OF THE DAILY MIRROR

J. Mattick, Fryston Road, Airedale, Yorks – asks:

Have you any idea when the West Indies first came to England to play cricket, and what year a player named Charles Ollivierre came over with them?

He stayed on to play for Derbyshire and became a great friend of my father. He was a good scholar and a clerk at a pit in Featherstone.

During the First World War my father got him a job at Wheldale Colliery. He played his last cricket for Pontefract, where he died some years ago.

Answer: It was in 1900 that a West Indies team first toured here – though official Test Matches between the two countries weren't played until 1928.

But your father's friend was on that first tour, and headed the batting averages. He qualified for Derbyshire in 1902 and two years later played a major role in a remarkable county match at Chesterfield.

After Essex had scored a mammoth 597, Derbyshire replied with 548, of which Ollivierre made 229. Then, after Essex collapsed for 97 in their second innings, he hit another 92 out of the 147 needed for Derbyshire to win.

Due to eye-trouble, Ollivierre retired from first-class cricket after the 1907 season, but continued at club level in Yorkshire.

Curiously, he later played a big part in developing the game in Holland, going there each year from 1924 to 1939 to coach schoolboys.

As you say, he died in Pontefract on 25 March 1949 aged seventy-two.

Mike Brearley Sums Up

Post-natal depression is fairly common for mothers, and students often have a similar experience after exams. There's also, I find, post-Test letdown even after we've won. A medal is a feeble symbol of the value of creative endeavour, and the pleasure of winning is mitigated by awareness of the fact that the gloom on our opponents' faces could so easily have been the feature of our own.

The process of winning is more significant, charged and absorbing, than the product. Anti-climax hits me immediately after the match (or even before that, if the conclusion has for a long time been foregone). As captain I'm taken off for interviews – two for TV and three for radio stations – and the press conference for cricket writers.

Meanwhile, the players, glum or glad, pack, sip champagne from the glass or lager from the can. After nearly a week of conflict and in-jokes, of exhausting work and exacting co-operation, the unit mustered at the selectors' whim but created (in its character) by its members, dismantles. The haphazard order of the dressing-room, the sprawling gear and hazy territories, of TV and fruit and autographs gives way to the littered disorder of wet towels, last bats to be signed, laundry wrappers and discarded hangers.

When I get back, half the players will be gone, to Scarborough or Taunton, Leicester or Hove. Relationships within the side will never be the same again. Loss, then, is involved in both winning or losing, but easier to put up with for the winners. I wouldn't have enjoyed my returning to Test cricket if we had lost every match. How then did we end up on top, albeit so narrowly?

The main factor was the return to form of Botham and Willis. Enough has been written about Ian, but Bob's transformation was – for half the Leeds Test right through to his injury on the second day at the Oval – equally crucial. For that time, Willis was the only really quick bowler on either side. He alone could on slowish pitches regularly force batsmen back on to the back foot, and pepper their fingers. Most batsmen are happier when they can 'come to' the ball, rather than when they have to play high up off the back foot. An exception is Bruce Laird, the gritty Western Australian who played so well against the West Indies. Hughes, Yallop, and to a lesser extent, Border, are twice as dangerous when they can get into a rhythm of forward play.

Willis's previous three series had been frustrating. In Australia in 1979–80, by the Third Test, his body refused to function for him, and his movements became staccato and dislocated. Last summer, against the West Indies, he bowled well for two Tests but in the third looked past it, and in the winter he had to fly home from the Caribbean for a knee operation. So it was a colossal physical and mental achievement not only to make his way back to the top, but also to bowl faster and better as the series went on.

Botham's bowling was also invigorated. The two of them, with invaluable support from Old, Dilley, Hendrick, Allott and especially Embury, gave the new thrust to our cricket. Certainly the most enjoyable aspect of captaining England was the fielding sessions when we bowled Australia out for low scores at Leeds, Birmingham and Manchester. It was a series in which class and experience counted for a lot. Boycott struggled through on the awkward pitches, always bearing the brunt of the fresh Lillee and Alderman. After Birmingham he was anxious and in need of reassurance. At last he fought through to calmer waters at the Oval and against Lillee bowling better than at any time during the summer.

Perhaps Lillee was only then fully recovered from his serious illness. At The Oval he bowled pretty quickly; he swung the ball out and in late enough for it not to be clear whether the movement was in the air or off the pitch. He varied his pace, and bowled some slower, deceptive leg cutters. He kept going to the very end. Has there ever been a bowler to equal him?

Marsh had a fine series behind the stumps, though like others he had a hard time with the bat. I have a great affection and regard for Hughes, but I'm surprised that Australia have never made Marsh captain. Tactically, he made many shrewd suggestions; knowledgeable, publicly overt; combative and privately warm. Marsh has always struck me as a man whom most cricketers would follow with a will.

Australia were unlucky with the weather early on; and with injuries to Lawson and Hogg. Somehow, Hogg never quite seems to be rated highly enough by the current hierarchy of players, is never made to feel important. He can, without question, be a superb bowler. Their absence, was, of course, largely compensated for by the skill and persistence of Alderman. Hughes told me that Alderman bowled a yard or two faster here than in Australia, an improvement which he couldn't explain. Alderman also hit the seam more than any of the other Australian bowlers, and caught fine catches in the slips.

I have not space to mention all the Australians, but I should like to say a word about Bright and Border. I did get tired of hearing 'traditionalists' talk as if Bright ought to be a doddle to play because he bowled slow left arm *over* the wicket. What nonsense! He drifts the ball in, and bowls from close to the stumps, so lbws are by no means ruled out. He was accurate, giving the batsmen a very little wide of the off-stump. If he pitched outside leg-stump, the only possible scoring shot (if there was any rough at all, as there usually was) was the sweep, but except for a genius like Knott, it is very hard to be sure that one can keep the ball on the ground, or to cut out the risk of the ball bouncing up off the glove.

Intikhab, Benaud and Gifford have all proved difficult to play when using this method. I have long thought it should have been more widely adopted.

Of all the Australian batsmen, Border most gave an impression of impregnability on a decent pitch. He is a correct and complete player who would have done even better if he had been able to bat at five or six all through. He rarely plays at wide balls unless he is certain that he can cut or drive with safety. He commits himself late to his shot. I made the mistake at Manchester of keeping a third slip rather than a short-leg; he tends when set to get outside the ball and be vulnerable to bounce, on the leg stump more than outside the off stump. He is a brilliant player of spin bowling, as is Yallop, and it's much to Embury's credit that he dismissed Yallop three times, and Border twice, in the series.

I'm conscious, in retrospect, of one or two mistakes, though not many are as clear cut as some commentators, with their second guesses, would have us believe. Judgement should be made on probability, not outcome. So, when Jim Laker writes on the Friday that it was a mistake to put Australia in at The Oval, one should know that his opinion, given to Paul Parker's father an hour before the start on Thursday, was that we should field. It is facile to refer to playing only four specialist bowlers as 'folly' only after three of them had broken down.

However, to get back to mistakes. At The Oval, with a depleted attack, we did well to reduce Australia to 109 for 4 in their second innings. This was done by trying all sorts of ploys and bowling changes, squeezing wickets out like blood from a stone. Then came the missed chance offered by Dirk Wellham just before lunch and I fear I was less resourceful, less able to convey to the bowlers the sense that they would find a way to get wickets. We fell back on defence too soon. There's nothing wrong with that, provided it is still *purposeful* defence, in which the side believe they can shut the batsmen out, and force them into a mistake.

Test matches – as their name implies – are indeed examinations. I was again disappointed with my efforts in the batting finals, and relieved and pleased to play a part with the bat in the last innings of the series. Having opened my Test career with a duck I had gloomy fantasies of ending it with a pair, and being forced to call my next book 'Full Circle'. (Private Eye once suggested that my favourite piece of music was Haydn's Duck Quartet.)

I still can't understand the size of the discrepancy between my record in Test matches, and my scores in all other cricket. It has been said that cricket is a game that one only learns how to play when one no longer can. Maybe I'll know a bit more by next summer.

SUNDAY TIMES, 6 SEPTEMBER 1981

Keen-Eyed Dickie Bird

BRIAN SCOVELL

Dickie Bird, one of the umpires in tomorrow's cricket Prudential World Cup Final at Lord's can remember little of what happened when he umpired the only previous World Cup Final in 1975.

Near the end, Australia's last man Jeff Thomson skied a catch to Roy Fredericks and was caught. Hundreds of ecstatic West Indian fans raced on to the pitch to mob their heroes but they'd failed to hear the umpire call 'no ball'.

There was such a babble of noise that it was impossible to hear anything. The game still wasn't over.

In the rush, Bird was accidentally struck on the back of the head and stunned.

'When the fans were finally cleared from the pitch, I found they'd frisked me,' he said.

'Everything had gone except the clothes I was standing up in – Thomson's sweater which I wore round my waist, my white cap, the spare bails, the spare ball, everything. All they wanted were souvenirs'.

Thomson and his partner Dennis Lillee had started to run. 'Come on', said Lillee, 'we can run 17 off this and win the game.'

The ball disappeared into the crowd as Fredericks overthrew trying to run Thomson out – another souvenir for a Brixton bus driver.

After order was restored, Tommy Spencer, the other umpire, came over to Bird and said: 'What the bloody hell is going on?'

It was a good question. No one knew. Had Thomson and Lillee run enough runs to win the game?

Bird and Spencer came up with the admirable British compromise: they awarded Australia four runs though the ball hadn't crossed the boundary line.

Umpires are like judges, they have to make these history-making improvised judgments sometimes.

Bird was paid a modest £100 for his 12-hour stint that day and he described the occasion as the pinnacle of his career. At the official presentation, Prince Philip said to him: 'Are you all right? I notice they've pinched your cap.'

'Yes sir, that's another one gone,' replied Bird. It wasn't the first time Royalty has noticed Bird's distinctive white cap, which was modelled on the one used by Yorkshire comedian Albert Modley.

'The Queen Mother once asked me why I'd taken it off during a Test match,' said Bird.

Bird will be paid £350 for umpiring in the West Indies *v* England Final.

But he would do it for nothing, in any case. Born in Barnsley (where he once opened the innings for Barnsley CC with Michael Parkinson) 46-year-old Bird is one of sport's supreme loyalists.

Presented with a Japanese car by a garage, he later returned it saying he ought to support the British car industry. He now runs a British car.

And two years ago, when top umpires were doing well if they earned £2,500 a year, he rejected a £10,000 a year offer from Kerry Packer's World Series Cricket.

Since joining the umpires' list in 1970, former Yorkshire and Leicester batsman Bird has made himself Britain's leading umpire.

His full name is Harold Dennis Bird. 'But since I was a kid, I've always been known as Dickie,' he said. He's one of the game's characters with his extravagant gestures. 'I make them because I'm nervous, not because I'm showing off,' he said.

Umpiring is one of the most highly-charged roles in sport. For, unlike the football referee who has two linesmen, the cricket umpire has no one to help him.

He is on his own when he makes a decision, and he's under acute pressure not only from the crowd and the TV cameras with their instant play-backs, but, increasingly these days, from the players.

Bird goes to bed before ten during Test Matches but admits he doesn't sleep well. He's not a person to share a room with because he often shouts: 'That's out!' or 'Catch it!' in his sleep.

Despite the tension which has turned him into a perpetual fidget, Bird hasn't lost his Yorkshire humour. He gets on well with the players.

During a Test at Trent Bridge in 1977, frustrated Australian Max Walker turned to him after bowling to Geoff Boycott in one of his obdurate moods and said: 'What do I bowl him next, Dickie?' 'A hand grenade,' said Bird. 'That's the only thing that will blast him out.'

There's probably more humour, especially written humour, in cricket than in any other sport and umpires are often at the heart of it.

One of the funniest of Bird's predecessor's was Alec Skelding, who used to remove the bails at the close of play and say, 'That gentlemen, concludes the entertainment for the day.'

Skelding liked a drink and one day he was having a night out in a pub. When it was closing time, he made towards the door which everyone else in the bar knew led to a telephone booth.

A few seconds later, he returned and said, 'I've inspected the light in there and it's unfit for play.'

Bird is so devoted to the sport he loves – he coaches abroad in the winter – that he hasn't had time to get married – though he confesses to three near misses.

He lives alone in a house called The Wickets at Barnsley, after his mother died last year.

Officiating with him tomorrow at Lord's is the former Gloucester wicket-keeper Barrie Meyer.

Umpiring for up to nine hours is a tiring business and can be a strain on the back – which is why Dickie Bird sometimes wears a brace.

That was one souvenir the West Indians missed in 1975.

DAILY MAIL, 22 JUNE 1979

MONSTROUS!

I was with Alex Bannister, cricket correspondent of the *Daily Mail*, at the Surrey *v* Sussex match at the Oval. Alex introduced myself and George Cox junior to a pleasantly quiet gentleman enjoying the sun and cricket – Boris Karloff, alias 'Frankenstein'.

Bursts out the cricketer, 'So you're the so-and-so who brought terror to my childhood!' ROY PESKETT